W9-BJD-617

JOHN J. SCHAUB
RESOURCE ROOM

DIVISION OF PROFESSIONAL STUDIES
ROBINSON BUILDING
GLASSBORO STATE COLLEGE
GLASSBORO, NJ 08028

Coming Back. . .
Or Never Leaving

Instructional Programming for Handicapped Students in the Mainstream

Anne Langstaff Pasanella
Cara B. Volkmor

University of Southern California

Contributions by Karl Skindrud
California State College, Dominguez Hills

Charles E. Merrill Publishing Company
A Bell & Howell Company
Columbus   Toronto   London   Sydney

Published by
Charles E. Merrill Publishing Company
A Bell & Howell Company
Columbus, Ohio 43216

This book was set in Optima and Times Roman.
The production editor was Jan Hall.
The cover was prepared by Will Chenoweth.

Copyright © 1977 by University of Southern California.
Copyright is claimed until 1982. Thereafter, all portions of this work covered by this copyright will be in the public domain.
This work was developed under a contract with the U.S. Office of Education, Department of Health, Education, and Welfare. However, the content does not necessarily reflect the position or policy of that Agency, and no official endorsement of these materials should be inferred.

Quotations in italic on pp. 9-11 are from:

Dunn, L.M. Special education for the mildy retarded—Is much of it justified? *Exceptional Children,* 1968, *35* (1), pp. 5, 11.

Quotation on p. 10 and adapted model on p. 12 are from:

Deno, E. Special education as developmental capital. *Exceptional Children,* 1970, *37* (3), p. 236.

These quotations are reprinted from *Exceptional Children* by their authors and by permission of The Council for Exceptional Children, copyright © 1968 and 1970, respectively.

Cover photo and photo for mediapak 1 by James Goff, Phoenix Productions.
Art for mediapaks 2-4 by Bob Galeotti and Leslie Galeotti, Galeotti Graphics.
Photo for mediapak 5 by Tim Williams.

International Standard Book Number: 0–675–08460–1
Library of Congress Catalog Number: 76–58243

3   4   5   6   7   8   9—82   81   80   79

Printed in the United States of America

preface

The last nine or ten years have been exciting and full of turmoil for special education. During this time, the whole approach to handicapped persons has undergone extensive change. In fact, the change has been so great that professionals who were trained ten years ago have had to completely re-orient themselves, and even those persons who graduated two or three years ago need specific professional development experiences in order to stay current and effective.

The following are some of the major changes which have been advocated, begun, or actually accomplished in the last decade:

1. A shift away from self-contained, all-day programming for special education students, including the mildly handicapped, and toward a variety of resource and support programs for all students having difficulties in school.
2. A shift from an emphasis on the two to five percent of the school population who require major modifications in their school programs and facilities, and toward an emphasis on the much larger group of

children showing specific and general learning, behavior, or aptitude difficulties.

3. An emphasis on working in and with regular education, which often involves new roles of consultation and inservice training for the special educator.

On the social level, we have found ourselves in the midst of a national experiment in racial desegregation and have been forced, on occasion, by legal judgments, to examine our assumptions and procedures of identification, classification, and programming for children whom we feel are in need of our services. At the same time, we have become increasingly involved with parents and community groups who have been asking for a greater say in educational decision making for their children.

Considering the range and the complexities of the problems facing educators of exceptional children in the mid-seventies, it is no wonder that many of our basic skills have had to be augmented. The administrator needs more than a thorough knowledge of the education code. The psychologist needs more than standardized tests. The teacher needs more than well-developed lessons and materials. This need to constantly learn and develop new ways of doing new jobs has kept our work interesting; however, with the excitement of a paradigm shift, sometimes we may have the feeling of not being completely sure of our professional ground. In a sense we are like surfers, making our way by using the uncontrollable waves of social movement. Also, like surfers, we stay upright by paying attention to the shifting forces which propel us, by maintaining a balance in our positions, and by making constant, delicate adjustments as we go along.

Anne and Cara, the authors of this book, with their well-developed sense of balance, are two of the better ''surfers'' in the business. In this volume they have done an important job of bringing together the practical ''nuts and bolts'' of programs which are being used across the country and unifying these concepts into a form which can be used to keep the rest of us above water.

In their chapter on identification and referral, you will find a variety of observation forms, screening devices, and checklists which have been validated in practice. Here, as in the rest of the book, the authors do not advocate a single procedure but will provide you with a selection of acceptable practices and some basis for choosing from among them. The practicality of this material makes it an excellent complement to the more theoretical *Issues in the Classification of Children* (Hobbs, 1975).

Similarly, you will find a rich resource of assessment procedures which can provide data leading directly to educational programming. The authors have sampled virtually all the better systematized assessment techniques presently in use, and they indicate some of the strengths and weaknesses of each.

Again, the emphasis is on balance and advocacy for the child, rather than on a particular theoretical approach.

The bottom line on educational efforts on behalf of children is always the actual learning experience and the effects which result. In mainstreaming mildly handicapped youngsters, such experiences have been the most difficult part of the process. On this topic the authors present a variety of programs, both in academic skill development and in social and affective areas. They show how published or locally developed programs may be refined and evaluated by means of one of several systems models. A truly amazing amount of work has been done in this mode since it was tentatively introduced to the field a little over a decade ago. The practitioner today no longer has to begin educational programming from scratch, but can build on patterns such as those presented here.

The final chapter of this volume will be useful to those who are responsible for the training of their peers and themselves. It provides access to many of the various training and support services which can help us catch the wave of progress and ride it to the next stage.

A fascinating aspect of this book, and of the stage of educational con- sciousness at present, is that which is not yet completely stated but clearly implied—the hints as to the possible next steps in improving our education of children in a dynamic democracy. When we really become skilled at the type of individualization of learning experiences discussed here, we approach the possibility of allowing learners—yes, even handicapped learners—to plan and carry out their own learning and to achieve their own objectives. Perhaps paradoxically, a highly structured analysis of learning programs can increase individual freedom and choice.

The possibility of developing and refining learner-directed programs, while retaining the strengths of the present behavioral and systems-oriented ap- proaches, provides enough challenge to carry us well into the 1980s. This volume should provide some of us with the grounding to allow us to push into this new area. I suspect the next decade will be as exciting as the last, if we can keep our balance while skimming through the waves of change.

Robert B. MacIntyre, Ph.D.
Ontario Institute for Studies in Education
Toronto, 1976

acknowledgments

Special thanks for their participation in the media portions of this program go to the following:

Santa Barbara School and High School Districts, Santa Barbara, Ca.: Thomas J. Murphy, director of Special Education; Ann Pierce, Victoria Brooks, and their students at *Dos Pueblos Senior High School;* Barbara Rollinson, Nancy Rood, Gerry Woodson, and their students at *Franklin Elementary School;* Joanne Freeman, Bill Straka, and their students, also, Frank Johnson at *Harding Elementary School;* Louise DeRose, Robin Acker, and their students at *LaCumbre Junior High School.*

Santa Barbara County Schools, Comprehensive Plan for Special Education: Larry Schram, assistant superintendent, special education, Joseph Pasanella, area manager—South County, Richard Windmiller, coordinator of evaluation.

Whittier Area Comprehensive Plan for Special Education, Whittier, Ca.: Larry Lindstrum, project coordinator, Jim Johnson, coordinator, Educational Assessment Service.

El Rancho Unified School District, Pico Rivera, Ca.: Mike Oldham, Susan Tinkley, Bob Guilland, Claudia Walter, Marie White, and their students at *Rivera Community School.*

Lowell Joint School District, Whittier, Ca.: Vonnie Di Cecco, Yvonne Fenaroli, and their students at *Olita Elementary School.*

The assistance and strong support of our colleagues at the California Regional Resource Center is also greatly appreciated. We express our thanks to: Andrea Carroll, Gabriele Gurski, Mary Male, Barbara Sarkis, and Marilyn Stem, who conducted the field evaluation with educators in Santa Barbara County, Sacramento City Schools, Humboldt and Del Norte Counties, Contra Costa County, and Stanislaus County.

And a special thanks to Keren McIntyre, who helped us uncover countless resources and gave much personal support, time and many suggestions; Cora Christion, who typed the original manuscript; and Linda Polin, who researched and edited.

contents

introduction   *1*

one

Mainstreaming, Resource Programs,
Training Models: An Overview   *6*

two

Identification and Referral   *36*

three

Assessment   *80*

four

Instructional Planning and Evaluation   *146*

five

Support Strategies for Children and Teachers   *212*

index   *252*

introduction

The title of this program, *Coming Back . . . or Never Leaving: Instructional Programming for Handicapped Students in the Mainstream,* alludes to a new way of looking at public education—education for all children, the average, the gifted, *and* the handicapped within the context of the regular school program. While our focus throughout is on the mildly handicapped, the title conveys our belief that the touchstone for effective educational programming for the handicapped is no longer the degree to which it is "special," but rather it is the extent of its continuity with regular education.

This book, the accompanying mediapaks, and training guide,* evolved out of our experience in a project designed to assist local education agencies in developing and implementing comprehensive plans for special education— plans capable of increasing articulation with regular education, and of providing appropriate services for all children within the public schools. Early in the project one objective was to develop a program to train or retrain special educators for the role of resource teachers to work with the

---

*Available from Charles E. Merrill Publishing Co., Columbus, Ohio 43216.

1

mildly handicapped in regular classes. As we read the literature, studied state guidelines, visited projects, and talked with people across the country, we became less and less clear as to how to meet this objective. The multifaceted role of the resource teacher (in relation to regular class teachers, handicapped learners, school administrators, and other professional educators) which we saw emerging out of the composite of all of our research suggested a need for a training program much greater in scope than we originally envisioned. For several weeks, we remained on a plateau of confusion and indecision. Suddenly we realized that what we wanted to say on the subject of mainstream instructional programming for the mildly handicapped needed to be said, not only to resource teachers, but to everyone who would be involved in working with these students, especially the regular class teacher and the principal. This program, then, was designed with this larger audience in mind. The underlying assumption is that the delivery of instructional programming services via a team approach rather than a role-specific approach will be of greater benefit to handicapped learners.

The program is essentially organized around the interrelated components of the instructional programming system shown in Figure 1.

The way in which this system can be operationalized at all grade levels for mildly handicapped students returning to, or continuing in, the regular school program is illustrated in the five mediapaks:

Part One: "Introduction to Mainstreaming"
Part Two: "Identification and Referral"
Part Three: "Assessment and Instructional Planning"
Part Four: "Coming Back: A Case Study"
Part Five: "Never Leaving: A Case Study"

Filmstrips one, two, and three provide an orientation to the programming steps required for successful mainstreaming of handicapped students, while filmstrips four and five document the assessment and planning phases of the process for two students, one in the fifth grade, and one in junior high school.

The chapters of this book attend to all of the components of the instructional programming system shown in Figure 1. Each chapter is correlated with a set of training tasks and activities.

We will begin with a chapter on the concept of mainstreaming and present a review of implementation techniques. This first chapter synthesizes the available literature and research for the purpose of heightening awareness, changing attitudes, and providing information on the critical issues involved in the education of the mildly handicapped. The next three chapters are intensely practical and represent a compilation of effective identification, referral, assessment, instructional planning, and evaluation techniques developed by practitioners. Chapter Five deals with inservice training and support strategies

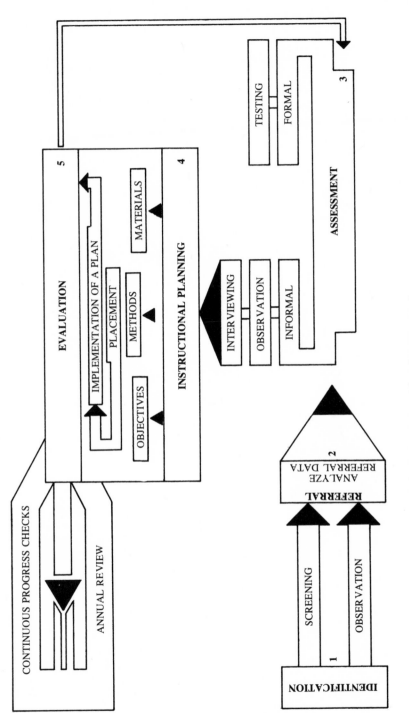

Figure 1. Instructional programming process.

as well as professional competencies necessary for communication, consultation, and teaching. The essence of this final chapter is the humanity, the energy, and the expertise that must go into the kind of instructional programming which respects the rights of individual learners and enhances their opportunity for success in the educational mainstream.

one

Mainstreaming, Resource Programs, Training Models: An Overview

. . . courts have ruled in principle that special education systems or practices are inappropriate if they remove children from their expanded peer group without benefit of constitutional safeguards . . . (Johnson, 1975)

It is a new language that suggests a new conception of the handicapped citizen, a new conception of that citizen's place in our society, a new conception of those obligations owed to him by those who act in place of the society . . . It is now a question of justice. (Gilhool, 1976, p. 21)

The preceding quotations strongly reflect the tenor of both recent court decisions and state and federal legislation regarding public education—all of which are providing a massive impetus for change in the nation's schools. Critical issues include *mainstreaming*, or placement in the "least restrictive environment"; due process procedures; confidentiality; nondiscriminatory testing; and individualized educational programming. Individual school districts now need to face these issues in order to comply with state and federal mandates for free, appropriate educational programs for *all* children.

6

While the requirement of *least restrictive environment,* or *placement alternative* (as applied by the courts), relates to all children, regardless of degree or complexity of handicap, our focus throughout this book is on that large segment of the school population traditionally labeled *mildly handicapped.* Included in this group are children who have been called *educable mentally retarded, educationally handicapped,* or *learning disabled.* Their common characteristic, as Lilly points out, is that "they have been referred from regular education programs because of some sort of teacher perceived behavioral or learning problem" (1970, p. 37). Though the bulk of the literature on mainstreaming addresses the needs of the disabled learner, the concept applies equally to students with physical or sensory deficits. Keeping the perspective of the mildly handicapped in mind, we turn now to a definition of mainstreaming.

Mainstreaming Defined

The mainstream philosophy has been described as a "transitional concept on the way toward unification of general and special education" (Rubino, Gal-

7

lagher, Scelza, & Toker, 1974, p. 24). Birch (1974) sees special education as a resource for the entire school population and therefore defines *mainstreaming* as an "amalgamation of regular and special education into one system to provide a spectrum of services for all children according to their learning needs" (1974, p. iii). He enumerates fourteen descriptive characteristics of mainstreaming which may be summarized as follows:

1. Handicapped children are assigned to regular classes where special education is provided for them.
2. Instructional procedures are broadened to allow all children to participate in regular programs to a level manageable by the individual student and teacher. The critical variable is the match between the child's needs and the capability of the mainstream program to meet them.
3. Mainstreaming may be accomplished at any level.
4. Handicapped pupils report to regular teachers and spend half or more of the day in a regular class, leaving the class only for essential instruction in small groups or on a one to one basis.
5. Special education personnel work in a special room, receiving students for specified periods, or as members of a school team providing educational assessment and instructional consultation for pupils with learning problems.

Beery (1972) suggests that mainstreaming implies a continuum of programs, including reduction of programs which "pull" a student *out* of the mainstream and "Educational Specialists" who work much of the time in the regular classroom.

Kaufman, Gottlieb, Agard, and Kukic (1975) state that definitions such as those of Beery and Birch are elusive and that a more concise definition encompassing the many complexities of mainstreaming is necessary. These authors point out that:

. . . definitions and comments pertaining to mainstreaming which appear in the literature have focused more on administrative considerations (e.g., the amount of time spent in regular classrooms) than on instructional variables (e.g., the instructional activities in which the child should participate when he attends the regular class). Quite possibly, the emphasis on administrative concerns reflects the prevailing view among researchers and practitioners that mainstreaming is primarily an administrative arrangement and is only secondarily, if at all, an instructional approach. (p. 4)

Accordingly, Kaufman et al. define the structure of mainstreaming as encompassing three major components: (*a*) integration, (*b*) educational planning and programming, (*c*) clarification of responsibility. *Integration,* as used in this definition, includes three interdependent elements—*temporal integration,* meaning time spent in the regular classroom; *instructional integration,* or sharing in the instructional environment of that class; and *social integration* and acceptance by classmates. The educational planning and programming component of mainstreaming is the ongoing cycle of assessment, instructional planning, and evaluation processes. Mainstreaming also involves articulated planning and programming by both regular and special educators at all levels of the system; thus clarification and assignment of responsibilities is the third component.

Note that these three components of mainstreaming are interactive; that *integration,* while critical, is not synonymous with *mainstreaming,* which, in the words of Kaufman et al., "represents one of the most complex educational service innovations undertaken to date by the educational system" (p. 11).

Meyers, MacMillan, and Yoshida (1975), referring to the above definition of *mainstreaming,* state: "It is paradoxical that nowhere in the definition is there a call for delabeling of the child since the labels were one of the major targets of criticism in the previous delivery system—i.e., the self-contained class" (p. 27). These authors point out that such a modification of the Kaufman et al. (1975) definition has subsequently been proposed in the literature.

In the following section we will attempt to review some of the factors which give rise to the mainstreaming movement of the 1970s and to discuss mainstreaming in the context of a continuum of educational services for all children.

Mainstreaming: The Issue

Birch (1974) lists 11 motivating factors providing impetus to the mainstreaming movement. These factors may be categorized as: the determination of professional educators; court decisions; governmental policies. For an indepth review of these factors and a greater historical perspective, the publications by Deno (1970), Hobbs (1975), Lilly (1970, 1971), Kaufman et al. (1975), Meyers et al. (1975), and Weintraub et al. (1976) are helpful.

Influence of Professional Educators

Criticisms of, and concerns about, special education services are expressed in the literature as far back as the 1960s. Johnson's article (1962) questions the validity of segregated classes for educable mentally retarded students. Dunn's celebrated article (1968) may be seen as a turning point for special educators. He prefaces this article with the statement:

In my view, much of our past and present practices are morally and educationally wrong . . . . Let us stop being pressured into continuing and expanding a special

education program that we know now to be undesirable for many of the children
we are dedicated to serve. (p. 5)

Lilly (1970, 1971) extended Dunn's view. Motivated by his review of the
current efficacy studies which he found to yield inconclusive and conflicting
evidence concerning special programs, he recommended drastic changes to
the special education delivery system. Solutions viable in the past were seen
by many critics to now be creating problems; the forces of change began to
move in. Deno (1970) challenged special educators to face the issue of
"whether they are justified in continuing to try to fix up the children that an
inadequate instructional program has maimed so they will fit better into a
system that should be adjusting itself to the learning needs of the children"
(p. 231). She stated a belief that the special education system could serve as
"developmental capital" in a major effort to upgrade all of public education.
Her words are strong:

> It is suggested that the special education system abandon its long standing
> assumption that its success can be judged by how many more children are enrolled
> in special education programs this year than were enrolled last year or 10 years
> ago. We suggest judgment by criteria which indicate: (*a*) to what extent special
> education is serving those children who cannot reasonably be accommodated in a
> good regular education program and (*b*) how the children it serves are progressing
> toward socially relevant goals. We suggest that special education resources be
> mobilized to serve as an experimental cutting edge to help education move itself
> along the path toward truly individualized or personalized instruction so that
> children who are different can be increasingly accommodated in a hospitable
> educational mainstream. (p. 236)

Meyers et al. (1975), in an extremely comprehensive review of the literature on the efficacy of special class placement, raise the question of failure to
control for the teacher variable as a serious problem in the reported attempts to
evaluate special classes. These authors take the position that "any particular
low-IQ child placed with the 'right' teacher, regardless of the administrative
arrangement, (special class; regular class) is likely to benefit," going on to
add, "unfortunately the reverse is just as true" (p. 9).

The concern for the children who were being inappropriately and in-
adequately served in special classes brought with it a recognition that a
worthwhile goal for special educators might be to enable regular teachers,
through support and training, to become more self-sufficient in managing the
instructional programs of the mildly handicapped. This philosophy underlies
the concept of a "continuum" or "cascade" of educational alternatives, and
is a critical component in effective resource programs for the mildly handicapped.

Mainstreaming should be viewed as one aspect of a continuum of educational services and alternatives. As a process it is not synonymous with the total abolition of self-contained special classes which may still be an appropriate placement for many children who are found to be profoundly retarded or sensorily handicapped, severely emotionally disturbed, or multiply handicapped.

Mainstreaming is not an isolated change in special education, but rather a basic change in the educational system, for special education cannot realistically be changed without a concomitant effect on mainstream education. "The burden for adaptation, which, previously, had rested unproportionately upon the child now shifts to the main system" (Meisgeier and Perez, 1973, p. 96). Dunn's 1968 article, referred to previously, appears now like a forecast of what we are grappling with in the late 1970s:

> *There is an important difference between regular educators talking us into trying to remediate or live with the learning difficulties of pupils with which they haven't been able to deal;* versus *striving to evolve a special education program that is either developmental in nature, wherein we assume responsibility for the total education of more severely handicapped children from an early age,* or *is supportive in nature; wherein general education would continue to have central responsibility for the vast majority of the children with mild learning disabilities—with us serving as resource teachers in devising effective prescriptions and in tutoring such pupils* (p. 11).

In Figure 2, the adaptation of Deno's "cascade" model (1970) represents the developmental approach Dunn describes. This graphic representation of a continuum of educational services illustrates the meaning of the term *least restrictive alternative*—a concept originally applied to the institutionalized mentally retarded—which is now being seen to have applicability to all persons classified as having exceptional needs. Stemming from the principle of a person's fundamental liberty, this term, when applied to education, "means that among all alternatives for placement within a general education system, handicapped children should be placed where they can obtain the best education at the least distance away from mainstream society" (Molloy, 1974, p. 5). Such a system is designed to make available a full range of special educational services and environments which are appropriate for individual students at a given time. For students who require special placement, the goal is integration or reentry into the mainstream. "The concept is that there is one system of public education for *all* children, not one for the handicapped and another for everyone else" (Abeson et al., 1975). Such an approach to educational programming means that the majority of handicapped students (those with the least amount of learning handicap) will be served in regular classrooms where their program can be modified or supplemented to

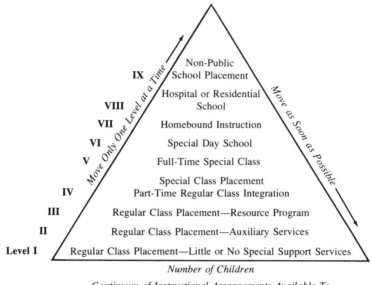

Number of Children

Continuum of Instructional Arrangements Available To
Public School Handicapped Children

Figure 2

meet their individual needs. Students with more severe handicaps, who are significantly fewer in number in the special education population, will be served in more restrictive settings such as special class or institutions. As Deno so aptly states, "It [the cascade model] gives opportunity for a two-pronged approach—care for the already wounded while moving ahead at the mainstream boundary to help prevent further wounding" (1970, p. 235).

Closely related to the "cascade" system which addresses the needs of the total range of exceptional individuals is Lilly's (1971) "zero reject" model, which places the responsibility for failure to educate the *mildly* handicapped on the teacher rather than on the taught. *Zero reject* means "that once a child is enrolled in a regular education program within a school, it must be impossible to administratively separate him from that program for any reason" (Lilly, 1971, p. 745). Problems must be dealt with by those most directly involved, and not referred to separate and isolated programs for treatment, though such services may still be the most appropriate for the severely handicapped.

The "Fail-Save" model, developed by Van Etten and Adamson (1973), focuses on how to keep a child with special needs from being held in a service plan that is ineffective and provides an operational basis for Deno's "cascade'' system. The "Fail-Save" model limits the amount of time that a child can spend in any program phase, thus forcing program accountability and ensuring that individual students have every available opportunity to demonstrate success in the mainstream. The model has four phases and an alternate placement provision:

Phase I. *Consultation:* Service always begins here with referral from the classroom teacher. A Methods and Materials Consultant/Teacher coordinates the diagnostic process which includes observation. Based on the assessment, one specific task is targeted for programming. During this time parents attend a training sequence on behavior management. For 5–6 weeks the consultant provides on-the-job training to the teacher, assisting with the educational prescription and needed revisions. If at the end of 10 weeks the child has shown appropriate (for him/her) progress, the direct service of the consultant to the teacher can be terminated. If the change in the child's performance is not satisfactory, Phase I may be repeated or the child may be moved to Phase II.

Phase II. *The Resource Room/Regular Class:* A more in-depth diagnosis is conducted and an educational plan designed. The child is assigned to the resource room for short periods of the day which do not interrupt participation in important regular class activities. The resource teacher provides consultation services to the child's regular teacher. At the end of 90 school days a progress check is made and either the special services are terminated or the student is returned to Phase I. If the rate of achievement has not been satisfactory, the child can repeat Phase II once or be transferred to Phase III.

Phase III. *Special-Classroom/Resource Room Program:* Here the child spends most of the day in a special class and part in the resource room. Intense programming is provided and the goal is to return the student to the regular class. Based on the child's academic progress and/or social development, the child can be returned to Phase II or referred to Phase IV.

Phase IV. *The Special Classroom:* Placement here suggests either total failure by the system or that the child's problems make it impossible for him/her to function in any other setting. At the end of 36 weeks an alternate may be considered.

Phase IV. *Alternate:* A special residential or day school placement.

Students in Phase IV for long-term placement or in a special facility would be given the chance to reenter the "Fail-Save" system at any point. Notice that a student cannot be moved away from the mainstream more than one phase at a time. Placement decisions are made by a group of professionals who know the child, with parents playing a vital role. Success of the model depends more on the skill and dedication of trained personnel than on administrative design.

Court Decisions

Until very recently, the law offered parents of handicapped children relatively little assistance in resolving their most pressing educational problems. In increasing numbers, however, handicapped citizens and their parents are turning to the courts to secure their rights, to secure under the law that which is due them (McClung, 1975; Gilhool, 1976). Lawyers have assumed a very active role in disputes over the adequacy of educational programs for the handicapped. The essence of the movement, which began two decades ago with the civil rights activists, is concern for individual rights in general. Resulting litigation has had a profound effect on educational goals and policy, and may, in time, have a dramatic, practical effect on the lives of handicapped children and their parents. The problem areas most frequently addressed by the courts have been: exclusion of handicapped children from the public schools; misclassification (labeling); and inappropriate programming. While cases centering around the problem of exclusion from public education programs are less relevant to the present discussion of mainstreaming for the mildly handicapped than are those cases dealing with misclassification and inappropriate programming, two such landmark cases will be included in the following brief account of recent litigation, since these cases demonstrate the impact which court decisions have had on the public school system.

The legal bases for the litigation involving the rights of handicapped children are the equal protection and due process clauses of the Fourteenth Amendment. The meaning of these terms as they relate to education is shown in Figure 3. Exercising their rights under the equal protection clause, thirteen retarded children and the Pennsylvania Association for Retarded Children (PARC) went to court in January 1971 against the Commonwealth of Pennsylvania on behalf of every excluded child in that state. They went to Federal District Court to secure access to a free public education in a state where the law said, on one hand, that a proper education for all of its retarded children would be provided, and on the other, that children who were "uneducable" or "untrainable" could be excluded from the public schools. The arguments of this group were based on the legal precedent set in a much earlier case (*Brown* v. *Board of Education,* 1954), which established education as a right, and on the fact, attested to by expert witnesses, that all children are able to benefit from an education (Gilhool, 1976). In the PARC case the state did not deny or try to defend the practices being challenged and the agreement reached provided that all retarded children between the ages of 4 and 21 years be granted access to a program of free public education and training appropriate to their individual capacities. The court further ordered that access was to be

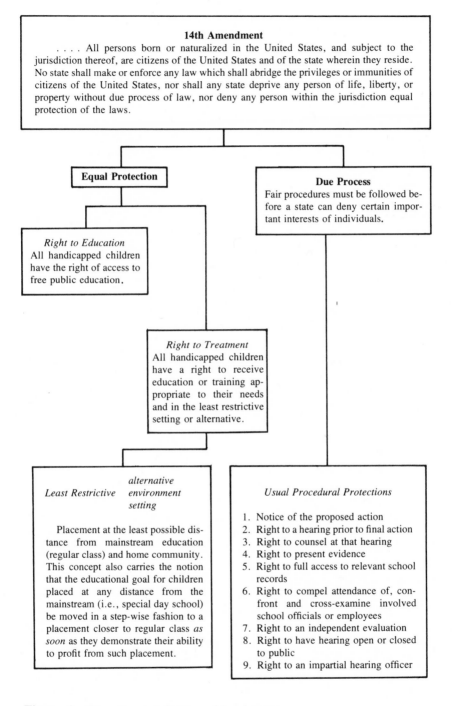

14th Amendment
. . . . All persons born or naturalized in the United States, and subject to the jurisdiction thereof, are citizens of the United States and of the state wherein they reside. No state shall make or enforce any law which shall abridge the privileges or immunities of citizens of the United States, nor shall any state deprive any person of life, liberty, or property without due process of law, nor deny any person within the jurisdiction equal protection of the laws.

Equal Protection

Due Process
Fair procedures must be followed before a state can deny certain important interests of individuals.

Right to Education
All handicapped children have the right of access to free public education.

Right to Treatment
All handicapped children have a right to receive education or training appropriate to their needs and in the least restrictive setting or alternative.

Least Restrictive   *alternative environment setting*

Placement at the least possible distance from mainstream education (regular class) and home community. This concept also carries the notion that the educational goal for children placed at any distance from the mainstream (i.e., special day school) be moved in a step-wise fashion to a placement closer to regular class *as soon* as they demonstrate their ability to profit from such placement.

Usual Procedural Protections

1. Notice of the proposed action
2. Right to a hearing prior to final action
3. Right to counsel at that hearing
4. Right to present evidence
5. Right to full access to relevant school records
6. Right to compel attendance of, confront and cross-examine involved school officials or employees
7. Right to an independent evaluation
8. Right to have hearing open or closed to public
9. Right to an impartial hearing officer

Figure 3. Educational definition of legal terms.

accorded those children within the context of "least restrictive alternative," and with due process safeguards.

Similar results were obtained in the case of *Mills* v. *D.C. Board of Education*, where the court extended the right to education to all students previously denied (including emotionally or physically handicapped and those with behavior problems), ruling that no child can be excluded from public education because of handicap. The decision also included due process hearings to determine classification and placement. Also of interest is the fact the court found unacceptable the Washington, D.C. School District's claim of insufficient funds, asserting that funding limitations cannot burden handicapped pupils more than it does normal students.

The courts have also inquired into the quality and appropriateness of publicly supported programs for the handicapped. In *Wyatt* v. *Stickney* (1971), the judge of the northern district of Alabama ruled that citizens residing in state schools and hospitals have the right to a humane physical and psychological environment and the right to an educational program which is individually designed to meet their needs. Furthermore, the court ruled that these individuals have the right to receive this treatment in the "least restrictive" setting—in the community or a public school, rather than in an institution.

The Supreme Court decision in the case of *Lau* v. *Nichols* (1974) was that the San Francisco schools' failure to provide Chinese-speaking students with an education in Chinese or instruction in the use of the English language, was a violation under the Civil Rights Act of 1964. Equal treatment of unequals, said the Court, did not result, in this case, in equal protection, and an appropriate program should be made available to the Chinese children.

The problem of misclassification, which is very critical to programming for the mildly handicapped, is related to the criteria or standards used to determine special education placement and, therefore, to due process. Two California cases illustrate this issue as it relates to the placement of minority group children. The background for these cases is the demonstrated overrepresentation (meaning more highly represented in special classes than would be expected based on population statistics) of black and Chicano students in special classes. Many of these children are so placed on the basis of their scores on IQ tests designed for the white middle-class culture.

Beginning with the cases of *Diana* v. *State Board of Education* (1970) and *Larry P.* v. *Riles* (1972—has not yet reached final settlement), and followed by similar suits in other states, the courts have ruled: against the use of group IQ tests; against the use of tests which are biased or culturally inappropriate for the child being tested; that children be tested in their primary language; that black children may not be placed in classes for the retarded on the basis of currently used IQ test scores; and that students may not be assigned to special education without parental consent.

In both *Diana* and *Larry P.,* the legal arguments centered around the equal protection and due process provisions of the Fourteenth Amendment. As noted earlier, *PARC* and *Mills* cases also relate to the right to due process of law. Due process, as stated in the definition given in Figure 3, provides individuals with the right to question official decisions. It is a tool for keeping officials accountable for their actions. Procedural protection, also listed in Figure 3, must now be afforded to handicapped students and their parents whenever special education placement is being considered. The procedure typically begins with the requirement that parents be notified that an assessment of their child's performance is going to be made by the school.

In summary, the courts have taken the position that the burden of proof rests with the school system to demonstrate that the exclusion of a child from participation with his/her peers in the educational mainstream is in the child's best interests and is not a violation of his/her personal rights. Specifically, schools have been required to conform to certain standards regarding the ethnic balance of students in special programs, to refrain from placing black children in classes for the retarded on the basis of current IQ test scores, and to ensure due process of law in placement decisions.

Legislation

At both the state and the federal levels, legislation has recently been enacted which attempts to remedy the problems of exclusion, inappropriate programming, and misclassification, and which, therefore, contributes to the rise of mainstreaming. For example, between the years of 1969 and 1972 in California, a succession of legislative enactments which followed court mandates led to the reduction of registration in classes for the educable mentally retarded (EMR) within the state by over 11,000 cases. This reduction was based, not on educational need, but on legislated changes in the guidelines for cutoff IQ scores for admission to EMR programs. Most of the decertified EMR students were returned to regular classes. Most received, at least on a limited basis, "transition" assistance in the form of resource teachers or aides. Meyers et al. (1975), in a document entitled *Correlates of Success in Transition of MR to Regular Class,* report on a large-scale project to investigate the current status of these decertified EMR students and to compare them with both normal peers and nondecertified EMR students. The report of Meyers et al. should be required reading for all educators responsible for, or involved in, mainstreaming of the mildly handicapped. It revealed that achievement scores of the average decertified student were below those of his/her matched "normal" classmates of the same sex and ethnicity, but *above* EMR students of the same age, sex, and ethnicity. The decertified students did not become "average" students, but in the words of the researchers:

As an appraisal of mainstreaming, then, via the study of the transition program, we are able only to state that mainstreaming of these former EMR students did indeed work by the criterion that there were not wholesale droppings out of school. . . . By the criteria of achievement measures and marks awarded by teachers, the students were apparently surviving and learning nearly as well as the never-segregated regular class match cases. In that sense, whatever was done had to be deemed successful; one must keep in mind that some D [decertified] students had experienced no transition help at all, and perhaps some did not need it (p. 181).

Numerous examples of legislation calling for mainstreaming of handicapped students are found in state statutes which, in recent years, have become comprehensive in defining eligibility requirements, listing the range of educational services to be provided, and requiring due process procedures.

The following examples of state laws and practices typify this trend:

1. *California* Assembly Bill No. 4040 (1974) creates pilot comprehensive programs to serve all individuals with exceptional needs; mandates due process safeguards; and provides that special services be offered in programs which promote maximum interaction with the general school population.
2. *Massachusetts* Chapter 766 (1972), which became effective in September 1974, places a major emphasis on mainstreaming and requires that individual programs for students with special needs be aimed toward maximum integration.
3. *Michigan* Public Act 198 (1971) requires that specific individualized instructional plans for handicapped students be designed on the basis of assessed needs, and that special classes must be operated in regular schools. This Act also specifies parent rights and due process safeguards.
4. *Washington* Special Education Code WAC 392–45 (1974) specifies various placement options for special students, ranging from regular to self-contained classes, and including intermediate levels such as regular class combined with resource room support. Due process procedures and parent involvement are required.
5. *Texas* Senate Bill 230 (1971) provided the impetus for the adoption, by the State Department of Education, of regulations which allow alternatives for allocating funds for special education; incentives for mainstreaming are built in. The Texas plan provides a continuum of services to handicapped students including resource rooms and diagnostic classrooms.

Special education legislation, similar to that cited above, can be found in the statutes of many other states. It is interesting to note that the period of expansion and revision of state laws regarding the education of the handicapped corresponds with the beginning of the litigative movement described earlier.

The third and last legislative attempt to improve the nature and quality of services to handicapped children which we will report here is Public Law 94–142, the "Education for all Handicapped Children Act," signed by President Ford in November 1975. This Act establishes a formula for federal funding to state education agencies and allows substantial "pass-through" of federal monies to local school districts, provided all requirements are met. Public Law 94–142 makes a number of critical stipulations which must be adhered to by *both* the state and its local school districts if they are to receive funds under this Act. These stipulations include:

assurance of extensive child identification procedures;

assurance of "full service" goal and detailed timetable;

a guarantee of complete due process procedures;

the assurance of regular parent or guardian consultation;

maintenance of programs and procedures for comprehensive personnel development including in-service training;

assurance of special education being provided to all handicapped children in the "least restrictive" environment;

assurance of nondiscriminatory testing and evaluation;

a guarantee of policies and procedures to protect the confidentiality of data and information;

assurance of the maintenance of an individualized program for all handicapped children;

assurance of an effective policy guaranteeing the right of all handicapped children to a free, appropriate public education, *at no cost* to parents or guardian;

assurance of a surrogate to act for any child when parents or guardians are either unknown or unavailable, or when said child is a legal ward of the state (Council for Exceptional Children, 1976, p. 4).

With regard to the "least restrictive alternative," this Act specifically requires the states to establish:

procedures to assure that, to the maximum extent appropriate, handicapped children, including children in private or public institutions or other care facilities, are educated with children who are not handicapped, and that special classes, separate schooling, or other removal of handicapped children from the regular educational environment occurs only when the nature or severity of the handicap is such that education in regular classes with the use of supplementary aids and services cannot be achieved satisfactorily [Sec. 612, D (5)].

In conclusion, it is clear that mainstreaming, or placement in the "least restrictive alternative," is no longer a service option to be implemented in selected school districts at the determination of certain administrators. Placement in the least restrictive environment is a legal mandate.

Resource Programs and Training Models

The preceding discussion has provided a framework within which to examine the process of mainstreaming as well as a historical perspective and review of the major issues, both philosophical and legal, involved in this new special education delivery system. With the emphasis on providing special education services to the mildly handicapped *within* the regular school program came the need for a new kind of special educator, and a new special education service—the resource teacher and the resource program. At this point it seems appropriate to discuss some of the characteristics of resource programs and training models which have been developed and implemented across the country in response to the challenge of improving the interface between regular and special education.

Resource Programs

Resource programs have developed rapidly in response to the trend towards keeping mildly handicapped students in the mainstream. Jenkins and Mayhall (1973) have observed that various programs seem to differ along at least three dimensions:

1. Direct versus indirect service by resource teachers;
2. Ability versus skill (diagnostic-prescriptive) orientation;
3. Resident versus itinerant delivery of resource-teacher services.

The dimensions that resource programs seem to have in common, again in the perception of Jenkins and Mayhall, are:

1. Identified criterion performance—success of a program is how well it helps the handicapped remain in the mainstream;
2. Daily instruction and assessment—continuous objective feedback;
3. Individual instruction;
4. Management of individual programs—peer and cross-age tutors.

The direct or indirect services dimension of resource programs relates to the percentage of time the resource teacher, usually a special education teacher with advanced training, spends instructing students, as opposed to the amount of time spent consulting with and training regular class teachers. Advantages of the latter approach are discussed more fully later in this chapter. The skill versus ability distinction is perhaps less obvious and should be explained before examining the specifics of the resource program. In *skill*-oriented programs, educational prescriptions "are based on a task analytic diagnosis of skills and subskills" (Jenkins and Mayhall, 1973, p. 35); the focus is on basic school tasks such as reading and arithmetic. Differential psychological diagnosis is the basis for *ability*-oriented programs; the emphasis here is on perceptual, motor, and psycholinguistic abilities—sometimes called central processing mechanisms.

Putting philosophical orientation aside for the moment, let's examine the rationale and implementation of resource programs more closely. Sabatino (1972) calls resource rooms the "renaissance in special education" since they represent a first step toward facilitating team effort in the education of the handicapped. Hammill and Wiederholt (1972) see the resource room as providing a middle path between the nearly exclusive reliance on special classes and their complete disbandonment. They define a resource room basically as "any instructional setting to which a child comes for specified periods of time, usually on a regularly scheduled basis" (p. 13). A project currently being implemented in South Carolina (Region V, Educational Services Center, 1975) describes the resource room as "a classroom designed for diagnosis and remediation of mildly handicapped students," and a place where the student can "enjoy being ordinary—not exceptional" (p. xi). Since the resource program is within the local school, it is most often the classroom teacher who determines a particular student's need for such services, although in secondary level programs students may be self-identified. The goal of the resource program is to provide needed instructional support to the student and his/her teacher so that the student can continue to grow educationally and personally in the mainstream.

Though resource rooms have been established on a categorical basis, to serve only emotionally disturbed students, for example, Hammill and Wiederholt (1972) advocate their implementation on a noncategorical basis; in this way, most of the children in the school who need help may be served and the effects of labeling or classifying are reduced. These authors list fourteen advantages of resource programs:

1. Pupils can benefit from specific resource room training while remaining *integrated* with their friends and age-mates in school.
2. Pupils have the advantages of a *total remedial program,* which is prepared by the resource teacher but may be implemented in cooperation with the regular class teacher.
3. Resource rooms are *less expensive* to operate than tutoring, remedial reading, and special class programs.

4. More children can be served under the resource room arrangement than can be served by the present system.

5. Since the resource teacher is assigned to a particular school, he is less likely than the school psychologist, remedial reading therapist, speech correctionist, or other itinerant staff to be viewed as an "outsider" by the other teachers in the school.

6. Because young children with mild, though developing, problems can be accommodated, later severe disorders can be *prevented.*

7. Because disability diagnoses are not necessary for placement purposes, pupils are *not labeled* in any way as handicapped.

8. Because labeling and segregation are avoided, the stigma invariably associated with receiving special attention is *minimized.*

9. Since most elementary schools are large enough to accommodate one or more resource rooms, pupils can receive help in their neighborhood school; thus the necessity of busing "handicapped" children across the town or county to a school housing an "appropriately labeled" class or resource room is eliminated or minimized.

10. Pupils are the recipients of flexible scheduling in that remediation can be applied entirely in their classrooms by the regular teacher with some resource teacher support or in the resource room itself when necessary; also, the schedule can be quickly altered to meet the children's changing situations and needs.

11. Because placement in the resource room is an individual school matter, involving the principal, the teachers, and the parents, *no appreciable time lapse* need occur between the teacher's referral and the initiation of special services for the child.

12. Under this alternative, medical and psychological work-ups are done only on the school's request rather than on a screening-for-placement basis; thus the school psychologist is freed to do the work he was trained to do instead of being relegated to the role of psychometrist.

13. Since the resource room will absorb most of the "handicapped" children in the schools, the special classes will increasingly become instructional settings for "truly" handicapped pupils, i.e., the children for whom the classes were originally intended.

14. Because of the resource teacher's broad training and experience with many children exhibiting different educational and behavioral problems and varying maturational levels, he is likely to become an "in-house" consultant to his school (pp. 35–37).

Along with all of the above positive features of resource programs, there are some problem areas. These include:

1. Complexity of scheduling junior high and high school students into the program.
2. Lack of sufficient articulation between instruction in the resource room and in the regular classroom.
3. The role of the resource teacher in assessment which may be perceived negatively by school psychologists.
4. Efficient student use of the resource room (homogeneous grouping of students throughout the day can help).
5. Resistance of regular class teachers and/or lack of administrative support.

Most of these problems can be minimized through intensive, relevant professional development programs and through consultation and support provided by skilled resource teachers. Approaches to professional development are reviewed below. Skills and techniques related to the consultative role of the resource teacher are discussed in depth in Chapter Five.

Changing the System by Changing the Teachers: Approaches to Professional Development

Several articles have been written on models for professional training, at both the pre- and inservice levels, necessary for the successful implementation of mainstreaming programs. A critical need is support for the regular class teacher who will carry the major responsibility for mainstreaming. The following review is presented as a backdrop for the descriptions of specific mainstreaming implementation models which are presented at the end of this chapter. All three of the training models described focus on the consultative role of the special educator.

Lilly (1971), along with the "zero reject" concept described earlier, also proposed a training-based services model wherein special educators would function in a supportive role to regular teachers. Special educators, called instructional specialists, would provide these teachers with the necessary training to be self-sufficient—to be able to handle problem learners. These specialists would be available, upon request, to serve teachers who refer problem situations and would instruct the teachers in how to handle behavioral and academic problems in their classes. The instructional specialist's job would be to change the behavior of teachers—not to work directly with students. The instructional specialist would be skilled in educational diagnosis, individual and small group instruction, and behavior management techniques; and would act as a knowledgeable colleague of regular class teachers within a school.

Shaw and Shaw (1973) take Lilly's approach further, proposing a teacher-centered inservice program which focuses on those aspects of the teacher's classroom which she/he considers inadequate. Thus inservice would be, first, at the teacher's request, and, second, related to specific teacher needs. These authors see the teacher and instructional specialist working very closely together on any or all of the following: pinpointing the problem; designing problem solutions; implementation; and evaluation. The teacher would actually experience the diagnostic-prescriptive process and begin to transfer learned skills to his/her work with other students, as opposed to merely being the recipient and implementor of an educational prescription prepared by an "expert." Acceptance of the instructional specialist would increase as the immediate usefulness of the inservice experience became apparent (satisfied teachers) and regular teachers would gradually become more self-sufficient in meeting the needs of handicapped students in their program.

Shaw and Shaw (1973, p. 65) emphasize that the validity of such an inservice strategy rests on three assumptions or conditions which must be present:

1. teachers can change their teaching behavior;
2. they can become self-sufficient in teaching the basic skills;
3. they want to be competent in these areas.

A systematic application of Lilly's training-based services approach is seen in the work of Cartwright and Cartwright (1972); Cartwright, Cartwright, and Ysseldyke (1973); and Ward, Cartwright, Cartwright, Campbell and Spinazola (1973). These authors propose two decision models—an identification model and a diagnostic teaching model—which can be followed by regular teachers, in consultation with special educators, to identify mildly handicapped students and to provide services to these children within the educational mainstream. The identification model specifies the competencies the teacher needs in order to be able to make informed decisions about students in his/her class: whether or not to request assistance from the special educator in order to maintain the student in regular class, or to refer the student for an alternative placement. The diagnostic teaching model specifies eight competencies: identify relevant attributes of the learner; specify learning objectives; select instructional strategies; select instructional materials; test the strategies and materials with students; evaluate performance; determine if the goal was met; and, if so, select the next goal and repeat the sequence. This model can be used to train instructional specialists to provide regular teachers with the skills to handle learning problems in their own classes.

Notice that all of the above approaches to professional development are primarily aimed at extending the skills of the regular teacher so that the instructional responsibility for mildly handicapped students remains with that teacher. Removal of the handicapped student from the regular class to the resource room without concurrent consultation, support, and training for the student's regular teacher does nothing to prepare the regular teacher to become more effective in meeting the needs of that particular student or of other similar students in the future.

As Mann (1974) states, "training programs must be child-centered, humanistic, individualized, and task oriented" (p. 43). We hope in this book to provide a basis for the design of such training. We share with Hammill and Wiederholt (1972) the belief that:

> The argument that regular class teachers do not have the skills and materials necessary to teach mild to moderately involved children is a folklore of special education that can easily be refuted by providing the teacher with some basic information (p. 39).

Required competencies and behaviors for *both* resource teachers and regular teachers who work with the mildly handicapped within the mainstream include:

1. Demonstrating positive attitudes toward the handicapped;
2. Participating in a team approach to identification and remediation;
3. Conducting systematic behavior observations and classroom screening;
4. Using behavioral and task analysis to assess learner behaviors;
5. Planning individualized instructional programs which include a broad range of instructional strategies and techniques;
6. Evaluating learning outcomes.

In addition, resource teachers will require training in effective communication skills. It is the intent of this book to help teachers acquire these competencies.

Success Strategies for Mainstreaming

The following list of success strategies is presented for consideration by educators who are interested in designing or participating in programs to change the future of the educational experience for all children:

1. Take into account the power structure of the total educational system.
2. Create administrative arrangements and staffing patterns which permit communication and interface between regular and special educators at all levels.
3. Enlist the support of building administrators; build their role as change agents and educational leaders.

4. Employ personnel from the educational mainstream as supervisors and coordinators of new programs to provide special education services.
5. Focus on external variables in the system or in the learning environment which can be changed, not on "defects" in the students.
6. Design programs which allow exceptional pupils to really participate in the instructional and social activities of the mainstream.
7. Remember that the degree to which all exceptional children can be integrated is more a function of adaptability of the curriculum, instructional materials, and teaching procedures than of handicap.
8. Allow the regular and special education staff to cooperatively design and make decisions on local policies and procedures for mainstreaming. They will have an investment in its success.
9. Do a needs assessment prior to initiating inservice.
10. Use creative, innovative faculty members for leaders in building-level inservice programs.
11. Give the school staff a detailed description of how the mainstreaming program will work. *Before* the program begins, handle concerns of both regular and special educators, such as, "How will my professional responsibilities change?"
12. Give regular teachers inservice *before* you give them the exceptional students. Help them understand that handicapped students will only be placed in their class with their full understanding and agreement.
13. Build the confidence and competence of the regular class teachers so that they do not greet the atypical learner with rejection.
14. Remember that the regular class teachers will be more willing to accept handicapped students when they know that they will get support and that they can also refer nonhandicapped pupils with learning problems.
15. Provide help with the social and emotional development of exceptional children to insure that these students will be better accepted by the regular teacher and ready for academic instruction in the mainstream.
16. Keep the *responsibility* for the education of children with learning disabilities with the regular class teacher.
17. Alert teachers to the value of early detection and prevention of learning problems.
18. Make the teacher a central member of the treatment team.
19. Improve the capacity of the regular teachers to provide for the diversity of children's needs by showing them effective ways to individualize instruction.
20. Be aware that the attitudes of special educators toward mainstreaming influence the reactions of regular educators.
21. Encourage resource persons to at all times take into account the student's "real world" of the regular classroom.

22. Provide opportunities for cross-fertilization—for teachers to share, exchange ideas, and visit other classrooms within and across school district boundaries.
23. Make record keeping, monitoring of pupil progress, and reporting of program results as simple as possible—communication will be enhanced!

Abstracts of Mainstreaming Programs and Training Models

Without exception, the following resource programs and training models are based on the premise that, "Master teachers are at the heart of an effective program for children with mild to moderate learning difficulties—master teachers skilled at educational diagnosis and creative in designing and carrying out interventions to remediate the problems that exist" (Dunn, 1968, p. 15). Some of the programs described below focus on the preparation of noncategorical special educators whose primary function is to consult with regular class teachers; some concentrate on resource teacher models; and still others deal with strategies for changing the structure of the educational system. All of the models described have, of course, many overlapping characteristics. Their point of divergence is along the dimension of direct versus indirect service to children. Program descriptions are drawn from the following sources; a source code letter appears with each, and full bibliographic data appear in the references section of this chapter. (*A*) Birch, J. W. (1974); (*B*) Deno, E. (1973); (*C*) Mann, P. H. (1974); (*D*) South Carolina, Region V Educational Services Center (1975).

CARE (Computer Assisted Renewal Education, Pennsylvania State University) (*C*)

This program is based in a mobile unit which is used for training regular teachers. The computer assisted graduate level courses are: CARE 1, which emphasizes training skills in identification and screening for handicapped in early grades; CARE 2 and 3, which are designed to train regular teachers to work with learning disabled children (Diagnosis and Prescription) and include specifying objectives, and selecting materials; and CARE 4, Education of the Visually Handicapped.

Consulting Teacher Program (Vermont) (*B,C*)

Consulting teachers are trained in a two year course in behavior theory, individualized instruction, practicum, training, and consulting methods. Regular teachers are trained by consulting teachers to define and measure behaviors, specify objectives, and implement and evaluate. They are trained also in teaching/learning procedures.

Diagnostic Prescriptive Teacher (DPT) Program (The George Washington University) *(B)*

The DPT is a specially trained, school-based special educator who serves as educational diagnostician—consultant to regular class teachers in an effort to improve their capacity to provide, within the mainstream, for the diversity of children's needs. These persons also work cooperatively with other ancillary specialists but do not provide direct services to students.

General Special Education Resource Teacher Model (The Seward University Project, Minneapolis) *(B)*

This model operates in a single elementary school to develop flexible, integrated, and cross-categorical special education services. Using a resource system approach, Special Education Resource Teachers (SERTs) develop and evaluate individualized programs for exceptional children in regular classes. Students spend a minimum amount of time in resource room activities, such as tutoring. SERTs coordinate the assessment process and develop program modifications. Direct instruction and program management is quickly turned over to the regular teacher or paraprofessional. SERTs continue to monitor student progress. The professional education component (pre and inservice) includes a resource teaching practicum which is cross-categorical. Emphasis is placed on observing and diagnosing a student's performance within the curriculum areas of the mainstream.

Harrison School Center (University of Minnesota and Minneapolis Public Schools) *(B)*

This is a program to develop mainstream placement alternatives for elementary EMR students and to train teachers to function in a variety of service delivery settings including a resource program setting. Learning-disabled and hearing-impaired children are included in the Resource Center, which serves as the training base. Resource and regular teachers participate in a team approach to assessment and prescription and resource teachers provide support to the teachers who maintain the children in regular classes for the major portion of the day. Student trainees are assigned to the Resource Center where they prepare individualized programs for their caseload. Students are trained in diagnostic techniques, instruction by objectives, remedial instruction, behavior management, and consultative skills. This cooperative program has resulted in a significant reduction in special classes in the Minneapolis schools.

Houston Plan (Houston, Texas) *(B,C)*

Under this plan, regular teachers are retrained in Teacher Development Centers in the areas of applied behavior analysis, learning centers, peer and cross age tutoring, strategies for individualized instruction, and continuous progress curricula. The focus of change is on the program regularities of the main system. Precision Learning Centers in elementary schools provide high intensity support service for teachers and all types of students. The plan is designed to bring about major, long term, system-wide change.

Kanawha County, West Virginia (A)

In 1971 the consultant for EMR classes formally proposed a mainstreaming plan. The proposal was accepted and supported at the top administrative levels. Selected elementary schools were involved in the initial stages. Later these project schools disseminated information on mainstreaming and helped faculties identify problems and potential solutions. Teacher-to-teacher inservice sessions at the local level are encouraged. Instructional sequences and curriculum materials for regular and special pupils are now integrated into learning packages which teachers may use as the basis for instruction. Some integration of pupils is now taking place at the secondary level also.

Learning Problems Approach (University of Miami) *(B)*

Regular class teachers participate with special education teachers and students in a one-year program based on a learning problems or task analysis approach to teaching children with learning disabilities. Regular teachers are trained in educational diagnosis and remediation and as trainers of other teachers; special education teachers graduate as resource teachers. The program has had great impact on local school systems where trainees function as change agents, demonstrating that the needs of the exceptional learner *can* be met within the mainstream system.

Louisville, Kentucky (A)

In 1972 the Kentucky Department of Education authorized a Resource Room for EMR students and Louisville began ·to move ahead rapidly. At the secondary level, EMR pupils are intermingled with other pupils on class rolls. Individual schedules are based on pupils' strengths and weaknesses. Special teachers work with EMR pupils on instructional tasks designed to meet their needs. The mainstreaming plan was introduced during a system-wide inservice session and the support of all the teachers and principals involved was obtained prior to initiating changes in a few school sites. Gradually other schools indicated an interest in converting their programs to a mainstreamed plan. One result is that regular and special teachers have learned to appreciate each other's strengths and limitations and there is greater rapport between the two groups.

Plano, Texas (A)

In all elementary schools, special education teachers are members of teaching teams covering two or more grades. The majority of the district's EMR pupils now receive special education support within the mainstream; other types of handicapped pupils are also integrated. Teachers describe students in terms of their educational needs and strengths—not in terms of labels. A team approach is used in making a psychoeducational study of the child. A "lead" teacher functions on each campus as head of the special education teachers and divides his/her time between indirect teaching of children and consulting and assessment activities. Each grade grouping of regular teachers also is headed by a "lead" teacher. Early identification of handicapped children is emphasized; services are available for three-, four-, and five-year-olds. Resource rooms have been established in junior and senior high schools.

Portland Public Schools' Prescriptive Education Program (C)

A multidisciplinary approach provides services to children with learning and behavior problems. Teachers are central members of the treatment team. Efforts are made to tailor each student's program to his/her needs.

Richardson, Texas (A)

Special education services are decentralized and building administrators have control over resources; thus they assume responsibility for arranging educational programs for all children in their school—handicapped or not. Staff development funds are divided equitably across regular and special education. Each school has an assessment and placement committee. Four instructional arrangements can be made for handicapped pupils; only one of these is special class placement. Regular teachers request assistance from special education teachers. Teacher acceptance of mainstreaming has increased over the years since the plan was initiated in 1969. Special and regular education have also merged at the administrative level.

South Carolina (D)

A federally funded program at the Educational Services Center, Region V, Lancaster, South Carolina, implements a resource room model for learning disabled students. The purpose of the program is to return children to the regular class on a full-time basis. Students from regular classes are scheduled into the resource room for specific training or remedial instruction during the day. Referrals are made primarily by regular teachers. Comprehensive inservice programs are provided for teachers.

Stratistician Model (Rocky Mountain Regional Resource Center, University of Utah) *(B)*

Stratisticians are special educators trained to function as resource persons to regular teachers. Operating within selected schools, these persons respond to teacher requests for diagnosis and remediation of problem behaviors. Their services to teachers include class screening; observation; program and curriculum evaluation; design of educational interventions; and program planning. Additional support in the form of workshops, information, and consultation is provided by the Regional Resource Center. Teachers in participating schools receive orientation prior to the beginning of school.

Tacoma, Washington (A)

This city began mainstreaming in 1958, and today special and regular education are functionally merged. Regular teachers accept the responsibility for handicapped students and receive help, as needed, from special education and support personnel. Inservice for faculty is provided through the Micro-College. Professionals from the mainstream are employed by special education leaders as supervisors and program coordinators, demonstrating a commitment to blending the two systems.

Tucson, Arizona (A)

Mainstreaming began in 1969, and in 1970 special education was reorganized and named Adaptive Education. EMR students are programmed into regular classes for part of the day, receiving remedial help from special teachers. Resource rooms are available at both the elementary and secondary levels. Self-contained classes maintain a small percentage of EMR students who are not able to be integrated. Prior to the move toward mainstreaming, the help of regular teachers was enlisted, special teachers were prepared for a change in role, and the administration was involved. Close contact with parents, through personal conferences and letters is a salient feature of Tucson's program. Parents and teachers appear to be extremely supportive.

Study Questions and Activities

1. Mrs. Haverford, a sixth grade teacher for 12 years, rushes into the teacher's lounge and says, "I just heard the district is going to return all handicapped children to regular classes next fall. How can we possibly cope with the handicapped in addition to our regular 35 pupils?" Provide Mrs. Haverford with a more realistic explanation of mainstreaming than she has apparently been given. Role play your interaction with Mrs. Haverford until you, your instructor, and your student colleagues are satisfied with your explanation.
2. Discuss the assumptions underlying traditional segregated placement of the mildly handicapped. How do these assumptions differ from those underlying the mainstreaming models presented in Chapter One? (See

the description of Deno's "cascade" model, and the Van Etten and Adamson "fail-save" model in Chapter One.)

3. Kaufman (1975) and his colleagues see "instructional integration" as a more critical component of mainstreaming than "temporal integration." What do they mean by "instructional integration"? What are the implications of such integration for the regular classroom if instruction is to serve *both* regular and special pupils?

4. Visit a neighboring school district. Interview the director of special education and outline the special services provided for the mildly, moderately, and severely handicapped. Compare these services to the continuum of services described in Chapter One. (See the adaptation of Deno's "cascade" model and the "fail-save" model.) Identify any major gaps between the services offered and the services required under Public Law 94–142 for placement in the least restrictive alternative.

5. Visit a special education resource room operated by an experienced resource teacher. Ask permission to interview the teacher regarding the following: (1) criteria for placement of pupils in the resource program; (2) assessment of pupils for instructional planning; (3) coordination of instructional planning and evaluation with the pupil's regular teacher and parents; (4) consultation and/or inservice training provided regular teachers regarding learning and behavior problems; (5) reevaluation and placement of pupils following one year in the resource program; and (6) the attitude of regular teachers and parents toward the resource program.

References

Abeson, A., Burgdorf, R. L., Casey, P. J., Kunz, J. W., & McNeil, W. Access to opportunity. In N. Hobbs (Ed.), *Issues in the classification of children* (Vol. II). San Francisco: Jossey-Bass, 1975, 270–292.

Beery, K. (Ed.). *Models for mainstreaming*. Sioux Falls, South Dakota: Dimensions (division of Adapt Press), 1972.

Birch, J. W. *Mainstreaming: Educable mentally retarded children in regular classes.* Reston, Va.: The Council for Exceptional Children, 1974.

Brown v. *Board of Education*, 347 US 483, 493; 74 S Ct 686; 98 L Ed 873 (1954).

California State Legislature, Assembly Bill No. 4040, August 1974.

Cartwright, G. P., & Cartwright, C. A. Gilding the lilly: Comments on the training based model. *Exceptional Children*, 1972, *39* (3), 231–234.

Cartwright, G. P., Cartwright, C. A., & Ysseldyke, J. E. Two decision models: Identification and diagnostic teaching of handicapped children in the regular classroom. *Psychology in the Schools*, 1973, *10* (1), 4–11.

Council for Exceptional Children. *The Education for All Handicapped Children Act: Public Law 94–142.* (Mimeo) Reston, Va.: Author, 1976.

Deno, E. Special education as developmental capital. *Exceptional Children*, 1970, *37* (3), 229–237.

Deno, E. (Ed.). *Instructional alternatives for exceptional children.* Reston, Va.: The Council for Exceptional Children, 1973.

Diana v. California State Board of Education, Civil Action No. C–70–37 RFP (ND Cal 1970).

Dunn, L. M. Special education for the mildly retarded—Is much of it justified? *Exceptional Children,* 1968, *35* (1), 5–21.

Gilhool, T. K. Education: An inalienable right. In F. J. Weintraub, A. Abeson, J. Ballard, & M. L. LaVor (Eds.), *Public policy and the education of exceptional children.* Reston, Va.: The Council for Exceptional Children, 1976.

Hammill, D., & Wiederholt, J. L. *The resource room: Rationale and implementation.* Philadelphia, Pa.: Buttonwood Farms, 1972.

Hobbs, N. (Ed.). *Issues in the classification of children* (Vols. I & II). San Francisco: Jossey-Bass, 1975.

Jenkins, J. R., & Mayhall, W. F. Describing resource teacher programs. *Exceptional Children,* 1973, *40* (1), 35–36.

Johnson, G. O. Special education for the mentally handicapped—A paradox. *Exceptional Children,* 1962, *29* (2), 62–69.

Johnson, R. A. Model for alternative programming: A perspective. In E. Meyen et al. (Eds.), *Alternatives for teaching exceptional children.* Denver: Love Publishing, 1975.

Kaufman, M. J., Gottlieb, J., Agard, J. A., & Kubic, M. B. Mainstreaming: Toward an explication of the concept. *Focus on Exceptional Children,* 1975, *7* (3), 1–12.

Kreinberg, N., & Chow, S.H.L. (Eds.), *Configurations of change: The integration of mildly handicapped children into the regular classroom.* Sioux Falls, S.D. Adapt Press, 1973.

Larry P. v. *Riles,* Civil Action No. 71–2270; 343 F Supp 1306 (ND Cal 1972).

Lau v. *Nichols,* 94 S Ct 786 (1974).

Lilly, M. S. Special education; A teapot in a tempest. *Exceptional Children,* 1970, *37* (1), 43–49.

Lilly, M. S. A training based model for special education. *Exceptional Children,* 1971, *37* (10), 745–749.

MacMillan, D. L. Special education for the mildly retarded: Servant or savant. *Focus on Exceptional Children,* 1971, *2* (1), 1–11.

Mann, P. H. (Ed.). *Mainstream special education: Issues and perspectives in urban centers.* Reston, Va.: The Council for Exceptional Children, 1974.

Massachusetts State Legislature 1972. Ch. 766 approved July 17, 1972; incorporated in Massachusetts State Laws, Title II, Chapter 15, Sec. IM–IQ.

McClung, M. The legal rights of handicapped school children. *Educational Horizons,* 1975, *54* (1), 25–32.

Meisgeier, C. H., & Perez, F. I. An integrated behavioral–systems model of accountability for education. In N. Kreinberg & S.H.L. Chow (Eds.), *Configurations of change: The integration of mildly handicapped children into the regular classroom.* Sioux Falls, S.D.: Adapt Press, 1973.

Meyers, C. E., MacMillan, D. L., & Yoshida, R. K. *Correlates of success in transition of MR to regular class.* Final Report, Grant No. OEG–0–73–5263, U.S. Office of Education, Bureau of Education for the Handicapped, Nov. 1975.

Michigan State Department of Education, *Special Education Code* (under the provisions of Public Act 198 of 1971), Lansing, 1973.

Michigan State Legislature, Public Act No. 198 (House Bill No. 4475), Lansing, 1971.

Mills v. *Board of Education of the District of Columbia,* Civil Action No. 1939–71; 348 F Supp 866; (DC Cir 1972).

Molloy, L. *One out of ten: School planning for the handicapped.* New York: Educational Facilities Laboratories, 1974.

Pennsylvania Association for Retarded Children v. *Commonwealth of Pennsylvania,* Civil Action No. 71–42; 343 F Supp 279 (ED Pa 1972).

Rubino, T. J., Gallagher, N., Scelza, C., & Toker, A. *Learning disabilities teacher-consultant handbook.* Trenton, N.J.: New Jersey State Department of Education, 1974.

Sabatino, D. Resource rooms: The renaissance in special education. *Journal of Special Education,* 1972, *6* (4), 335–347.

Shaw, S. F., & Shaw, W. The inservice experience plan: Changing the bath without losing the baby. In Evelyn N. Deno, *Instructional alternatives for exceptional children.* Reston, Va.: The Council for Exceptional Children, 1973.

South Carolina Region V. Education Services Center. *The resource room: An access to excellence.* Lancaster, S.C.: South Carolina Region V Education Services Center, 1975.

Texas Education Code, Chapter 16 Foundation School Program, Subchapter C. Professional Units, Subsection 1616 Comprehensive Special Education Program for Exceptional Children. Austin, Tex.: Texas Education Agency, 1971.

United States Public Law, P.L. 94–142, *Education for All Handicapped Children Act,* 1975.

Van Etten, G., & Adamson, G. The fail-save program: A special education service continuum. In Evelyn N. Deno (Ed.), *Instructional alternatives for exceptional children.* Reston, Va.: The Council for Exceptional Children, 1973.

Ward, M. E., Cartwright, G. P., Cartwright, C. A., Campbell, J., and Spinazola, C. *Diagnostic teaching of preschool and primary children.* University Park, Pa.: Pennsylvania State University, 1973.

Washington State Administrative Code. Chapter 392–45: Special Education Program for Children with Handicapping Conditions, 1974.

Weintraub, F. J., Abeson, A., Ballard, J., & La Vor, M. L. *Public policy and the education of exceptional children.* Reston, Va.: The Council for Exceptional Children, 1976.

Wyatt v. *Stickney,* 344 F Supp 387 (MD Ala 1971).

Resources

Abeson, A. A., Bolick, N., Hass, J., *A primer on due process*. Reston, Va.:
The Council for Exceptional Children, 1975. Details the rights of children
and parents in the educational decision-making process.

Council for Exceptional Children. *PL 94–142: The Education for All Handicapped Children Act*. Reston, Va.: Council for Exceptional Children,
1976. Three filmstrips and accompanying tapes detailing PL 94–142: I,
"Introducing PL 94–142," hits the silent issues covered by PL 94–142, e.g.
labelling. II, "Coping with PL 94–142," concerns the legally binding
responsibilities of local and state educational agencies and the US Commis-
sioner of Education. III, "PL 94–142 Works for Children," covers parent
due process procedures and rights using three case study examples.

Gilhool, T. K. *The right to education*. Reston, Va.: Council for Exceptional
Children, 1973. A tape cassette of a speech providing an overview of
litigation relevant to the education and rights of exceptional children.

two

Identification and Referral

> If handicapped children can be identified while they are still young, it may be possible to prevent the occurrence of a more serious handicap later on. Handicapping conditions are usually cumulative; that is, if a child has an educational problem that goes unidentified, he is likely to fall farther and farther behind his peers in school. Eventually, his lack of progress will be obvious, but by then it may be too late for him to catch up (Cartwright and Cartwright, 1972b, p. 1).

The focus of this book is instructional programming for mildly and moderately handicapped students in regular classrooms. We are not talking about severely handicapped children whose problems are so obvious and so profound that they are unable to enter the mainstream when they begin school, though many of the techniques in this book are very effective with this group also. Rather, we are looking at two other populations of children:

1. those students who have been removed from regular programs and placed in special education because they are slow learners, have IQs below average, have not learned the basic skills, or are behavior problems; and

2. those students who are in the mainstream but who are potential candidates for special services.

With the first group, we are concerned with their preparation for successful reentry into mainstream education with adequate support services to insure growth; with the second, we are interested in demonstrating techniques for early identification, remediation, and continuance in regular education. Several authors—Cartwright and Cartwright (1972a); Cartwright, Cartwright, and Ysseldyke (1973); and Mann (1974)—assert that regular teachers must be sensitized to the need for early identification of learning problems and enabled to identify and assess the severity of such problems. When identifiable problems are beyond what can be successfully handled in the regular program, supportive services, such as a resource program, should be made available for further assessment, instructional planning, or both. For resource programs to be successful in meeting the needs of children and regular teachers, teachers will need to know how to identify learning problems and when to request additional help. The purpose of this chapter is to briefly review the learning characteristics of high risk students; to present some techniques for in-class identification and criteria for determining when to refer a child; and to suggest specific referral procedures and considerations. The relationship of the identification and referral phases to the total process of instructional programming is shown in Figure 4. The content of this chapter is primarily addressed to regular teachers and resource teachers. The chance for early identification and remediation rests with these people.

Characteristics of Children with Learning Problems

Children are constantly generating behavioral data in the classroom which, when precisely observed and effectively used, can enable us to detect deviations that are, or may become, learning handicaps. There are two basic determiners of what constitutes a learning problem: (a) the extent to which the child's behavior deviates from what may be considered "normal" or typical for children of his/her age or grade level; and (b) the teacher's tolerance for and ability to deal with behavioral and academic differences.

While it is beyond the scope of the book to present information on developmental stages and norms for various skill areas, several excellent resources on these topics are listed at the end of this chapter. Our emphasis here is on observable characteristics which may signal, or provide an initial description of, a learning problem which requires attention. Since identical behaviors may be demonstrated by children with different handicaps and a certain handicap may produce different behaviors in different children (Cartwright and Cartwright, 1972b), we are of the opinion that knowing the etiology of a problem does not necessarily facilitate effective instructional planning. Therefore, we have not organized the information on characteristic problems according to the traditional categories of handicap. It should also be noted that one child may display one or more of these characteristics and not require special services, while another child may. Finally, many children with potential or actual learning problems display various combinations of the characteristics which follow. Hewett and Forness (1974) have observed that:

> The normal child succeeds in school because he looks and listens, readily tries, follows established routines, has learned about the physical properties of the environment, gains the approval of others, and acquires knowledge and skill. The exceptional child assumes his educational uniqueness because he falters along one or more of these behavioral dimensions (pp. 219–20).

Accordingly, the following sample problem behaviors are those primarily associated with the areas of information processing, storage and retrieval, language, perceptual-motor, speech, vision, hearing, and social-emotional functioning.

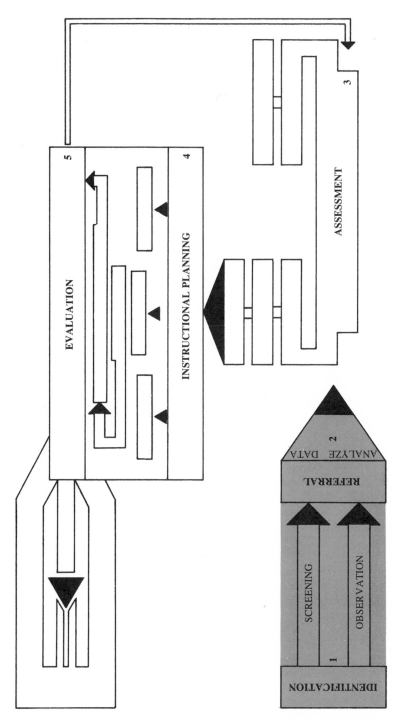

Figure 4. Instructional programming process.

1. Evidences of Information Processing, Storage, and Retrieval Problems*

slow rate of learning

level of learning is below age expectancy

forgets quickly

does not transfer a learned skill or concept to a new situation where it is also appropriate

performs concrete tasks better than abstract ones

does not profit from incidental learning

performs poorly on tasks related to verbal learning

has difficulty establishing a "learning set"—tackling problems in a systematic manner

2. Evidences of Language Problems

difficulty with verbal learning tasks—receptive and/or expressive

words often pronounced correctly in isolation, but incorrectly in sentences

words run together

unusual vocal rhythms or volume

speech problems (see Section 4): emphasis on gestural, rather than vocal expression

poor oral reading ability, but good comprehension of what is read

3. Evidences of Perceptual-Motor Problems

inability to correct errors spontaneously

reversals

awkward physically

inability to discriminate shapes, sizes (visual discrimination)

inability to differentiate sounds (auditory discrimination)

poor visual memory

poor auditory recall

poor handwriting

poor reader (reads one word at a time; loses place; skips words, lines, and so on)

difficulty with fine motor tasks

4. Evidences of Speech Problems

articulation errors (omissions, substitutions, distortions—as opposed to pronunciation)

stuttering

inappropriate pitch, loudness, quality of voice

non fluency

---

*Behavioral descriptors in sections 1–7 were adapted from Cartwright, C.P. and Cartwright, C.A., 1972b.

5. Evidences of Vision Problems

poor motor coordination, awkward
physical tension of the body
tilting head to one side
moving head excessively when reading
cries, becomes ill or feigns illness, is tense, unwilling to participate when
    called upon for tasks requiring good vision
unable to distinguish colors
physical abnormalities of eyes (crossed, red, swollen, drooping lids) when
    present over a long period of time and/or in combination

6. Evidences of Hearing Problems

frequently says "What?", "Pardon?"
speech problems
makes inappropriate or inconsistent responses
unusual concentration on speaker's face
shyness
bizarre or silly responses

7. Evidences of Social-Emotional Problems

bizarre or inappropriate responses occur frequently or consistently
short attention span
inconsistent behavior
loses control—fighting, temper tantrums
mood swings
hyper or overactive
lethargic
complains about health excessively
overreacts to fear or has irrational fears
delayed speech or speech problems
excessive verbalization
relates poorly to other children and/or adults
poor academic achievement
nail-biting, thumb-sucking, or facial twitching

It is obvious that the above categories are not mutually exclusive, nor are
they inclusive of all samples of problem behavior. Extreme caution should be
used in interpreting behavior. It is the frequency, intensity, and clustering of
discrete behaviors that provide evidence of a problem. The above lists are
intended only to *alert* you to potential learning problem areas. All of the
characteristics may be observed directly and systematically through the in-
depth observation techniques presented in Chapter Three.

Screening for Identification

Screening Process

Effective educational decision making depends on surveying all of the students in the class to identify those who display behaviors interfering with present learning (inattention, poor self-concept, inadequate study habits), as well as those students who are deficient in the basic skills (reading, math, social interaction) required for future learning. It is critical that the teacher routinely observe students in the classroom setting. The most effective procedure is to set up a continuous schedule whereby each student is evaluated every few weeks. The resource teacher should provide information and assistance to the classroom teacher in designing and using a screening process. Initial screening can be accomplished in two ways. One is through the use of systematic observation methods described in Chapter Three; the other is via the use of various screening devices described below. Screening provides a starting place for in-depth educational assessment. It is unlikely that more than one or two children will be screened out for further assessment at any one time.

Screening Techniques

Checklists and rating scales are the two most common approaches to educational screening. The teacher should be knowledgeable about the characteristics of both types of instruments so that the most appropriate screening tool may be selected. Checklists provide the maximum amount of observer structuring; the behaviors to be noticed are established at the time the checklist is constructed. The observer simply checks those items listed which are descriptive of a particular child. Note that checklists are necessarily limited to those specific aspects of behaviors upon which observers can readily agree. Brandt (1972) points out that they are "especially appropriate when the behavior alternatives with respect to a given problem are somewhat limited, mutually exclusive, and readily discernable to observers" (p. 95); for example, "reads at grade level," "counts by tens," and "responds when name is called." Checklists allow us to quickly and systematically examine a wide range of behaviors. The extent to which the checklist items are behaviorally stated increases its usefulness as a screening device.

Rating scales are a more discriminating type of checklist since they call for observer *interpretation* of behavior. In completing a rating scale, the observer must make a judgment about the presence, absence, or extent of certain characteristics. The observer may be required to assign a numerical value, according to a high-to-low scale, to a specific trait, such as "dependence," or simply to mark the appropriate word to describe the frequency of a given behavior (alway, sometimes, never).

It should be noted that rating scales suffer some inherent weaknesses. One is the ambiguity of the characteristics or traits being rated; what one person judges to be dependent behavior another does not. Another problem is the "halo" effect; when a rater feels positive toward an individual she/he tends to rate that person high on positive attributes and to play down the person's negative traits. Finally, some judges tend to avoid both extremes when rating, giving every person an average rating. This tendency precludes the identification of individual students who deviate from the group. Rating scales which include operational definitions of the trait to be rated are to be preferred. Also, it is a good practice to rate all students on the same item before moving on to the next variable. For example, the teacher would individually rate all students on item 1 "asserts own opinions" before going to item 2 "enjoys trying new things." This procedure minimizes the halo effect.

Brandt (1972) notes that, "The difference between checklist data and ratings is primarily a matter of the kind of judgment required of the observer. With checklists, he classifies behavioral events. His judgment is qualitative. . . . In contrast to this type of judgment, ratings represent a quantitative assessment of the degree to which some quality is present" (p. 118). Both checklists and rating scales are imprecise tools, however, and should only be used to obtain organized descriptions or impressions of behavioral functioning which can later be verified through systematic observation.

Screening Instruments

Following is a representative list of available screening instruments. Before selecting an instrument for use with your students, you should review it carefully to determine whether it is expedient to administer, score, interpret, and most of all, whether it is suited to your purpose. Some screening devices are quite broad; others focus on a narrow range of behavior. Inclusion of a particular item in the list below does not imply its formal evaluation or endorsement by the authors. Annotations for each instrument listed here may be found at the end of this chapter along with actual copies of two additional screening instruments. In view of the emphasis on early identification, a sample preschool checklist is included.

1. *A Basic Screening and Referral Form for Children with Suspected Learning and Behavioral Difficulties,* by Robert Valett.
2. *Academic Readiness Scale,* by Harold Burks.
3. *Behavioral Index of Communicative Disorders,* by F. Stewart and S. F. Vasa.
4. *Classroom Inventory of Teacher Estimates for Special Service (CITES),* by Calvin C. Nelson.
5. *DIAL,* by Carol Mardell and Dorothea Goldenberg.

6. *First Grade Screening Test,* by J. E. Pate and W. W. Webb.
7. *Individual Learning Disabilities Classroom Screening Instrument,* by John Meier, V. O. Cazier, and Marian Giles.
8. *Pupil Behavior Rating Scale,* by Nadine Lambert, University of California, Berkeley.
9. *Screening Checklist for Classroom Teachers,* Department of Learning Disabilities, University of the Pacific.
10. *Teacher Rating Scale for the Identification of Handicapped Children,* Arizona State Department of Education.
11. *Walker Problem Behavior Identification Checklist,* by H. Walker.

Decision Points

The purpose of using screening techniques and instruments is to gather initial information on learner characteristics. Such information should be recorded carefully so it is available for reference at all times. In surveying the students in a classroom we are looking for those whose behavior or performance is significantly deviant from the group. These are the students we will need to study further. Screening test results should be combined and compared with other information known about the student.

Teachers are best able to identify problem learners when they have a solid background in normal child development and when they are alert to the educational relevance of the characteristics described earlier in this chapter. Keep in mind that everyone deviates from the "norm" or "average" in some way; for most children, observed differences in their behavior or performance will fall within normal limits. Cultural, social, and educational practices and expectations are all relevant here. Children may also display differences from one behavioral area to another; this is not necessarily cause for great concern.

If, as a result of a classroom screening, there do not appear to be students with notable problems, then the periodic evaluation of individual children's progress simply continues (see Chapter Four). Any child who is "screened out" of the group should receive in-depth assessment. The teacher must try to obtain as much information about the child as possible. Depending on the time available to the teacher, availability of support services, teacher skill, and nature or severity of the problem, the teacher must make a decision as to whether or not it is necessary to refer the student to the resource teacher or school appraisal team. If the teacher decides that a specialist is not needed, she/he conducts a more precise assessment of the student's functioning (see Chapter Three). The next step is to use all of the known information and data on the student to develop an appropriate instructional plan (see Chapter Four). If the teacher decides, however, that a specialist *is* required, the next appropriate step is to gather all available screening and diagnostic information and complete a referral statement. Cartwright (1972b) summarizes the decision process as follows:

A teacher continually *surveys* the data for the total group in order to *screen* out those children with deviations.

The children who have deviations are then involved in *diagnosis*.

On the basis of data gathered in diagnosis, a decision is made to either *modify* the child's educational program or to *refer* the child to a specialist for more intensive diagnosis (p. 53).

Sometimes it is appropriate to design and implement an instructional plan for a period of time, then return to the decision point—should this child be referred, or is she/he making progress? The following section presents some suggested referral procedures, including a variety of formats for teacher referral statements and guidelines for completing them. Note that completion of a referral form can be an extremely helpful step even if the student is *not* going to be referred, since it can be used as a set of guidelines for designing the instructional plan.

Referral Procedures

The Referral Form

A referral form represents a statement of concern about a student's rate of learning. In schools where resource programs are available, the referral statement is often the initial basis of communication between the classroom teacher and the resource teacher. The referral form should be clear, concise, and easy to complete. Hammill and Wiederholt (1972) emphasize that referral forms should not be too demanding of the teacher, either in terms of assessment skills or in terms of time needed to complete. If the referral form is too sophisticated and detailed, some teachers will feel inadequate and will fail to refer children who really need additional help. These authors suggest:

> The forms should instead request information on such factors as the child's level of performance in basic academic skills, his ability to benefit from group instruction, and his classroom behavior, and should include a section for any comments the regular classroom teacher might care to make (p. 52).

The resource teacher should provide regular teachers with specific information and guidance on how to complete referral forms. The following five items are basic:

1. *The child's presenting problem should be stated precisely.* Expressions such as "decreasing academic ability"; "low academic achievement"; and "displays social problems" are vague and generalized and do not zero in on the problem. Referral statements should be specific and should attempt to delimit the problem, for example: "reading achievement scores have dropped over the past 18 months while math scores

remain at or near grade level''; ''achievement in all basic skill areas is below age and grade level expectation although language skills have shown improvement recently''; ''refuses to join in group activities and frequently cries when classmates tease him.''

2. *Include specific comments on learner strengths.* This places the emphasis on the positive aspects of the learner's behavior, and can provide valuable ideas for planning remediation.

3. *Avoid making inferences as to why the child behaves in a certain way; include descriptions of what the child* actually does (*not your interpretation*). Saying that a student is ''hyperactive,'' ''aggressive,'' or that she/he is ''suspected to have mild cerebral palsy involvement'' does not describe the actual behaviors that concern us as teachers. When a student is being referred for assessment, every attempt should be made to describe his/her behavior in functional terms: ''does not sit at desk for more than two minute intervals; talks while others are talking; starts an activity before directions have been given; punches children on the playground; talks loudly; always tries to be first in line, or to use equipment; speaks in a halting manner; has difficulty using pencil, scissors; frequently requires help with buttoning, shoelaces.'' These are examples of *behavioral* descriptions of students' problems.

4. *Provide as much supportive documentation of the problem statement as possible (test scores, baseline performance data, tried materials and methods, and so on.* The extent to which the problem statement is supported by data which the teacher has gathered will help to point to specific assessment strategies and avoid duplication of effort.

5. *Include accurate identifying information: age, birthdate, date of referral, date testing was done, and so forth.* This may seem an obvious point, but it is amazing how often referrals are submitted without these data being completed. Since the referral form will become part of the student's file, it is important that careful records be kept.

Sample Referral Forms

Sample A, which follows, is an example of a completed referral form which illustrates many of the points discussed above. Notice that the reason for referral is stated in fairly precise terms and is supported by actual test scores. The referring teacher has also commented on the student's strengths. The form itself provides the teacher with a structure for quickly recording referral information.

Compared to sample A, sample B (page 48) is much less structured. The teacher is not directed, by the form, to supply *specific* data on the student's performance. Lack of structure in the design of the referral form contributes to

Sample A
Student Referral Form*

Name: Thomas Barton   Birthdate: 6/15/67 C.A.8:5 Date of Referral 11/17/75

School: Starlight Elementary   Teacher: Mrs. Sharon Lake   Grade: 3

PARENT/GUARDIAN: Mrs. Nettie Thomas   ADDRESS: 1214 E. Walnut

PHONE: 737-2101

Reason for referral: Reading and math skills are below grade level; Tommy seems to try hard but gets few results. He very seldom responds in group situations and is kind of a "loner." I'm concerned about his reading comprehension and social adjustment.

Describe program and materials used with student in the classroom:
Lately Tommy has been using the manipulative materials in the math center with some success. I have tried some reading drill techniques but Tommy gets tense and seems confused.

Areas of strength: Tommy is very attentive; he follows directions and seems motivated to try hard. He enjoys drawing and painting and is very interested in cars.

Math–Text and Skill Level: Greater Cleveland; SRA Achievement Test (arithmetic) given 9/24/75 grade placement score = 2.5. Errors in reading numbers and writing answers were noted.

Reading–Text and Skill Level: Bank Street Reader—California Reading Test, Upper Primary (9/19/75) score = 2.4. Comprehension skills are weak.

Social Adjustment:
Tommy is new in our school this year. He does not seem to have many friends and usually plays alone at recess or stands watching a group of kids. He responds well to adult attention.

Health:
Generally good though Tommy frequently appears tired and listless. Vision and hearing are normal.

Parent's Cooperation:
Mrs. Thomas seems very concerned about Tommy's school performance and says she would like to help but she is working on shifts and does not see Tommy when he comes home from school. Father is not in the home.

Other agencies involved with child:
None at present. I have suggested to Mrs. Thomas that she contact "Big Brother."

---

*Adapted from a form used in Humboldt-Del Norte Master Plan Project, Humboldt County Office of Education, Eureka, California.

Sample B
Student Referral Form

Name   Sandra Storia   Birthdate   2/8/69   Age

Referral Date   11/17/75   School   Camelia   Grade   1

Referred By   Mrs. Doolittle

Parent or Guardian   Mr. and Mrs. Storia

Address   939 Buttonwood   Phone

1. *Reasons for Referral:*
   Very disruptive in class, possible dyslexia

2. *Where in class is student deficient?*
   Reading and behavior

3. *What do you want to know about the student?*
   Why she can't learn to read

4. *Background Information:*
   a. *Past school history:* was in kindergarten at Martindale last year.
   b. *Family structure:* mother; father; two siblings and a grandmother.
   c. *Other information:* I have talked to the mother and she says they have a lot of trouble with Sandra at home too.

the reporting of vague information which is of little value in formulating an assessment plan.

The next three referral forms, Samples C, D, and E, are examples of more structured and detailed formats. The following features should be noted in the examples:

Sample C: 1. provides a space to indicate the student's primary language;
2. suggests that the parent be notified that the referral is being made;
3. asks the teacher to complete a screening checklist and prioritize problem areas;
4. encourages referrals from persons who know the student outside of the school situation;
5. asks for behavioral descriptions and test scores;
6. asks for comments on student's strengths.

Sample D: 1. requests baseline data (test scores);

      2. provides a checklist of behaviors, though the items are not all directly observable behaviors;

      3. allows the teacher to include personal impressions and observations of the student.

Sample E: 1. asks for use of behavioral terms to describe behavior;

      2. requests test results when available;

      3. provides behavior checklists in critical areas, focusing on both positive and negative behaviors;

      4. can be used both for screening and for informal follow-up evaluation.

Sample C

STUDENT REFERRAL FORM FOR SCHOOL APPRAISAL TEAM*

REFERRED BY: _____ DATE _____
                  NAME/POSITION

STUDENT'S NAME _____ BIRTHDATE _____
CHRONOLOGICAL AGE ____ SCHOOL _____
GRADE _____ TEACHER/COUNSELOR _____ SEX ____
NAME OF PARENT (or guardian) _____
ADDRESS _____ TELEPHONE _____
LANGUAGE SPOKEN AT HOME: ☐ ENGLISH ☐ SPANISH
☐ BOTH ☐ OTHER _____

I SPECIFY REASON FOR REFERRAL:

    PARENT NOTIFIED: ☐ YES   PARENT AGREES: ☐ YES
                  ☐ NO   ☐ NO

II DESCRIBE ANY ATTEMPTED INTERVENTIONS (Educational, Psychological, Medical, etc.)

III KNOWN SIGNIFICANT HEALTH PROBLEMS:

IV OTHER AGENCIES INVOLVED WITH STUDENT:

*Developed by Santa Barbara County Comprehensive Plan for Special Education, Santa Barbara County Schools, Santa Barbara, California, 1975.

V   PAST AND/OR CURRENT SPECIAL EDUCATION PLACEMENTS:

Where referral is initiated from outside of school, principal/designee contacts students' classroom teacher and/or counselor to complete the following section:

CLASSROOM TEACHER/COUNSELOR

PLEASE COMPLETE CITES SCREEN AND ANSWER FOLLOWING QUESTIONS:

1. CHECK, RATE, AND PRIORITIZE FOLLOWING AREAS OF CONCERN:
   A. Check areas of concern.
   B. For each area identified, assign a "1" or "2" rating.
   C. When all areas of concern have been checked and rated, go back and assign a priority number for each area.

AREA	A	B	C
1. Speech and Verbal Communication			
2. Visual Behaviors			
3. Visual Perception			
4. Auditory Behaviors			
5. In-Class Social Behavior			
6. Out-of-Class Social Behavior			
7. Work Habits			
8. General Motor Behaviors			
9. Discrepancy Classwork & Test Score Data			
10. Attentional Behaviors			
11. Absenteeism/Tardiness			
12. Conformity to Values			

2. INDICATE SPECIFIC OBSERVED BEHAVIORS FOR ABOVE AREAS CHECKED:

3. DESCRIBE PROGRAM AND MATERIALS USED WITH STUDENT:

4. CURRENT GRADE LEVEL AT WHICH STUDENT IS FUNCTIONING:
READING: _____ MATH: _____

5. CURRENT TEST INFORMATION:

6. AREAS OF STRENGTH AND/OR INTEREST OBSERVED IN STUDENT:

_____   _____
TEACHER'S/COUNSELOR'S SIGNATURE   DATE

Sample D

REFERRAL FOR SPECIAL SERVICES*

It is the desire of the special services staff to have the most complete picture possible of the student referred in order to better understand the problem and to provide assistance as soon as possible. This form has been made succinct and therefore must be filled in *completely* before services can be provided.

DATE _____ SCHOOL _____

STUDENT _____ ADDRESS _____

AGE _____ BIRTHPLACE _____

PARENT _____ PHONE NO. _____

GRADE _____ REPEATED GRADE _____

RECENT TEST SCORES:
    NAME OF TEST   DATE OF TEST   SIGNIFICANT RESULTS

_____ _____ _____

_____ _____ _____

_____ _____ _____

SPECIFIC AREA OF ACADEMIC WEAKNESS:
    SUBJECT   DESCRIPTION OF PROBLEM

_____   _____

                  _____

_____   _____

                  _____

*Adapted from *The Resource Room: An Access to Excellence*. South Carolina Region V, Educational Services Center, 1975, pp. 167-69.

REMEDIAL ASSISTANCE AND APPROACHES I HAVE TRIED:

_____

_____

_____

_____

CHECK THE SPACE BESIDE THE STATEMENTS THAT BEST DESCRIBE
THE STUDENT:

ADJUSTMENT:

___ well poised   ___ tense   ___ moody   ___ lazy

___ at ease   ___ anxious   ___ hostile   ___ shy

___ courteous   ___ excitable   ___ eager for praise   ___ cries often

___ cooperative   ___ easily upset   ___ sensitive   ___ depressed

___ cheerful   ___ unhappy   ___ needs frequent reassurance

RESPONSIVENESS:

___ alert   ___ hyperactive   ___ indecisive   ___ deliberate

___ prompt responses   ___ impulsive   ___ withdrawn   ___ daydreams

___ industrious   ___ confused   ___ hesitant   ___ irrelevant or bizarre response

TEACHER OPINIONS—BEHAVIOR OBSERVATIONS: (Please comment on student's personality and general adjustment as you know him/her)

_____

_____

_____

_____

_____

RELATIONS WITH OTHERS:

___ outgoing: good natured   ___ friendly   ___ tolerant

___ has many friends   ___ independent   ___ jealous

___ has few friends   ___ patient   ___ tactful

___ seeks attention

___ enjoys group activities

___ plays alone

___ high degree of conformity to peer group expectations

___ conscientious

EFFORT, APPLICATION:

___ careful   ___ careless   ___ distractible   ___ readily fatigued

___ gives up easily   ___ works at rapid   ___ works at slow   ___ spontaneous
                     tempo   tempo

                                                   ___ creative

SELF-CRITICISM:

___ extremely critical of self   ___ boastful, in spite of lack of success

___ healthy recognition of own mistakes   ___ does not seem bothered by poor efforts

___ downplays own inadequacies

ATTENTION:

___ listens carefully   ___ inattentive to most instructions

___ waits until instructions are completed   ___ seems to understand most instructions
before beginning task

___ begins to work impulsively without
listening to instructions

PERSEVERANCE:

___ works constructively on long tasks   ___ easily distracted after short periods
                                               of concentration

___ distracted only by unusual   ___ does not complete many tasks
circumstances

MOTIVATION:

___ eager   ___ resistant, sullen   ___ guarded, suspicious

___ indifferent   ___ apathetic   ___ excessive concern with
                                                  results

VERBALIZATION:

___ talkative   ___ difficulty in expressing him/herself

___ expresses him/herself well   ___ offers frequent comment

SELF-CONCEPT:

___ seems self-centered   ___ forceful

___ lacks self-confidence   ___ submissive

___ seems self-confident

How do you see this child? _____

_____

_____

_____

                                       _____

                                             Signature of Person Initiating
                                                Referral and Position

Sample E

TEACHER REFERRAL STATEMENT*

Name of Student _____ C.A. _____ Report Date _____
School _____ Birthdate & Grade _____
Teacher(s) _____ Consultant _____

   I. Achievement Data
     Describe the student's typical performance in each area. Use behavioral terms so
     that the description is precise. Cite any available test results. If not observed or
     sampled, mark N/O.
     A. Oral Language _____
          _____

          Written Language _____
          _____

     B. Reading Comprehension _____
          _____

          Word Analysis Skills_____
          _____

     C. Mathematical Comprehension_____
          _____

          Computation Abilities _____
          _____

     D. Other_____
          _____
          _____
          _____

  II. Learning Behaviors Checklist
     Place a check mark next to the statements which describe behavior *usually*
     exhibited by the student. Use the comment space to elaborate on your choice and
     to provide supporting information.
     A. Behavior Related to Inputs
          __ is attentive during most activities
          __ is attentive only during his/her favorite activities
          __ rarely pays attention
          __ indicates a preference for material received through the
               __ auditory channel
               __ visual channel
               __ combination
          __ is able to use tactile sensations
          __ exhibits unusual behavior during activities which require good hearing
          __ exhibits unusual behavior during activities which require good vision

---

*Adapted from Cartwright and Cartwright, 1972b, pp. 308–15.

Comment:_____
_____
_____

B. Behaviors Related to Information Processing
 — organizes tasks and materials so that time is used efficiently
 — has short-term retention for most learning areas
 — has long-term retention for most learning areas
 — can recall information for only some selected learning areas
 — does not remember information
 — discriminates between sounds
 — discriminates between shapes and figures
 — discriminates between letters, numbers, words
 — can make associations
 — can recognize associations
 — can make generalizations
 — can differentiate between generalizations and specific facts
 — translates from concrete experiences to abstractions
 — is able to profit from incidental learning
 — finishes (or attempts to finish) tasks s/he starts
 — is easily distracted regardless of task
 — follows instructions directed to a group
 — follows instructions directed to him/her individually
 — follows one direction but not a sequence of directions
Comment:_____
_____
_____

C. Behaviors Related to Outputs
 — volunteers comments, answers, etc. during group activities
 — speaks spontaneously on a one-to-one basis to other child and/or adults
 — speaks only when called on or when conversation is initiated by another person
 — must be urged to speak
 — shows specific speech problem (describe)
 — performs gross motor skills in coordinated fashion
 — performs fine motor skills in coordinated fashion
 — is clumsy and awkward in most motor activities
 — exhibits involuntary repetition when making a motor response
 — exhibits involuntary repetition when making a spoken response
 — uses a vocabulary typical of older children
 — uses a limited vocabulary typical of children his/her age
 — uses a limited vocabulary
 — uses only simple sentences
 — uses single words and some phrases, but not complete sentences
 — reverses some letters and/or numbers when writing
 — prefers right hand for most activities
 — prefers left hand for most activities
 — uses either hand with about equal dexterity

Comment:_____

_____
_____
_____

D. Behaviors Related to Feedback
   Place a check mark next to the events which are rewarding for the student.
   __ tangible rewards such as tokens which can be traded for free time
   __ physical attention such as a hug, a pat on the back
   __ symbolic rewards such as grades, stars
   __ competitive rewards such as being named the winner
   __ comments of approval (verbal praise) from an adult
   __ comments or indications of approval from peers
   __ opportunities to pursue activities of his/her own choosing
   __ knowledge of results such as being told an answer is correct
   Place a check mark next to statements which apply to the student.
   __ exhibits a strong preference for a certain type of reward;
      if so, specify _____
   __ does not display a preference for any one type of reward but works well for
      a variety of rewards
   __ needs to be rewarded several times during completion of a task
   __ can delay receiving reward until completion of task
   __ can delay receiving reward until several tasks are completed

Comment: _____

_____
_____
_____

III. Physical Symptoms Checklist
   Place a check mark next to the statements which apply to the child. Use the
   comment space to elaborate and provide supporting information. Attach any
   medical reports which are available.
   __ is often absent
   __ is usually tired
   __ is overly active
   __ is listless, lethargic
   __ is underweight
   __ is overweight
   __ complains of headaches, dizziness
   __ has unusual posture when doing visual tasks
   __ has unusual posture when standing
   __ has unusual gait
   __ appearance of eyes is abnormal
   __ has frequent earaches

Comment:_____

_____

_____

_____

_____

IV. Social-Emotional Behaviors Checklist
Place a check mark next to the statements which apply to the child. Use the comment space to elaborate and provide supporting information.
— prefers working with others
— prefers to work by himself
— exhibits about equal willingness to work with others and alone
— gets along with others in work situations
— gets along with others in play situations
— refuses to participate in group activities
— adapts easily to changes
— needs to be carefully prepared and gradually introduced to change
— behavior in group activities is predictable
— is more easily excited than others his age
— has temper tantrums (kicks, screams, beats on floor, etc.)
— makes a deliberate attempt to be by himself
— exhibits an unusual amount of persistence
— gives up and moves to another activity when he experiences difficulty
— is aggressive (fights, kicks, hits, verbal insults, etc.)

Comment:_____

_____

_____

_____

Resource teachers often receive informal referrals from teachers in their school(s) who desire a ''second opinion'' or some specific teaching suggestions for a student in the regular program. Sample F is the type of form which could be adapted for use in this situation.

In summary we feel it is important to structure referral forms very carefully so that the teacher, or other referring agent, is encouraged to provide precise information about the student's performance which is based on observable behavior. When descriptions of what the student *can* do and what efforts (methods, materials) have been made by the teacher to meet the student's needs are provided, this information, analyzed in relation to the problem statement, enables the resource teacher to make preliminary suggestions for program modifications. The process of actually filling out the referral form allows the teacher to check whether the information which has been gathered about the student is as adequate and as complete as possible.

Sample F

DIAGNOSTIC/PRESCRIPTIVE TEACHER PROGRAM*
REFERRAL FORM

Student's Name ——————————————— Age ——— Sex ———
Grade/Team/Subject ——————————————— Room No. ———
Date of Referral ——————————— Referring Teacher ———————

Please complete this form and return both copies to the Diagnostic/Prescriptive Teacher's mailbox.

1. What is the specific behavior that led to this referral?

2. What methods have you tried to solve the problem?

3. What do you see as the student's particular strengths?

4. When is a convenient time for us to talk?

——————————————
Referring Teacher

Specific Suggestions for Processing Resource Program Referrals**

1. Noncategorical resource programs are advantageous since any student who has a significant problem in the regular classroom can be referred and admitted; students do not have to be diagnosed and labeled as having a specific handicap.
2. Referrals by classroom teachers are a reliable and efficient way of locating potential learning disabled students; therefore, teacher requests should be given high priority. Resource teachers and regular teachers should cooperatively make the major decisions on admissions policies. With older students, self-referral can be encouraged.
3. The students who need help the most should be given first consideration for entry into the program.
4. Care should be taken to avoid admitting more students to the resource program than can be adequately served.
5. Referrals should be processed through the building administrator who can then keep track of the number of referrals, which teachers are referring, and who *over*-refers.

*The Diagnostic/Prescriptive Teacher Program, The George Washington University.
**Many of the following ideas were adapted from Hammill and Wiederholt (1972) and Wiederholt (1974).

Analyzing Referrals

A significant feature of the Resource Program for mildly handicapped students, and therefore of the informal assessment methods presented in Chapter Three of this book, is the potential availability of these services at the local school level. For this reason, every effort should be made to keep the whole referral process as streamlined as possible. Quick turn-around time from initial referral to scheduling the student for services is necessary. An accurately completed referral form, submitted by the teacher, is the first step. The second is for the responsible person, often the resource teacher, to review the referrals and respond to the referring teacher. This is best accomplished by conferring with the teacher and by arranging to observe the student in the classroom. At this time the student's teacher and the resource teacher can discuss how, together, they may try to deal with the identified problem behavior, and a detailed plan can be drawn up for more in-depth assessment.

To assist in the process of analyzing referrals and planning assessment strategies, the Referral Analysis Chart*, shown on page 61, may be used. A blank form has also been included. At the end of this section you will find referral forms and completed Referral Analysis Charts which serve as an introduction to two case studies which are continued in Chapters Three and Four.

General Directions for Completing the Referral Analysis Chart

1. Begin with the box in the upper left corner—"Information Provided by Referral" as to the "Referring Agent."
2. Complete the boxes in the first column, taking information from the referral form itself.
3. Continue with columns 2–4. In column 2, write any other relevant information known about the student.
4. In column 3, write questions to be checked out in order to specifically determine the "what," "when," "where," and "how" of the student's academic and/or behavioral characteristics.
5. In column 4, write a method for investigating the questions listed in column 3—who will investigate; what methods (e.g., interviewing) or materials (tests, etc.) will be used?

More detailed instructions have been listed on the chart itself.

---

*Developed by Gabriele Gurski, Educational Program Specialist, California Regional Resource Center, School of Education, University of Southern California, 1975.

Referral Analysis Chart and How to Complete It

	1. Information Provided by Referral	2. Other Information Known	3. Resulting Questions to be Explored	4. Persons, Materials, Strategies for Investigating Questions
Referring Agent	Information which identifies the person making the referral (i.e., name, grade level taught, etc.)	Information which you, through your past experience, can add to the information provided. (curriculum responsibilities, etc.)	Information which you might need in order to interact with the referring person effectively.	Information on strategies which answer the questions of "what, when, where, how and who" for answering questions to be explored.
Student Referred: Identity	Information which identifies the pupil referred (i.e., name, grade level, age, etc.)	Information which you, through your past experience, can add to the information provided. (grade level expectancies, etc.). This column may not be applicable if you do not know the student.	Questions about the pupil generated by the previous two columns and which are not provided for by the body of the referral.	Same as above, relating to this row.
Academic	Any descriptive terms or information provided by the referral about the pupil's academic learning progress.	Behavioral definitions which you can generate on the basis of your past experience for the descriptive terms in the previous column. These could vary widely for individuals.	Questions generated by your attempts to define the descriptive terms behaviorally. Any other information you would want to know about this student's learning/academic progress.	Same as above, relating to the content of this row.
Behavior	Any descriptive terms or information provided by the referral about the pupil's behavior.	Behavioral definitions which you can generate on the basis of your past experience for the descriptive terms in the previous column. These could vary widely.	Questions generated by your attempts to define the descriptive terms behaviorally. Any other information you would want to know about this pupil's behavior.	Same as above, relating to the content of this row.
Other (Possible reinforcers, etc.)	Any other descriptive terms or information provided by the referral that are not listed above.	Behavioral definitions which you can generate on the basis of your past experience for the descriptive terms in the previous column.	Questions generated by your attempts to define the descriptive terms behaviorally. Any other information you might want to know about the pupil.	Same as above, relating to the content of this row.

Referral Analysis Chart

	1. Information Provided by Referral	2. Other Information Known	3. Resulting Questions to be Explored	4. Persons, Materials, Strategies for Investigating Questions
Referring Agent				
Student Referred: Identity				
Academic				
Behavior				
Other (Possible reinforcers, etc.)				

Planning for Assessment

When the Referral Analysis Chart is completed, you will have an initial assessment plan prepared which includes a list of items to be covered in the assessment, and persons responsible for obtaining the information. At this point, diagnostic, or assessment, sessions for the student should be scheduled, following notification of the student's parents.

The referral forms and completed Referral Analysis Charts shown on the next few pages are based on actual case data. These case studies will be continued in Chapter Three, where the assessment results will be reported, and in Chapter Four, where the instructional plans designed for these students are presented.

Case Study I: Leonard

PUPIL REFERRAL

Name: ___Leonard T.___ Grade: _8_ Birthdate: ___11/7/61___ Sex: _M_

Classes: ___Reading; P.E.; Math (Regular) & 3 periods in special class___

School: ___Moore Junior High___

Past grades and/or teacher comments: ___Leonard has been in a special class (Educable Mentally Retarded) since the 4th grade; this fall he was integrated for reading lab, P.E., and math. His teachers report no problems. I feel that Leonard functions at a higher level than the other students in my class.___

Reason for referral: ___Leonard seems ready for full-time integration in the regular program with resource teacher support. He has made good progress in the special class, but resents being in it and does not get along well with my other students— seems to feel superior.___

Standardized test data:

Achievement:	*Test*	*Date*	*Scores*	
	Wide Range	10/75	Reading:	3.2
			Spelling:	3.0
			Math:	4.4
Aptitude:				
	WISC	10/74	VIQ:	71
			PIQ:	85
			FS:	75

Health Information: ___Excellent health: vision and hearing screening 9/15/75 = Normal___

Any other relevant data in cumulative record folder or otherwise known to teachers (absences, tardies, etc.): ___Has history of poor peer relationships with students in special class; gets in fights with them. With regular students he seems to know___ his limitations and doesn't push it with those kids. Will need special help in reading, spelling, and language (understanding directions; self expression).

Parent contacts: Interview with mother 11/1/75

Person Making Referral: Special Class Teacher

Signature: *D. Walker*

Date: 11/15/75

Case Study II: Richard

STUDENT REFERRAL FORM FOR SCHOOL APPRAISAL TEAM*

REFERRED BY: J. Bates   Classroom Teacher   DATE   9/30/75
                              NAME/POSITION

STUDENT'S NAME   Richard A.   BIRTH DATE   6/1/64

CHRONOLOGICAL AGE   11:4   SCHOOL   Cordova

GRADE   5   TEACHER/COUNSELOR   J. Bates

SEX   M   NAME OF PARENT (or guardian)   Mr. and Mrs. A.

ADDRESS   1876 Hollister Ave.   TELEPHONE   964-2811

LANGUAGE SPOKEN AT HOME: ☒ ENGLISH ☐ SPANISH ☐ BOTH
☐ OTHER

I SPECIFY REASON FOR REFERRAL:

Richard performs significantly below grade level expectation in both reading and spelling. He has great difficulty with all academic areas related to reading. In two years he has shown less than a year's growth in reading. This seems to affect his feelings about himself; he worries about his poor reading.

PARENT NOTIFIED: ☒ YES   PARENT AGREES: ☒ YES
                 ☐ NO   ☐ NO

II DESCRIBE ANY ATTEMPTED INTERVENTIONS (Educational, Psychological, Medical, etc.)

Richard has been receiving extra help in reading since last fall, but is not making progress. Receives medication to control attention and behavior; this seems to help.

---

*Form developed by Santa Barbara County Comprehensive Plan for Special Education, Santa Barbara County Schools, Santa Barbara, California, 1975.

III KNOWN SIGNIFICANT HEALTH PROBLEMS: None

IV OTHER AGENCIES INVOLVED WITH STUDENT: None

V PAST AND/OR CURRENT SPECIAL EDUCATION PLACEMENTS: Special class— learning disability 9/72 to 10/74

Where referral is initiated from outside of school, principal/designee contacts students' classroom teacher and/or counselor to complete the following section:

CLASSROOM TEACHER/COUNSELOR

PLEASE COMPLETE CITES SCREEN AND ANSWER FOLLOWING QUESTIONS:

1. CHECK, RATE, AND PRIORITIZE FOLLOWING AREAS OF CONCERN:
   A.   Check areas of concern.
   B.   For each area identified, assign a "1" or "2" rating.
   C.   When all areas of concern have been checked and rated, go back and assign a priority number for each area.

AREA	A	B	C
1. Speech and Verbal Communication			
2. Visual Behaviors			
3. Visual Perception	✓	1	1
4. Auditory Behaviors	✓	2	1
5. In-Class Social Behavior			
6. Out-of-Class Social Behavior			

AREA	A	B	C
7. Work Habits			
8. General Motor Behaviors			
9. Discrepancy Classwork & Test Score Data			
10. Attentional Behaviors			
11. Absenteeism/Tardiness			
12. Confirmity to Values			

2. INDICATE SPECIFIC OBSERVED BEHAVIORS FOR ABOVE AREAS CHECKED:

   Has difficulty remembering names of people and things; reads in a halting manner. Word attack skills are poor, does not seem to hear beginning sounds.

3. DESCRIBE PROGRAM AND MATERIALS USED WITH STUDENT:

   Sullivan; SRA

4. CURRENT GRADE LEVEL AT WHICH STUDENT IS FUNCTIONING:
   READING: _____2_____ MATH: _____4_____

5. CURRENT TEST INFORMATION:
   Wide Range Achievement 5/27/75: Reading = 2.5; Spelling = 2.9; Arithmetic = 4.2

6. AREAS OF STRENGTH AND/OR INTEREST OBSERVED IN STUDENT:

   Richard is an active participant in sports during the physical education program and in after school sports. He has many friends and his peer group admires him tremendously.

   _____*J. Bates*_____   _____9/30/75_____
   TEACHER'S/COUNSELOR'S SIGNATURE   DATE

Referral Analysis Chart Completed for Leonard

	1. Information Provided by Referral	2. Other Information Known	3. Resulting Questions to be Explored	4. Persons, Materials, Strategies for Investigating Questions
Referring Agent	D. Walker—Special Class Teacher	Apparently concerned about Leonard's social development; recognizes he will need special help to succeed in regular program.	Does Leonard have friends? Are they in regular classes? What suggestions can be made to regular teachers?	Teacher consultations (all Leonard's teachers)
Student Referred: Identity	Leonard T. CA: 14:0 Grade 8: 3 regular (rdg., math, P.E.) classes; 3 special ed. classes	Partial integration in regular classes	What other regular classes should be considered? Are parents concerned, involved?	Teacher consultation Consultation with counselor Talk to Leonard Home interview
Academic	WRAT 10/75 Reading 3.2 Spelling 3.0 Math 4.4 Seems ready for full integration; has made good progress in special class. Regular teachers report no problems.	Achievement low for 8th grade placement	What specific skills does Leonard have/need? Were regular teachers contacted at time referral was made?	Skill testing (criterion referenced) Teacher consultations
Behavior	History of poor peer relations with special class students; with regular class kids seems to know his limitations and doesn't push it. Resents being in special class—seems to feel superior.		What contacts has school counselor had with Leonard? What specific behaviors does he demonstrate with regular class peers? Is there acceptance, interaction?	Classroom observation Talk to Leonard Consultation with counselor Teacher consultations
Other (Possible reinforcers	Hearing/Vision normal WISC 10/74: Verbal = 71 Performance = 85 Full Scale = 47	No strengths or possible reinforcers noted on referral form. Possible self-concept problems.	What are some motivations for Leonard? Interests? How does he feel about his school	Home interview Classroom observation Talk to Leonard.

Referral Analysis Chart Completed for Richard

	1. Information Provided by Referral	2. Other Information Known	3. Resulting Questions to be Explored	4. Persons, Materials, Strategies for Investigating Questions
Referring Agent	Bates—5th grade teacher	Arranges for extra help in reading	What extra reading help is provided? What are teacher's goals for Richard?	Teacher consultation.
Student Referred: Identity	Richard A. CA = 11.4 5th grade pupil	Lives with father, mother, older brother. Older than most 5th graders	Ethnic/language factors involved in learning problem? Retained in the past? How long in this school district?	Home interview. Teacher consultation Cum folder
Academic	Extra help in reading but no progress, below grade level in reading and spelling; has difficulty with all academic areas related to reading; less than 1 yr. growth in 2 yr. Math = 4.2 (WRAT 5/27/75) difficulty remembering names of people and things	Difference between reading and math achievement *might* suggest language problems	Test results prior to 1975? Retest? Language assessment? Is he more successful with concrete-type tasks and work?	Cum folder Informal assessment Diagnostic testing Classroom observation Talk with student
Behavior	Reads in halting manner; poor word attack skills. Lacks progress in reading; seems to affect feelings about self. Worries about poor reading. On medication to control attention and behavior—seems to help.	Parents evidently sought medical help.	What indicators are there of lowered self-concept; worries? What medication? How long?	Classroom observation Teacher consultation Home interview
Other (Possible reinforcers etc.)	Active participant in sports Many friends; admired by peer group Has been in special class (learning disability)	Shows strengths which could facilitate success in regular program	Does teacher select reading materials related to sports? How can peer reinforcement be used? Why was Richard returned to regular program?	Teacher consultation Cum folder

Study Questions and Activities

1. Analyze sample referral forms A and B in Chapter Two using the Referral Analysis Chart shown in the text. What specific questions were generated by your attempts to behaviorally define the descriptive terms of each referral? Which of the referral forms was easier to translate into behavioral terms? Why?

2. Outline an inservice workshop for regular classroom teachers explaining how to identify pupils with special learning and/or behavior problems and how to prepare appropriate referrals for special services.

3. Mrs. James, a fifth-grade teacher, habitually refers one-third of her class for special services. By contrast, Mr. Perez, the other fifth-grade teacher, has yet to submit his first referral. (There are no differences in the composition of Mrs. James' and Mr. Perez' classes.) How should a resource teacher deal with the problems of over- and under-referral noted here?

4. Discuss additional screening or assessment procedures required for minority children from non-English speaking homes. (See current films on identification of minority children for special education services, e.g., *Entre Dos Mundos, 1975*.)

5. Develop a referral form from the samples presented in Chapter Two. Interview a half dozen regular class teachers (as a class project) and complete referral forms on their two most difficult learning and/or behavior problem pupils (anonymous referrals, of course). Establish some criteria for determining which students qualify for special services. Role play a school appraisal team composed of the principal, the resource teacher, the school nurse, and the referring regular class teacher, meeting to determine: (a) which referrals qualify for placement in the resource room; (b) which referrals should be maintained in the regular class with assistance from a resource consultant; (c) which referrals require more intensive assessment by an interdisciplinary team (if any); (d) which appear unable to qualify for any special services; and (e) which referrals require additional information from the referring teacher before placement decisions can be made. Recommend revisions in the referral form used on the basis of your "field test" of the form.

References

Brandt, R. M. *Studying behavior in natural settings.* New York: Holt, Rinehart and Winston, 1972.

Cartwright, G. P., & Cartwright, C. A. Gilding the lilly: Comments on the training based model. *Exceptional Children,* 1972, *39* (2), 231-234. (a)

Cartwright, G. P., & Cartwright, C. A. *Computer assisted remedial education: Early identification of handicapped children.* University Park, Pa.: Computer Assisted Instruction Laboratory, College of Education, the Pennsylvania State University, 1972. (b)

Cartwright, G. P., Cartwright, C. A., & Ysseldyke, J. E. Two decision models: Identification and diagnostic teaching of handicapped children in the regular classroom. *Psychology in the Schools,* 1973, *10*, 4–11.

Hewett, F. M., & Forness, S. R. *Education of exceptional learners.* Boston: Allyn and Bacon, 1974.

Hammill, D., & Wiederholt, J. L. *The resource room: Rationale and implementation.* Philadelphia, Pa.: Buttonwood Farms, 1972.

Mann, P. H. (Ed.). *Mainstream special education: Issues and perspectives in urban centers.* Reston, Va.: The Council for Exceptional Children, 1974.

Region V Educational Services Center. *The resource room: An access to excellence.* Lancaster, S.C.: Region V Educational Services Center, 1975.

Wiederholt, J. L. Planning resource rooms for the mildly handicapped. *Focus on Exceptional Children,* 1974, *5* (8), 1–10.

Resources

Child Development

Elkind, D. *A sympathetic understanding of the child: Birth to sixteen.* Boston: Allyn and Bacon, 1974.

Ginsburg, H., & Opper, S. *Piaget's theory of intellectual development: An introduction.* Englewood Cliffs, N.J.: Prentice - Hall, 1969.

Hawkes, G. R., & Plase, D. *Behavior and development from 5 to 12.* New York: Harper and Brothers, 1962.

Lazerson, A., Estrada, J., Rosler, M., (Eds.). *Developmental psychlogy today.* Del Mar, Calif.: Communications Research Machines, 1971.

Screening Instruments

1. *A Basic Screening and Referral Form for Children with Suspected Learning and Behavioral Difficulties,* by Robert Valett. This device is designed to survey social-personal, conceptual-cognitive, language, perceptual-motor, sensory-motor, gross-motor behaviors, direction following, and simple academic skills of students in kindergarten through grade 8. Problem descriptions can be written in the booklet; behaviors are rated from 0–2 (no concern, 0; to primary concern, 2). Normative data for rating scales is not provided. Administration time is approximately 1–1½ hours per student. Available from Fearon Publishers, Palo Alto, California.

2. *Academic Readiness Scale,* by Harold Burks. These 5-point scales test readiness for first grade in the areas of motor; perceptual-motor; attention; academic; and social behavior, and provide a profile of skill level. Test items have moderate to high predictive validity. Estimated administration time is 20-25 minutes per child. Available from the Arden Press, PO Box 844, Huntington Beach, California 92646.

3. *Behavioral Index of Communicative Disorders,* by F. Stewart and S. F. Vasa. This instrument is a developmentally based, behaviorally oriented informal tool designed to assist in the initial identification of learning and behavior strengths and weaknesses. Behavior is measured in nine categories, including language, reading, math, and emotional. There are a total of 150 items. Administration and scoring is simple; testing requires about 40 minutes per student. This test appears suitable for the elementary grades. A Teacher Activity Code sheet which allows the teacher to make note of various intervention activities tried and the amount of time spent in each is included. Available from the Center for Research, Service and Publication, Laramie, Wyoming.

4. *Classroom Inventory of Teacher Estimates for Special Service* (CITES), by Calvin C. Nelson. Designed as a class rating device for school-wide screening, this instrument lists twelve behavioral categories (including speech and verbal communications, visual perception, work habits, and social behavior) with sample descriptors. The teacher rates all students on a scale from 0 (does not require special services) to 2 (requires immediate attention); a rating of 1 is assigned if the student exhibits a problem which does not presently interfere with his classroom functioning. CITES is most appropriate at the elementary level. The experimental edition was produced for Santa Barbara County Schools, Santa Barbara, California (1974).

5. *DIAL,* by Carol Mardell and Dorothea Goldenberg. This screening test is for identifying prekindergarten children with potential learning problems (ages 2½–5½). It is designed for administration by a team of professionals and/or trained paraprofessionals; 6-8 children can be screened per hour. Four areas of functioning are assessed: gross motor, fine motor, concepts, and communications. The test was normed on a population of 4,400 children. Available from DIAL, Inc., Box 911, Highland Park, Illinois 60035.

6. *First Grade Screening Test,* by J. E. Pate and W. W. Webb. This is a group test designed to identify children who will probably have difficulty learning at the first grade level. The test yields a single, composite score; a cutting score divides the group of scores into two; children who score at or below the cutting score should be considered for more in-depth assessment. Available from American Guidance Service, Inc., Publisher's Building, Circle Pines, Minnesota 55014.

7. *Individual Learning Disabilities Classroom Screening Instrument,* by John Meier, V.O. Cazier, and Marian Giles. This scale is designed to assist classroom teachers in identifying elementary school students (K-6) with potential learning handicaps. A total of 80 items provide indices of the child's functioning in areas such as: auditory perception, visual perception, sequential memory, and social-emotional. Pupil work samples are also scored. Student behaviors are rated on a 4-point scale (unobserved to severe); cut-off scores for each area of behavior are suggested. Specific remedial suggestions are offered. Available from Learning Pathways, Inc., Evergreen, Colorado 80439.

8. *Pupil Behavior Rating Scale,* by Nadine Lambert, University of California, Berkeley. Designed as a classroom screening device for grades K-6, this scale consists of 11 nonintellectual behavioral attributes; each student is assigned a unique score on each attribute, relative to others in the class. Scores can be combined, yielding a composite score for each student. The purpose is to identify children requiring further attention; no cut-off criteria are provided. Available from the test author.

9. *Screening Checklist for Classroom Teachers.* This checklist is organized into the following areas: discrepancies (better in arithmetic than reading); auditory difficulties; visual difficulties; kinesthetic or motor difficulties; and behavior symptoms. Items appear appropriate for the elementary level and use of the form to accompany a referral statement would be very appropriate. This checklist was developed by the Department of Learning Disabilities, University of the Pacific at Pacific Medical Center, California.

10. *Teacher Rating Scale for the Identification of Handicapped Children.* Eleven separate scales sampling a wide range of problem areas (social, academic, emotional, and so on) are included in this scale for K-8 students. The individual student is rated on 75 items: *1* = does not exhibit; *5* = consistently exhibits. Scores are obtained on each of the 11 scales; estimated administration time is 20–40 minutes per child. Available from the Arizona State Department of Education, Phoenix, Arizona.

11. *Walker Problem Behavior Identification Checklist,* by Hill Walker. This checklist can be used as a screening for identification or to accompany a referral; it contains 50 items which sample behaviors, such as acting out, immaturity, distractibility, withdrawal, and so forth, and yield raw scores—*T* scores for each area as well as a total score. Cut-off scores are provided. Administration takes approximately 30 minutes per student in the elementary grades (age level for which the test was constructed). Available from Western Psychological Services, Los Angeles, California.

Checklist For Classroom Teachers (Grades 7–12)*

Name of Student _____ Birthdate _____ Age _____

Grade _____ School _____

Teacher/Counselor _____ Date _____

I. Please check only those items which are appropriate.

INDICATORS OF VISUAL DIFFICULTIES

— Visually confuses or is slow to recognize letters or words which appear similar, as ra*m*-ra*n*, etc.

— Reverses or inverts letters such as p-q, c-p, m-w, u-n.

— Transposes letters such as saw-was, stop-spot.

— Art and drawings are immature and lacking in detail.

— Prefers auditory activities such as class discussion, or more verbal activities.

— Does not do well in activities which require reading instructions.

— Confuses identification of right/left on pencil/paper assignments, and/or when moving about the room or a building.

— Difficulty learning order of the days of week, or seasons of the year.

— Inability to read graphs, maps, globes or floor plans.

— Difficulty judging distances.

— Difficulty spacing letters and/or words appropriately.

INDICATORS OF AUDITORY DIFFICULTIES

— Difficulty understanding spoken directions.

— Does not form phrases and/or sentences correctly in spoken language.

— Speech not as clear as should be for age level.

— Quiet, not talkative.

— Difficulty "finding" words for speech; substitutes words like "thing" for nouns.

— Difficulty or slowness in organizing thoughts for expression.

— Uses phrases or single words rather than sentences.

— Difficulty discriminating consonant sounds; hears *mat* for *bat*, *tab* for *tap*, etc.

— Difficulty discriminating and learning short vowel sounds.

— If given a word, has difficulty sounding it out, sound by sound, as *cat* is k-ă-t.

— Difficulty relating printed letters to their sounds (as "f," "pl," "ide").

— Cannot separate sounds which make up blends, as "fl" has sounds of f-f. . .1-1.

— Spells and reads sight words more correctly than phonetic words.

---

*Adapted from forms prepared by the Special Education Master Plan for Stanislaus County, Stanislaus County Department of Education, Modesto, California (1975).

__ Has difficulty sequencing syllables or letters in speaking and/or reading and/or oral spelling as, *pas*ghetti for *spa*ghetti; *cala*pillar for *cater*pillar.
__ Written spelling slightly superior to oral spelling.
__ Prefers visual activities (art, sports).
__ Difficulty learning syllabication and accent.
__ Silent reading better than oral reading.
__ Comprehension of reading material below reading ability.

INDICATORS OF KINESTHETIC OR MOTOR DIFFICULTIES

__ Poor coordination.
__ Poor balance.
__ Does poorly on any pencil/paper task or will not attempt these.
__ Written spelling significantly lower than oral spelling.
__ Inarticulate or mumbled speech.
__ Cannot remember how to write letters, although can remember what they look like.
__ Poor pencil grasp.

II. Check those behaviors that the pupil exhibits more often than other members of the class.

__ Upset by changes in routine.
__ Easily excitable, over-reacts.
__ Behavior unpredictable from one hour to the next.
__ Seems more immature than majority of classmates.
__ Considerable evidence of uncooperative behavior.
__ Relates poorly to other students.
__ Appears generally unhappy.
__ Easily frustrated in social situations.
__ Impulsive behavior, poor self-control.
__ Daydreams, sometimes seems in another world, withdraws.
__ Does not seem able to perceive thoughts and feelings of others.
__ Does not comply with class rules.
__ Aggressive, irritable, then remorseful.
__ Aggressive, not remorseful, remains angry.
__ Does not seem to profit from previous experience; repeats same inappropriate behavior.
__ Is often unaware that his/her behavior is annoying to others.
__ Erratic (some days alert, other days not).
__ Seldom completes assignments in the allotted time.
__ Requires more individual teacher time than can be offered.
__ Does not follow directions independently.
__ Easily distracted.
__ Seems to lack motivation.
__ Easily upset or frustrated by academic activities.

___ Requires constant help; cannot complete work independently.
___ Unable to sit still, inattentive.
___ Sluggish, complains of being tired.
___
___
___
___
___

III. List the student's strengths and interest areas.

_____
_____
_____
_____

Attach to Referral Form

Preschool Evaluation Form*

CHILD'S NAME _____

MALE _____ FEMALE _____ BIRTHDATE _____

EVALUATION DATE _____

	YES	NO
I. SOCIAL		

I. SOCIAL   YES   NO

1. Child responds to social stimulation.
2. Child smiles when being held, talked to, played with, etc.
3. Shows an interest in object or person for at least 30 seconds.
4. Child looks at self in mirror.
5. Shows desire for attention by reaching for people, cooing, etc.
6. Reaches for familiar object offered him/her.
7. Responds to peek-a-boo game w/teacher.
8. Plays independently w/toys or other materials unattended.
9. Plays alongside one other child w/t aggressive behavior for 10 seconds.
10. Responds to departure farewells.
11. Shares toys or objects with others during play or work projects.
12. Plays simple games (ball rolling, tossing) with another child in cooperative manner.
13. Differentiates between boys and girls.
14. Uses please, thank you, you're welcome, appropriately.
15. Goes to and returns from other rooms in building without assistance.
16. Accepts absence from parent/guardian.
17. Follows predetermined rules when participating in an activity (waiting turns, etc.) 75% of time.
18. Refrains from publicly engaging in inappropriate activities (nosepicking, masturbation).

II. CONCEPTS
1. Identification of body parts (Receptive)

a. head	f. ear
b. arm	g. nose
c. leg	h. mouth
d. foot	i. stomach
e. eye	j. hand

*Prepared by Judy Bancroft, Santa Barbara County Comprehensive Plan for Special Education, Santa Barbara County Schools, Santa Barbara California (1975). Based on materials from the Oregon State Department of Education.

2. Identification function of object. Show me what you do   YES   NO
   with this.
   a. comb
   b. toothbrush
   c. washcloth
3. Demonstrates understanding of spatial relationships.
   a. Put block on top of box.
   b. Put block under box.
   c. Put block behind box.
   d. Put block in front of box.
   e. Put block in back of box.
   f. Put block beside box.
4. Demonstrates understanding of polar opposites.
   Show me the one that is:
   a. big/little
   b. long/short
   c. full/empty
5. Matches shapes, "Show me the one that looks like
   this." ○ □ △

6. Identifies shapes (receptive) "Show me the
   __○ □ △__   ."

7. Matches colors. Place red, yellow, blue blocks in front
   of the child. Teacher holds up a block and says, "Show
   me the one that looks like this."
8. Identifies colors. Teacher presents 3 blocks at a time
   and says, "Show me _____."
9. Identifies own printed first name with distractors.
10. Identifies printed first name of classmates.
11. Identifies lowercase letters; uppercase.
12. Identifies left and right. "Show me your _____
    arm."
13. Marks on paper.
    a. finger paint
    b. crayon (with model and spontaneously)
    c. pencil (with model and spontaneously)
14. Traces printed shapes.
    a. vertical | d. cross
    b. horizontal | e. square
    c. circle | f. triangle
15. Reproduces lowercase letters with model.
16. Prints name, first, last.
17. Discriminates more and less.
18. Constructs set of 1 object; 2 objects; 3 objects.
19. Counts orally to 3; to 10.

20. Matches groups having equal number of objects to 10. YES NO
21. Reads numerals (1, 2, 3) to 3; to 10.
22. Matches numbers with appropriate point on number line.
23. Counts out a set number of objects on command from 10 objects.

III. EXPRESSIVE LANGUAGE

IV. TOILETING
   1. Uses toilet when placed on it.
   2. Indicates need to go to bathroom
   3. Is toileted with assistance.
   4. Tends to toileting procedure independently.

V. EATING
   1. Eats strained or liquified food from spoon.
   2. Eats mashed foods from spoon presented by teacher.
   3. Drinks from cup with help.
   4. Chews and swallows semi-solid foods.
   5. Picks up and eats finger foods.
   6. Drinks from cup unassisted.
   7. Uses spoon to scoop foods.
   8. Chews and swallows solid foods (raw carrot, apple).
   9. Drinks from glass; with help; without help.
   10. Uses fork.
   11. Drinks liquid with straw.
   12. Refrains from grabbing food from another's plate.

VII. GROSS MOTOR
   1. Turns head from side to side while lying on back.
   2. Lying on stomach, raises head to 90° angle.
   3. Lifts head and chest off floor and is supported by forearms.
   4. Rolls from stomach to back.
   5. Holds head steady while held in a sitting position.
   6. Holds head steady when pulled to sitting position.
   7. Sits on floor with legs spread (45° angle from body midline) for 10 seconds.
   8. Rolls from back to stomach.
   9. Sits in chair for 30 seconds with back supported.
   10. Moves independently on stomach 3 feet (crawls).
   11. Creeps on hands and knees 10 feet.
   12. Stands, bearing weight on 2 feet for 1 minute.
   13. Pulls to standing position.
   14. Gets to sitting position from lying down.
   15. Cruises (walking with help of holding onto furniture).
   16. Walks without support for 15 feet.

17. Throws (tennis size) ball 3 feet.   YES   NO
18. Stoops and recovers to standing position.
19. Walks without support, maintaining correct posture.
20. Walks backwards.
21. Runs (10 yards).
23. Kicks ball.
24. Catches 6" diameter ball.
25. Jumps with both feet.
26. Walks downstairs.
27. Jumps down.
28. Balances on one foot for 5 seconds.
29. Hops.
30. Throws ball 5 feet.

VIII. FINE MOTOR
1. Follows moving object with eyes from midline to left and right, while on back (2" to left and right of head).
2. Follows moving object w/eyes 90° left and right.
3. Reaches for bottle.
4. Touches hands together in midline.
5. Holds bottle without assistance.
6. Grasps toy when touched to fingers.
7. Grasps with palmar grasp 1" square block.
8. Takes block from table and holds with palmar grasp.
9. Releases 1" block; releases into cup.
10. Transfers toys from one hand to the other.
11. Grasps with pincer grasp.
12. Builds tower of blocks.
13. Places graduated size rings on peg.
14. Builds bridge of 3 blocks. T models.

15. Strings large beads.
16. Replaces round and square shapes on form board.
17. Works puzzles.
18. Builds with toys requiring fit.
19. Cuts with scissors, the following: | O △

IX. DRESSING
1. Undressing skills
    a. removes socks   d. removes shirt—pullover and fastened
    b. removes pants   e. removes shoes
    c. removes jacket
2. Dressing skills
    a. puts on socks   d. puts on jacket
    b. puts on pants   e. puts on shoes
    c. puts on shirt

3. Uses fasteners   YES   NO
   a. zips/unzips   c. unsnaps/snaps
   b. buttons/   d. ties/unties
      unbuttons

three

Assessment

One of the most controversial problems in education is too little vs. too much assessment (Sabatino, 1972a, p. 343).

Varying orientations and philosophies have led special educators to coin an array of terms for the process of identifying and analyzing learner characteristics and variables in the learner's environment. Such terms include:
educational diagnosis
psychoeducational study
psychological evaluation/assessment
formal/informal testing.
We use the term *educational assessment* inclusively, to accommodate all such terms and approaches, to the extent that their goal is not the labeling or categorizing of children, but the identification of learning needs. We regard the description we apply to the process as relatively unimportant; what is critical is the relationship of that process to instructional planning. Assessment, diagnosis, and evaluation must lead to action. This point is argued very clearly by Cromwell, Blashfield, and Strauss (1975) in their discussion on the

characteristics and validity of diagnostic constructs. Essentially, these authors suggest four components of a diagnostic category:

  A. historical-etiological data
  B. assessment of present behavior
  C. defined treatments or interventions
  D. predictive outcomes.

They emphasize that in obtaining A and B data, the situational and cultural context must be considered, and that it is actually components C and D which determine the usefulness and validity of diagnosis. "Diagnostic constructs that include C and D data (ACD, BCD, and ABCD) have clearly defined intervention procedures and prognostic statements. They are typically the most valid diagnostic constructs" (Cromwell, Blashfield, and Strauss, 1975, p. 11). Constructs derived from C and D data alone (CD), or from A and B data alone (AB), may be important but are not valid in diagnosis.

Educational assessment must be viewed as a continuous process which provides the rationale for specific planned instruction; instruction may itself provide a vehicle for further assessment. The assessment and planning phases flow on into evaluation as shown in Figure 5. Measures of pupil growth and change determine the validity of our instructional plan for a student and the accuracy of our assessment.

> The handicapped child's education is dependent upon a continuously changing instructional pattern, based upon his needs and functions. There is no one diagnostic statement that can cover any more than one educational planning period. In short, then, the term diagnostic-prescriptive implies that diagnosis should have an immediate relationship to teaching if it is to have any instructional value. The problem is that educational diagnosis is dynamic, continuous. The one-shot approach to psychoeducational child study sadly lacks the capability to validly sample behaviors leading directly to the instructional management of handicapped children (Sabatino, 1972a, p. 344).

Given the intimate relationship of assessment to instructional planning, it is difficult conceptually to separate them; we do so in this book merely to allow a logical sequencing of the content variables in these two areas. The diagnostic teaching model, developed by Cartwright and Cartwright (1972), which has the purpose of preventing or correcting learning problems and enhancing learning assets, provides a decision framework for the assessment approaches described in this chapter and the steps involved in instructional planning, which are presented in Chapter Four. This model has five essential steps. These steps or activities always occur in sequence (Ward et al., 1973, pp. 15–17):

Step 1: identify the relevant attributes or characteristics of the student; focus on those which are related to the behaviors of most concern to the teacher and on those which indicate a need for special teaching or management techniques.

Step 2: specify teaching goals; translate these goals into instructional objectives.

Step 3: select instructional strategies which will insure accomplishment of stated objectives and which will be appropriate to the known attributes of the learner.

Step 4: make and/or select appropriate materials related to specific strategies for instruction.

Step 5: test the strategies and materials; the ultimate test is, "Does it work with the child?" If the objective is reached, the next objective is specified; if not, steps 1–4 are repeated in sequence.

Certain Step-1 activities were discussed in Chapter Two; this chapter will attempt to present the more in-depth and extensive assessment activities which might be necessary in Step 1 above. These activities include:

observation
interviewing
examining school records
testing

These activities may, or may not, occur in this sequence, depending upon the individual child being studied. Not all of these activities are required for an adequate assessment of each child. Whether to begin with testing or with observation, or to include interviewing, can be determined only by a thorough analysis of the referral information which, as we noted in Chapter Two, culminates in the development of an initial plan for conducting the assessment. In any event, parents must be notified prior to the school beginning any assessment related to special educational programming. Such due process procedures are mandated by federal legislation (Public Law 94–142, 1975).

There is a growing trend toward educational assessments being conducted by a team of professionals, as opposed to being the, more or less, sole responsibility of the school psychologist. In many states where comprehensive plans for delivering special education services are being implemented, there is a two-level assessment process. The first level is provided by a team at the local school level, and a second level assessment team operates in the district, county, or larger region. The second level is usually reserved for complex and difficult cases which may require more extensive and detailed assessment. Since this book is addressed to meeting the needs of the mildly handicapped, we are concerned in this chapter with assessment techniques which are most appropriate for the local school assessment team. You will note, therefore, a heavy emphasis on the use of the more "informal" procedures as opposed to the standard diagnostic measures. In particular we have stressed the use of observation and interview methods, focusing both on the student and on environmental events—often neglected areas of assessment. As you review this chapter it will also become apparent that we see the classroom teacher as playing a critical role in the assessment process.

Observation

To observe is to take notice, to pay attention to what children do and what they say (Almy, 1959, p. 25).

Observation is a fundamental assessment technique which involves "systematically looking at and recording behavior for the purpose of making instructional decisions" (Cartwright and Cartwright, 1974, p. 3). By definition, observation occurs when someone, other than the student, notices and documents student behavior. In this way observation differs from testing—a situation in which the student makes his/her own record (writing answers on a

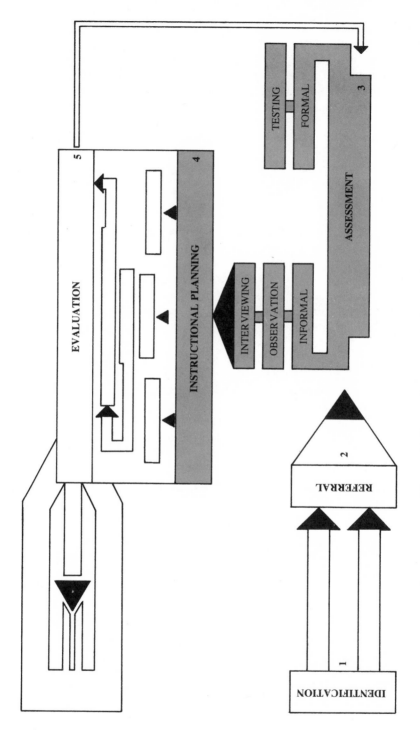

Figure 5. Instructional programming process.

test). There are many behaviors exhibited by students about which we might want to gather information and which cannot be studied through testing; for example, showing respect, sharing, playing with a group of peers. Direct observation methods allow us to assess such variables as:

> group participation and responsiveness
> individual behavior in a group
> attitudes toward academic work
> peer dynamics
> classroom structure and organization
> teaching methods and materials
> teaching style
> learning environment
> student-teacher interactions
> learner's history of success (entry behaviors).

Observation also plays a critical part in evaluation where the focus is on recording evidences of student achievement of objectives, and of the success of instructional interventions. Although it is not by any means a sufficient approach in all cases, observation has several distinct advantages over other assessment methods:

1. Observation provides us with a direct measure of behavior in natural settings; unlike psychological test results, observation data "speaks for itself" and does not need to be "translated" for the teacher.
2. The observer's attention is focused on facts as opposed to impressions and judgments.
3. Observation is an assessment process which can be conducted during ongoing instruction in the classroom.
4. The success of intervention techniques, educational methods and materials can be assessed on the basis of observation data; thus observation can increase teaching effectiveness.
5. Observation can itself be an intervention, bringing about change in student behavior.
6. Observation can result in a very precise assessment of student performance relative to the behaviors we expect the student to transfer to everyday situations. This is often a more reliable form of diagnosis than is psychological testing since the learner is usually performing without distraction or interruption.
7. While observing a particular target behavior, we may recognize previously unnoticed problems or side-effects.
8. Observation can provide teachers with hunches as to how learning may be facilitated.

Semmel (1975) argues that if we are to be able to select the teaching activities and conditions which are most likely to be effective in modifying the behavior and performance of a particular student, we must be able "to discriminate the state of a classroom or pupil at a given point in time during an educational interchange" (p. 258). For this reason, the starting point for the assessment process should be classroom observation, unless this has been thoroughly covered in the identification phase.

The classroom teacher is in a position to observe more of a student's learning behavior than anyone else on the assessment team and should therefore be seen as a primary contributor to and interpreter of assessment results (Hammill, 1971). With a little training and practice, we can all learn to observe behavior more objectively and precisely, thus becoming more able to interpret behavior diagnostically rather than judgmentally. Observation has a very long history in the field of child study; there are many very sophisticated methods, some old, some new, which can be used, including film, video, and/or audio tape techniques. Such methods are not reviewed here since they are too complex and time-consuming for typical classroom situations. The intent of this section is to provide information which will increase the skill of classroom teachers as educational decision makers. Simple systems for gathering information—anecdotal records, participation charts, frequency and time sampling—will be discussed, as well as additional uses for checklists and rating scales. Guidelines for selecting an observation approach and some cautions regarding the limitations of observation approaches, along with suggestions for off-setting these, are presented. First, let's outline some basic skills or prerequisites to the use of any particular observation method.

Observation Skills

Although there are definite situations where one approach is appropriate and another not, the effectiveness of all observation methods depends on the skill of the observer. Here are some suggestions:

1. *Select and define the target behavior*. If a student is "screened out" and referred for further assessment, it means that there is a general category of behavior (often several behavioral areas) of concern to the teacher. Focus at first on the most critical in the perception of the teacher. Define, or describe, that behavior precisely and in such a way that most people would be able to agree that they had seen an instance of it. Saying that Todd is "constantly trying to attract attention" doesn't tell us much about what Todd does that really bothers us. What does Todd actually do? Does he "make faces"; shout answers when it's not his turn; bring presents to the teacher; or crawl under his desk?

Todd's actual observable behaviors must be listed in order to define "attracting attention."

2. *Note the setting for, and events following, the demonstration of target behavior.* This may be difficult at first, but through practice in immediately recording what you see it beomes easier. Analysis of Todd's behavior might reveal, for example, that Todd resorts to attention-seeking behavior following verbal reprimands from the teacher, or only in large group situations. Noticing the events that repeatedly follow the behavior, such as peer approval or teacher recognition, may suggest ways to control or change the target behavior. The setting includes such things as time of day, date, classroom activity, work assignment, people and materials involved, and behavior of others. Awareness of any or all of these items may help you determine what triggers the behavior being studied. Since the classroom teacher is so close to the situation it will often be necessary for a member of the school assessment team to assist in identifying the significant variables surrounding the behavior being studied.

3. *Be thoroughly informed about the purpose underlying the observation.* This will influence your choice of observation method and recording procedure.

4. *Be as unobtrusive as possible.* Your presence may alter the behavior being observed.

5. *Try to get lots of observation data.* Choose a variety of settings for data collection—the playground, independent study, group situations, and so on. Usually behavior patterns do not become evident in a short span of time. To notice change or growth, observational records must be kept over time. Remember there are cycles and trends in behavior; some observations will merely reflect a temporary deviation and we must look at a larger sample of behavior to determine what is typical for the student.

6. *Select or design appropriate data-recording procedures.* Recording should be quick, efficient, and easily understandable by another person.

7. *Experiment with the procedure and forms.* Practice various observation techniques several times before data gathering. Observe several learners in the same situation for comparison.

8. *Be precise.* Lack of precision in information-gathering leads to misinterpretation of data and faulty instructional decision making.

9. *Do a reliability check.* Have another person observe the same student; compare your records. The teacher and the resource teacher, for example, should "exchange notes."

10. *Interpret your data cautiously.* Avoid the temptation to try to determine "cause" and the pitfall of circular reasoning (saying that a child
who does not pay attention or sit still is "hyperactive," and then later
explaining to his/her parent or teacher that the problems of inattention
and restlessness are caused by hyperactivity). Make tentative inferences about process variables (such as feelings and attitudes) *only* on
the basis of accumulated evidence (patterns or clusters of specific
behaviors). Above all, don't jump to conclusions!

Types of Observation

1. *Anecdotal records* are reports of informal teacher observations of students
and are primarily used to provide a qualitative picture of certain aspects of
social functioning or adjustment (Thorndike and Hagen, 1955). Observations
of unanticipated behaviors or incidents should be recorded in the anecdotal
format. By recording a behavioral event immediately after it occurs we gather
dependable data that cannot become warped or distorted in our memory. "A
set of such records provides stable evidence on which later appraisals can be
based" (Thorndike and Hagen, 1955, p. 484). We can look for recurring
patterns and progressive changes in a student's behavior and relate the anecdotal data to other information known about a student. Note that comments in
"cum" folders are *not* anecdotal records since they are not based on direct and
immediate observation; rather, they are subjective appraisals of the student.

Thorndike and Hagen (1955) state that a well-prepared and useful anecdotal
record has the following features:

a. It provides an accurate description of a specific event.
b. It describes the setting sufficiently to give the event meaning.
c. If it includes interpretation or evaluation by the recorder, this interpretation is
separated from the description and its different status is clearly identified.
d. The event it describes is one that relates to the child's personal development or
social interactions.
e. The event it describes is either representative of the typical behavior of the
child or significant because it is strikingly different from his usual form of
behavior. If it is unusual behavior for the child, that fact is noted (p. 486).

At first you may find that your behavioral descriptions are too lengthy. Try not
to be discouraged; your observation reports will become more concise as you
gain skill in identifying the critical elements of behavior.

Two very helpful resources on the use of observation methods are the books
by Almy (1959) and Cartwright and Cartwright (1974) referenced at the end

of this chapter. Anecdotal records I and II are examples drawn from these books.

Anecdotal Record I

Name: Bryan G.	Date: 10/17/75
Observer: T. Melchor	Time: 10:30 a.m.
Setting: Math	

Incident: When it was time for Bryan to work with a group in the Math Center, he said, "I want to stay at my own desk."

Anecdotal Record II

Name: Bryan G.	Date: 10/20/75
Observer: T. Melchor	Time: 1:30 p.m.
Setting: Recess	

Incident: The whole class was out on the playground, engaged in various games and activities. Bryan stood by himself beside the swings where the younger children were playing.

Note the precise format used. Interpretations can be added, if desired, beneath the factual report of the incident. These two examples, when part of a sequence of such behaviors, can be interpreted to mean that the student, Bryan, avoids situations involving peer interaction.

Almy provides an example (A, which follows) of anecdotal data where the teacher has tried to describe a student's behavior clearly and without allowing her interpretation of it to creep into the report. She contrasts this with example B, following.

Example A:

Helen came into the room today and took her seat without speaking to anyone in the room. She maintained an attentive attitude throughout the class period but took no part in the class discussion. When asked for a contribution once during the period, she flushed, shook her head, and remained silent. She picked up her books when the bell rang and left the room alone (Almy, 1974, p. 49).

Example B:

Helen is a shy, reticent, unsocial girl who does not make friends easily, who does not participate in class discussions, and who is alone much of the time (Almy, 1974, p. 50).

2. *Observations Involving Measurement.* Several approaches to observational recording which involve numerical outputs will be briefly described here. Included are: frequency (event) recording; duration recording; time sampling; and the "placheck" method. These techniques can be used efficiently and effectively in school situations to obtain baseline data—the measure of a behavior under a set of stable conditions. Gathering baseline data on the target behavior is essential if we are to accurately measure and evaluate behavioral changes which result from implementing various teaching strategies.

2.1 *Frequency or event recording* is simply a count of the *number of times* the target behavior occurs. The teacher might count and add up the number of times the student responded to verbal questions, or left his/her seat during a school morning or day. Counting devices, such as a wristband golf-counter, may be used, or simple tally marks written on a piece of paper will suffice. Frequency recording is used for counting behaviors which are single units: push-ups, talk-outs, thank-yous said, and hitting. Many behaviors of this type occur at a very high rate and are of short duration, making it difficult for us to recall their frequency when we rely on memory alone. Systematic recording can help us find out if Todd *really* gets out of his chair excessively, or if it only *seems* that he does. Low rate behaviors are those which occur more infrequently and which are more difficult to describe in discrete observable units (such as temper outbursts and stealing). To get information on low rate behaviors we would rely not on frequency recording, but, rather, on teacher reports or interviews with the student, teacher, and parents.

Frequency counts made on a regular basis also enable us to notice small improvements in behavior—and remember, behavior changes *slowly*. Precision Teaching is an observation and data-gathering system based on frequency counts which is particularly appropriate for assessing behavior change, and is one which students can learn to use for monitoring their own behavior. Information sources on Precision Teaching are included at the end of this chapter.

2.2 *Duration Recording* is a method for use when we are concerned with *how much time* is spent in a particular behavior. The amount of time a student is "on-task" might be of interest—or the length of time a pre-schooler engages in parallel play. To record these behaviors a conventional watch or clock can be used (a stopwatch, if available, adds precision). During any given observation period we simply note the time the behavior starts and when it stops, then record the elapsed time. We might, for example, observe a student for a total of 20 minutes each day for 5 days (100 minutes), recording the duration of each display of "on-task" behavior, and totaling the amount each day. Our data might look something like this:

Total minutes on task

Student:	Richard	Day 1	5
		2	7
		3	5
		4	8
		5	8
		Total	33

We would then have some evidence to show that the student is "on-task" only about one-third of the time. Duration recording is very time-consuming for the observer, but can be used efficiently when the teacher is assisted by a resource teacher or an aide.

2.3 *Time Sampling* is a technique which, like frequency recording, is very useful in observing high rate behaviors. The observation period is divided into equal time intervals—a 30-minute observation session might be divided into ten three-minute intervals—and the observer only records behavior at the *end* of the interval or, in this instance, every 3 minutes. What happens in the minute before or after is not recorded. In the following example, the observer recorded "out-of-seat" behavior every 3 minutes for 30 minutes, marking a + (plus) when the behavior was occurring at the end of a 3 minute period and − (minus) when it was not.

+ = out-of-seat
− = in-seat

−	+	+	+	+	−	+	−	+	+
3	6	9	12	15	18	21	24	27	30

minutes

The data show that the student was "out-of-seat" 70% of the time the observer sampled the behavior.

The time sampling method is especially useful for teachers in that it does not require their constant attention. In time sampling, shorter intervals generally lead to more accurate data; the observer must decide, however, on predetermined time periods within which to observe, based on past experience with the particular target behavior.

2.4 *Placheck* (Planned Activity Check) is a recording technique originally developed by Risley (1971), which is useful for teachers interested in observing *groups* of students. As described by Hall (1971), the procedure is as follows:

1. The observer scientifically defines the behavior (planned activity) he wishes to record in a group of children.
2. At given intervals (e.g., each ten minutes) the observer counts as quickly as possible how many individuals are engaged in the behavior, recording the total.
3. The observer then counts and records as quickly as possible how many individuals are present in the area of the activity.
4. The number of pupils present can then be divided into the number of pupils engaged in the behavior. By multiplying the result by 100, the observer finds the percent of those engaged in the behavior at a particular time (p. 4).

Hall provides the following example of how the "Placheck" method works:

. . . suppose a shop teacher wants to check on what portion of his class is working on an assigned woodworking project during a 50 minute period. Each ten minutes he quickly counts how many are working on the project. He then counts the number of pupils present. Let's suppose that during the first part of the period he finds that 10/20 and 15/20 are working. During the second part of the period, ten boys who had been excused to work on another project return to the class. He then finds 15/30, 30/30 and 20/30 of those present working on the assigned project. That is, 50 percent, 75 percent, 50 percent, 100 percent and 67 percent, or a mean of 68 percent worked on the assigned project during the class period (p. 4).

The book by Vance Hall from which the above excerpt was taken is listed in the references for this chapter and is an extremely practical resource on observing and recording behavior in school settings.

3. *Checklists and Rating Scales.* Several of the instruments mentioned in Chapter Two under screening devices, can be used to systematically record observed behaviors of individual students. A frequently neglected source of relevant data for instructional planning is the *environment,* or situational context, in which the behavior is displayed—the classroom, school, and home. Following are some specific approaches to observing the classroom and environmental events within it. We feel that the use of such approaches is

extremely critical in the assessment and determination of techniques to maximize the handicapped child's effective interaction with the regular curriculum, subject matter, peers, and adults.

Teachers of young children may find the *Evaluation Checklist* developed by Harms (1972) extremely useful in identifying strengths and weaknesses in their own classroom environment. This checklist consists of lists of questions organized into four categories: physical environment; interpersonal environment; activities to stimulate development; and schedule. Sample questions include, "Can quiet and noisy activities go on without disturbing one another?"; "Do the adults show children how to help themselves?"; "Do children do real things like cooking, planting seeds, caring for animals?"; "Are children involved in suggesting and planning activities?" (pp. 383–85).

The checklist shown on the following pages is an adaptation of one designed and used by these authors to determine physical and methodological changes made by elementary teachers in their classroom environments. Such a checklist, when completed, can give a useful picture of the environment in which the student being studied is expected to function, although it does not reflect individual student reaction to the environment. The checklist was originally designed to measure the extent to which "open education" concepts, such as student-directed learning in activity centers and individualized instruction and scheduling, were being utilized in combination with a structured behavior management system. Two additional checklists follow.

Classroom Environment Checklist*

DATE OF OBSERVATION _____

TIME OF OBSERVATION _____

NAME OF OBSERVER _____

NAME OF TEACHER _____

NAME OF SCHOOL _____

GRADE LEVEL _____

IS A TEACHER AIDE ASSIGNED TO THIS CLASS? _____

1. Room Arrangement:
   a. Furniture is arranged for use by:
      ( ) total group only
      ( ) small groups
      ( ) large groups
      ( ) individuals

---

*Developed by C.B. Volkmor, A.L. Langstaff, and M. Higgins, University of Southern California, 1971.

DRAW A QUICK SKETCH OF FURNITURE ARRANGEMENT:

b. Activity Centers Evident:

( ) LIBRARY   ( ) ACTIVITY-GAMES

___ Books (10 or more different)   (List 3 items present)

___ Other Reading Material

_____   _____

_____   _____

( ) AUDIO-VISUAL   ( ) ARTS & CRAFTS

(List 2 items of equipment)   (List 2 activities present)

_____   _____

_____   _____

( ) SCIENCE   ( ) OTHER _____

(List at least 1 item present)   (List 2 items present)

_____   _____

_____   _____

( ) OTHER _____

_____

_____

c. Children use Activity Centers without direct teacher supervision

( ) YES   ( ) NO

2. Room Environment

Objects NOT typical of classroom equipment:

( ) Easy Chair   ( ) Cushions   ( ) Other _____

( ) Lamp   ( ) Posters   ( ) Other _____

( ) Area Rugs   ( ) Mobiles   ( ) Other _____

( ) Individual Study
    Carrels

Comments: _____

_____

3. Rewards

a. Individual children rewarded for academic   ( ) Yes   ( ) No
   behaviors

b. Individual children rewarded for social behaviors   ( ) Yes   ( ) No

c. Teacher rewards appropriate group behavior   ( ) Yes   ( ) No

Comments: _____

_____

d. Types of Rewards: Available   Used During Observation

( ) Checkmarks   ( ) Touch   ( ) Tokens

( ) Praise, Smile   ( ) Stars

( ) Activities, Privileges ( ) Free Time

( ) Tangibles

Comments: _____

_____

e. Kids have opportunity to choose type of reward   ( ) Yes   ( ) No
Comments: _____

_____

4. Student Contracts
  a. Teacher or aide checks off child's work as soon as
    completed   ( ) Yes   ( ) No
  b. Free time or choice of activity immediately follows
    task completion   ( ) Yes   ( ) No
5. Individualized Instruction
  a. Students do different level tasks   ( ) Yes   ( ) No
  Comments: _____

_____

  b. Students have individual schedules   ( ) Yes   ( ) No
  c. Individual schedules include group tasks, individual
    tasks and reward time   ( ) Yes   ( ) No
  Comments: _____

_____

  d. Folders are used for daily work   ( ) Yes   ( ) No
  (If you marked "NO" above, explain how tasks were presented to students:

_____

_____

_____

6. Materials
  Check (✓) materials, equipment, or activities visibly available to children in classroom. Check twice (✓✓) those things you observe in use while you are in the classroom. Give examples if possible where space is provided.

ARTS AND CRAFTS
__ Chalk
__ Charcoal
__ Clay
__ Crayons
__ Collage and Paper Mache Materials
  (paste, paper, etc.)
__ Finger Paint
__ Macrame
__ Models
__ Mosaics
__ Origami (Japanese Paper Folding)
__ Painting
__ Stitchery
__ Woodwork
__ Other _____

_____

_____

AUDIO VISUAL
__ Camera
__ Cassette and Cassette Tapes
__ Films
__ Projector
__ Filmstrips
__ Viewer
__ Language Master
__ Overhead Projector
__ Records
__ Record Player
__ Slides
__ Projector or Viewer
__ Tapes
__ Tape Recorder
__ Other _____

_____

_____

If many, estimate # _____   If many, estimate # _____

GAMES   *SCIENCE*
Estimate Number _____   __ Animals _____
__ _____   __ Aquarium
__ _____   __ Chemistry Set
__ _____   __ Electricity Experiment
__ Puzzles (jigsaw, crossword,   (battery, etc.)
   shapes)   __ Herb Garden
__ Other _____   __ Magnets
   _____   __ Magnifying Glass
   _____   __ Measuring Instruments (measuring
                                             cups, spoons, rulers, yardsticks)
                                          __ Microscope
LIBRARY   __ Plants
                                          __ Terrarium
__ Magazines _____   __ Rock Collection
   _____   __ Shell Collection
   _____   __ Thermometer
__ Newspapers   __ Barometer
   _____   __ Weights
   _____   __ Other _____
                                             _____
__ Dictionary   _____
__ Encyclopedia
__ Recreational Reading Book
If many, estimate # _____   If many, estimate # _____

7. Were there unusual physical circumstances in the room? (Bolted down furniture, no
   wall space, small room, etc.) Explain:
   _____
   _____
   _____

8. Briefly describe what was happening in the class at the time of observation:
   _____
   _____
   _____

9. Do you consider that this was a valid assessment of what goes on daily in the
   classroom?   ( ) Yes   ( ) No   (If No, explain)
   _____
   _____
   _____

                                         _____
                                              Signature of Observer

The next two checklists are designed for recording observations of an individual student, functioning in the classroom environment. Note that the form calls for observation of teacher style and methods as well as student responses.

In-class Observation*

PUPIL NAME _____ SCHOOL _____

  I. A. Reason for Referral:
      B. Needs as seen by classroom teacher:
 II. A. Physical Environment (include lighting, sound, color, number of students, seating, organization of classroom, daily schedule):
      B. Instructional Materials Available (include those student is using):
      C. Time and duration of observation and activities observed:
III. A. Management and Instructional Techniques of the Teacher (use of positive or negative reinforcement. Note disruptive behavior and teacher-child interaction. Modality used by teacher in presenting material and type of follow-up, etc.):
      B. Behavior in Group Situations (large, small):
      C. Coping level, reaction to stress, frustration:
      D. Behavior in structured vs. non-structured situations:
      E. Degree of self-direction, ability to organize work, degree of independent functioning; ability to complete assigned work at school and home and ability to attend to task:
      F. Interaction with Peers:
      G. Academic functioning and skills in:
         Pre-academic:
         Reading:
         Written work:
         Math:
         Social studies:
         Motor—gross and fine:
         Learning style:
         Language:
      H. Areas of Interest:
      I. Additional Information

OBSERVER'S NAME _____

TITLE _____

---

*Developed by Santa Barbara County Comprehensive Plan for Special Education, Santa Barbara County Schools, Santa Barbara, California, 1975.

Classroom Observation*

Student's Name   Teacher's Name

School   Grade

Time of Day   Length of Observation (Minutes)

Classroom Setting: (Approximate number of students, room arrangement, etc.)

Specific Activity (Reading, Math, etc.—Size of group, etc.)

Observations of student interactions with peers as they affect functioning in the regular program.

Additional Comments:

———— ———— In the judgment of the classroom teacher, was the student's
 Yes   No   behavior during the observed period of time "typical" of his usual
                school performance?

Signature of the Observer
(Resource Specialist, Program Specialist, Psychologist)

Date

4. *Designing Your Own Observation Tools*. Rather than relying solely on published checklists, teachers or resource persons can design their own. Teacher-designed checklists are particularly relevant when the purpose is to assess the extent to which teaching has been effective (evaluation). Instructional objectives, or terminal behaviors, stated earlier for the student can simply be expressed as checklist items; for example, "Counts by 10's to 100" or "uses adverbs correctly." Cartwright and Cartwright (1974) suggest that

*Developed by Santa Monica Unified School District, Department of Special Services, Santa Monica, California, 1975.

teachers, through experience in working with students, can add checklist items which allow variations from the expected behavior to be noted. In this way, the diagnostic value of the checklist is increased. These authors point out that the checklist is used most efficiently when the items are listed by the teacher in the order in which s/he expects the behaviors to occur. Dates when the behavior is noted can also be placed beside the checklist items.

A useful technique for observing several students simultaneously is the Participation Chart. The names of the students are listed in a column and space is provided beside each name to record the sequence and frequency of each person's participation in group activities or discussions. The number of times each student participates is totalled and can then be compared with the others in the group. A teacher who is concerned that the same few students always dominate group discussions might use the Participation Chart approach to test out his/her hunch. The following sample chart showing hypothetical data on verbal interactions was adapted from Almy (1959, p. 30).

Sample Participation Chart

Observer: Ms. Anderson	**Date:** 1/12/76

Activity: Small group discussion following lesson on fossils.

TOTAL

Students:	
Manuel	0
Carla	1
Nettie	0
Raoul	0
Hughston	4
Maria	0
Laura	2
Sandy	3

Both Almy (1959) and Cartwright and Cartwright (1974) provide additional discussion and illustration of the use of Participation Charts.

Choosing a Method

Selection of one particular observation method over another depends largely on the target behavior itself and the instructional decision to be made. Hall, Hawkins, and Axelrod (1975) suggest some considerations in choosing a specific observation method:

the duration of the behavior being studied
how obvious the behavior is

the number of behaviors being recorded
the amount of behavioral change expected
the degree of precision desired in measurement
the amount of time and attention which can be devoted to recording the behavior
(p. 199).

In addition, examine whether the method focuses on positive as well as negative behaviors (many checklists do not), and whether data summaries, collected via the method being considered, are easily read by classroom teachers.

Limitations of Observation

1. *Observer bias*. The personal element in observation can never be completely removed; the way we see others grows out of our own experiences with people, and we do not see precisely the same things as the person next to us does.

2. *Halo effect*. This refers to the tendency to give a higher or lower rating to a behavior than it deserves as a result of a generally favorable or unfavorable impression already held by the observer toward the observed. We tend to rate children we like more generously—those who bother us, more severely.

3. *Logical error*. The observer makes an assumption about the relationship of two characteristics given knowledge of one characteristic, e.g., a child with articulation difficulties is presumed to have language comprehension lag.

4. *Limits of human memory*.

5. *Unreliability of observation data*. The data may not be truly representative of the student's typical functioning; this problem is often the result of making too few observations (the child may have been at a low ebb) and of arriving at conclusions too soon without considering the observation data in context. In addition, the observer is limited in the amount of time s/he can spend observing a single student or group.

Tips for Improving Observation

1. *Don't rely on memory*—make a record while the observation is being conducted.

2. *Record details objectively, accurately,* and as completely as possible without evaluating (unless using a predetermined rating system). Learn to sort out your feelings from the facts.

3. Where possible, *use several ratings,* taken by a number of different observers.

4. *Be aware* of the influence of "halo" effect and logical error and consciously monitor observation behavior to eliminate these biases.

5. *Operationally define behaviors* to be observed so that there is ready

agreement between two observers as to what constitutes an instance of *X* behavior.

6. *Design or select* recording instruments which focus on positive as well as negative behavior.

7. *Gather information over an adequate period of time* and a variety of situations to insure that a reliable, valid, and sufficient sampling of behavior is obtained prior to drawing conclusions.

8. *Look for patterns of behavior* that can be substantiated through other means of assessment.

9. Where possible, *have others observe the same behavior* and compare findings. Outside observers often pick up data that the teacher does not see because s/he is too close to the situation.

10. *Be as unobtrusive as possible* during the observation period to minimize the effect of the observer on the observed.

11. *Observe* during times when learners are working independently.

12. *Make use of time* when learners are being supervised by others, such as at recess or during team-teaching.

13. *Make prearranged schedules* for observation.

14. *Develop coding or shorthand systems* for recording information.

15. *Become selective in observations* and focus on behaviors which tend to be representative of behavior patterns.

16. *Decide* if another assessment procedure would yield the same information and be less time-consuming.

17. *Regard observation data as hypotheses* to be tested, not conclusive evidence about the child.

18. *Observe the child performing a particular task;* your job of drawing an inference is enhanced by the circumscribed nature of the task and the anticipated type of response (Meyen, 1972, p. 155).

19. *Observe the child within the curricular areas of the mainstream,* for "The assumption is that performance on mainstream curriculum tasks . . . is criterion performance and the handicapped child's failure to function typically on these tasks leads to his being considered a problem" (Deno and Gross, 1972, p. 118).

Outcomes of Observation

The use of systematic observation methods allows us to gather firsthand evidence on which to base educational decisions—decisions about further assessment, learner objectives, teaching procedures, instructional materials, behavior management, and classroom environment. Observation of baseline behavior and of environmental variables can suggest hypotheses to be tested in the instructional phase.

Observation techniques permit us to study some very critical kinds of learning which do not result in a permanent product, such as cooperating with members of a group, or doing daily chores. Through observation we can evaluate the extent to which such learned behaviors are transferred into everyday living. Problem behaviors can be detected much earlier by the teacher who uses a standard format for recording observation data, thus gathering information on the student's behavior patterns.

Observation is an efficient tool to use in evaluating learner achievement of stated objectives. Daily or weekly observation records may reveal small gains or improvements that would otherwise go unnoticed.

Depending upon your purpose, and the behaviors being studied, the rigorous application of observation methods may produce an almost sufficient data base for beginning to plan instruction. This is often true for affective, social, and management behaviors. For information processing and academic skill problems, the observational data will frequently point to specific areas which require more precise measurement or testing. The opposite is also true; formal assessment may be followed by "in situ" observation. Through observation of the student's behavior at school you may decide that it is essential to gather information from the home, perhaps through interviewing.

Interviewing*

> If you give a child a hammer, things to be pounded become the most important things around (Willems and Rausch, 1969, p. 45, on the "Law of the Hammer").

The "Law of the Hammer" dictates that our information is often limited by our choice of assessment tools. Systematic observation of behavior in the classroom, as noted earlier, may only be useful in the case of frequently occurring behavior problems. This is especially true where the method of observation is cumbersome and must be done by someone other than the classroom teacher. Consequently, exclusive reliance on systematic observation could cause us to focus too intently on common problems such as task-related classroom behavior, talk-outs, noncompliance with classroom rules, etc., and to ignore assessment of problems such as fighting with peers, lying, stealing, temper tantrums, poor achievement, etc. Systematic observation might also miss outside environmental events influencing student behavior, e.g., lack of breakfast before school, domination by an older sibling outside of school, illness, teacher-pupil interaction when the observer is not present, or major contingencies affecting student behavior of which the observer is unaware.

---

*The entire section on interviewing was developed and written by Dr. Karl Skindrud, School of Education, California State College, Dominguez Hills, Carson, California, 1976.

The "Law of the Hammer" implies that exclusive reliance on any single method of data collection is likely to bias the diagnostician. As will be shown later in the section on testing, reliance upon psychometric testing of cognitive processes has provided a limited scope for the remediation of academic problems.

Types and Uses of Interviewing

The interview offers some major advantages as an informal method of data collection. While various precautions must be exercised in its use, the resource teacher would be foolish to avoid interviewing school staff and the student him/herself as the initial assessment strategy, and indeed should conduct further interviews when systematic observation and psychometric testing have proven fruitless. The major advantage of the interview is its efficiency and almost unlimited scope. The types of information appropriately gathered by interview include:

assessment of teacher concerns about student behavior;
description of classroom rules and performance objectives (teacher expectations);
estimation of low base rate behavior problems not accessible to one-hour classroom observations;
assessment of parent concerns regarding student behaviors in the home and classroom;
description of home management and tutoring procedures (parent expectations);
description of provision for biological, developmental, and social needs in the home (sleep, diet, peer relations, etc.);
obtaining a history of early development (birth injuries, trauma, serious illnesses, attention, family constellation, etc.);
assessment of student motivational variables (interests, reinforcers, fears, expectations, cooperation, etc.);
negotiation of work contracts;
persuasion of the teachers, parents, or the student of the importance and/or possibility for improvement in student behavior, performance, etc.;
informal evaluation of attempts to remediate behavior problems or performance;
assessment of attitudes.

Approaches to interviewing vary from open to structured. The *open* interview has the advantage of allowing the informant to immediately share any major concerns about the student. Rather than seeking specific information, the interviewer uses the basic interviewing skills of attending, asking open-ended questions, paraphrasing and encouraging further conversation, reflection of feeling, and summarization.

Eventually, the interviewer will want to move into a *structured* format and begin probing for specific information so that the information gathered is not entirely biased by the informant's perceptions. The outline below has been suggested by Kanfer and Saslow (1968) for the comprehensive assessment of all possible environmental and developmental determinants naturally related to problem behaviors. Their outline has been adapted to the school situation by the present author:

1. *Analysis of the problem situation.* What are the behavioral excesses, deficits, and assets of the student as seen by the teacher? By his parents? By him/herself?

2. *Clarification of the problem situation.* Who objects to the problem behaviors? Who tends to support them? What events led to the crisis resulting in referral? What consequences does the problem have for the student? For the teacher? For peers? Parents? Siblings? What would be the benefits of removal of the problem for the student and others? Does the problem behavior occur in the classroom? On the playground? To and from school? At home? Does the problem only occur in reading, or math? During seatwork or group activities? With one teacher or all teachers?

3. *Motivational analysis.* How does the student rank various incentives in their importance to him/her? Which of the following reinforcing events are most effective in initiating or maintaining his/her behavior: adult approval; peer approval; choice of free activities following seatwork; group participation; competition; tangible reinforcers; independent projects; avoidance of teacher disapproval; peer disapproval; aversive consequences. Under what specific conditions do these motivational variables appear effective? Do they require parent approval or cooperation? Who or what has the most effective and widespread control of the student's current behavior? Can the student relate reinforcement contingencies to his/her own behavior, or does s/he fail to perceive the influences controlling his/her behavior? Which motivational variables and events are most accessible for utilization in the school?

4. *Developmental analysis.* What are the student's current biological limitations (physical defects, sensory limitations, results of serious illnesses)? What is the student's response to them? What is the student's relevant developmental history? How will these biological conditions limit response to remediation? What are the characteristic features of the student's present sociocultural milieu (ethnic and socioeconomic affiliation)? Are his/her attitudes congruent with his/her milieu? Have there

been changes in this milieu which are pertinent to current behavior? What are the most recent major changes in the student's behavior? Are any of these changes correlated with recent major changes in the student's developmental history or sociocultural milieu? Can the problem behaviors be traced to a model in the student's social environment from whom s/he has learned these behaviors?

5. *Analysis of environmental contingencies maintaining problem behaviors.* What conditions, persons, instructional settings or strategies, reinforcers, or contingencies tend to change his/her behavior? Can these conditions be maximized without deleterious effects to the student? Are there situations where the student manifests appropriate self-management of problem behaviors? How does s/he achieve such control—by manipulation of self or others? Are more severe problem behaviors subject to acceptable aversive consequences by others? Is there a correspondence between the student's verbalized self-control and observations by others? Is teacher and/or self-monitoring necessary to increase self-awareness or acquire additional information?

Many other structured formats are available for the collection of information on the classroom, learning and behavior problems, developmental histories, and so on. While the above format appears to comprehensively assess those critical environmental and developmental variables most functionally related to learning and behavior problems, any one area could deserve more in-depth probing. Often a school nurse has forms available for obtaining detailed information on the early developmental histories of children. Such medically-related information may be best obtained by her, unless she is unavailable. A general strategy is to look for immediate environmental causes. If adequate attempts to improve the environmental management of the problem behaviors are unsuccessful, then interdisciplinary assessment may be necessary to determine significant developmental deviations impairing progress.

Limitations of Interviewing

The major limitation of the interview as a data collection technique is its retrospective and interpretive nature. You are relying on the informant's memory of past events with all its susceptibility to selective recall. Recent research has determined that retrospective global judgments are more susceptible to bias than discrete behavioral observations (O'Leary, Kent, and Kanowitz, 1975).

Checking the information sought by interviews with several informants familiar with the problem situation may increase reliability. Interviews with the teacher, parent, and *student* are minimally required in any attempt to remediate serious learning or behavior problems.

Tips for Improving Interviews

Interviewing teachers, parents, and students who have learning and/or behavior problems at school is a useful method of data collection. However, as is often the case in working with individuals where there is a problem, the information provided may be consciously or unconsciously biased by the informant. How the resource teacher initiates and conducts the interview can significantly improve or interfere with the communication process.

Adopting a habitual role of "fact-finder" (seeking information, ignoring feelings), "fix-it specialist" (solving the problem for another), "advisor" (telling another what to do), "judge" (evaluating others' feelings), and "questioner" (always seeking more information) can turn off others to openly sharing the information they have. Seeking complete information from others in a problem situation is more productive where the interviewer recognizes the other person's strengths as well as weaknesses, presents himself/herself as having experienced similar problems and recognizes the other person's feelings (often expressed nonverbally). It may also be helpful to recognize how others tend to see you as an interviewer: Mr. Nice Guy (always friendly, but unassertive); Mr. Tough Guy (aggressive and domineering); Mr. Logical (objective, but lacking awareness of feelings). Self-awareness of one's own behavior patterns in interpersonal situations allows one to deal more effectively with others in an interview situation (Tubesing and Tubesing, 1973). Some tips on improving communication in the interview situation follow:

1. *Listen attentively to the informant.* Communicate this attentiveness through a relaxed posture, use of varied eye contact, and verbal responses, which indicate an attempt to understand the informant.
2. *Ask open-ended questions initially.* For example: "What is your major concern about Sally?" "What do you feel could be done to improve the situation?" "What has been done to deal with the problem?" You will obtain more information of potential usefulness through open invitations to talk (although more time may be required) than through the use of close-ended questions, e.g., "Is Billy a problem in math?" "Does he have difficulty relating to his peers during recess?" "Have the parents been cooperative during conferences?" Such specific questions can be directed to the teacher (parents, or student) *after* you have heard their interpretation of the problem.

    A typical problem with closed questions is that the interviewer leads the client to topics of interest to the interviewer only. Too often an interviewer projects his own theoretical orientation onto the information he is trying to gather. Often if the interviewer relies on closed questions to structure the interview, s/he is forced to concentrate so hard on thinking up the next question that s/he fails to listen and attend to the informant.

3. *Recognize and use nonverbal communication.* Learn to "read" body language as clues to another's true feelings about the problem situation. The voice: its loudness, tone, rate of speed, firmness, and phrasing. The face: its tenseness, eye contact, responsiveness, and willingness to smile. Body posture: orientation to the interviewer, amount of tension (clenched fist, sweaty palms, and so on). The language pattern: the nature of the topics discussed, outside information, personal feelings, beliefs a person holds very important, or perceptions.

 The nonverval cues, together with what is *not* said, may communicate more than a person's words taken alone. Often a teacher is really saying she's "had it" with a certain problem student, but she's unwilling to admit defeat and does not say it. Recognizing her true feelings may open the door to cooperative efforts in solving the problem.

4. *Paraphrase and summarize the informant's message.* If not done to excess, this conveys interest, crystallizes the message, and checks the interviewer's perception of the informant's intended communication. Paraphrasing is a restatement of the informant's communication in order to test your understanding of his/her comment. It is a statement in your own words of what the informant's comment conveyed to you. For example, *Teacher:* "I've got 35 students and they each have their own problems. Parents are coming in and asking me to give their child special attention. The administrator wants this, the reading specialist that, the social worker something else. They never offer to help with any of my problems." *Interviewer:* "You feel that everyone is making demands on you without being of assistance."

5. *Recognize different levels of communication and their effects* (Tubesing and Tubesing, 1973). Advice, interpretation, support, probing, and paraphrasing each elicit different responses in the informant. What may be appropriate at one point may be inappropriate at another. *Paraphrasing* is the least restrictive and encourages the informant to give his/her view of the problem. *Probing* gets information but limits areas about which the informant can talk. *Support* (e.g., "All people feel that way at times") tends to shift the focus from the feelings of the informant to those of the interviewer. *Interpretation* gives information but intellectualizes the conversation (moves away from the feeling level) and closes off further communication. It may be clear to the teacher that "interpretation" and "support" are attempts by a busy resource person to dodge helping the teacher with a pressing problem. *Advice* sets one person above another and may put the informant on the defensive.

Outcomes

The proposed framework for interviewing the teacher, the parent, other professionals, or the student, permits the resource teacher to determine possible environmental or developmental causes for the problem behaviors. The interviewer may see correlations between changes in the environment, the onset of developmental problems, student attitudes, and the occurrence of the problem behaviors. Environmental events which covary with the problem behaviors suggest possible avenues for appropriate intervention. Does the teacher always counsel the student following temper outbursts? What preceded the temper outbursts—no breakfast, lack of sleep, teasing by a dominant sibling? Has the student recently been promoted from a slow class where s/he was a "star" to a competitive class where s/he "feels like a nobody"? Would reducing task difficulty, increasing teacher attention, or improving home cooperation be sufficient to reduce problem behavior?

These are all hypotheses that need to be explored during the instructional period. The initial instructional plan will consist of these hypotheses to be "tested" and refined, as feedback is received from the teacher, parents, and the student. Only such continuous evaluation—often by the informal interview of these significant individuals—will permit the ultimate resolution of the problem.

School Records

An obvious and important data base for the assessment process is school records or "cum" folders—when available. Depending on the completeness of the student's file, valuable information may be found here which will give some historical perspective on the student's current problem, as well as some guidelines for further assessment. We are aware that there are some practitioners who prefer to begin their study of the child "cold"—to make their own measures, interpretations, and impressions without fear of being biased by prior evidence. There is certainly validity to this approach. However, we recommend that a thorough review of the child's educational history be made in advance of using in-depth educational, diagnostic, or psychological instruments. Frequently, with older students, one finds that they have been "assessed to death." Such a finding might influence your choice of test to be used this time, or your decision of whether to test (in the formal sense) at all. In addition, you may discover random pieces of information which need to be followed up, such as the child's referral to a community mental health agency. Was the referral completed? What were the outcomes? Initiating steps to obtain such data, concurrently with the assessment phase, may save valuable time.

It is useful to prepare a very *brief* chronological summary of the student's educational history, including test scores, achievement status, and pertinent comments, which will provide the assessment team with a framework for viewing the student's current functioning. Samples of such summaries are shown below for case studies I and II, which were introduced in Chapter Two.

Case Study I: Leonard

Educational History Summary

STUDENT: Leonard T. BIRTHDATE: 11/7/61 C.A. 14:1 DATE: 11/30/75
PRESENT PLACEMENT: Moore Junior High   Grade: 8 (Regular and Special Classes)

Leonard has been in the Larchmont School District since kindergarten. At the end of the 4th grade he was retained and placed in a class for the educable mentally retarded in September 1970. This placement was based on Leonard's low scores on mental ability tests and inadequate performance in learning basic skills. Special class placement continued until the middle of grade 7, when Leonard was integrated into the regular school program for reading lab, P.E., and math, remaining in the special class for three periods per day.

Current Test Scores: WISC (10/74): VIQ = 71 PIQ = 85 F.S. = 75
WRAT (10/75): Reading 3.2; Spelling: 3.0; Math: 4.4

Case Study II: Richard

Educational History Summary

STUDENT: Richard A. BIRTHDATE: 6/1/64 C.A. 11:4 DATE: 10/15/75
PRESENT PLACEMENT: Cordova Elementary   GRADE: 5 (regular)

Richard was in the regular school program in La Subida School District for kindergarten and grade one. It is reported that at the end of grade one he was retained for "immature behavior," "slow language development," and "short attention span." He then attended a class for the educationally handicapped. In 1972 he moved to Wrightway School District and entered a regular second grade. Parents sought medical help to control excessive activity and inattention. Richard was put on Ritalin. In January 1973 Richard was placed in a special class, and in October 1974 he was returned to the regular program since his reading and behavior problems had improved significantly.

Current Test Scores: WRAT   (5/27/75):   Reading = 2.5;   Special = 2.9;
Arithmetic = 4.2

Testing

Introduction

The assessment technique to be considered in this section is testing; testing is frequently categorized as a formal method, in contrast to observation and interviewing, which are usually considered informal assessment. Actually, the distinction between formal and informal assessment procedures is rather arbitrary, since many so-called "informal" tools are published, field-tested, instruments (System FORE, for example). Accordingly, when we discuss testing, we talk first about those tests that are designed primarily to tap *process* variables (intelligence, psycholinguistic abilities, and so on), and secondly about *skill* testing where the focus is on assessment of skill development (primarily academic), without regard to underlying abilities. We have placed more emphasis on the use of skill testing in conducting a pupil study for the following reasons.

1. *The growing disenchantment with ability testing.* Several authors, including Dunn (1968) and Hammill (1971), have argued that many of the psychometric tests used in the schools do not provide the teacher with precise information about a student's specific learning strengths and weaknesses. Analysis of student performance on a quantitative, normative instrument is not sufficient to permit the establishment of realistic goals, objectives, and an individualized prescriptive program. Even more significant is the fact that a disproportionately large number of students from minority groups have been placed in special education programs as a result of their performance on standardized tests of mental ability normed on the Anglo population (Mercer, 1975). While retaining the standardized test approach to assessment, Mercer argues for pluralistic assessment, using multiple measures (general academic readiness, adaptive behavior, health) and multiple normative frameworks, which will take into account the sociocultural identity of the child. Public Law 94–142 (1975) now mandates the use of culturally appropriate assessment procedures for handicapped children.

2. *The need for* Teachers *to be able to determine the special educational needs of students.* As we stated earlier, we believe that the probability of assessment information being translated into instructional action is increased when the teacher is enabled to participate in a meaningful way in the assessment. For the mildly handicapped student we need measurement tools which can be used by the teacher, in the classroom setting, to measure the discrepancy between that child's level of essential skills and the minimum level required to participate in mainstream education. When combined with information about the student's interaction with the environment, such data form the necessary basis for educational planning.

3. *The growing body of evidence which questions the remediation of*

auditory-perceptual, psycholinguistic, or visual-motor processes. Such remediation is typically planned on the basis of ability test scores. Numerous studies have shown that the contention that process remediation is a prerequisite for academic achievement cannot be supported empirically (Cohen, 1969; Ysseldyke, 1973; Hammill and Larsen, 1974 a, b; Hammill, Goodman, and Wiederholt, 1974). Ability training for the purpose of facilitating academic achievement appears, at best, to be in a highly experimental stage and not appropriate for widespread adoption by the public schools.

Process Testing

The tools used in process testing are usually considered "formal," in that they are standardized tests, administered by specially trained persons, in other than classroom settings (Hammill, 1971). Tests here include the well known Stanford-Binet, Wechsler Intelligence Scales, Illinois Test of Psycholinguistic Abilities, and the Frostig Developmental Test of Visual Perception, which, among others, are used to measure mental, language, and perceptual abilities. The value of such tests is in their objectivity, known reliabilities, validities, and national reputations (Hammill and Bartel, 1975).

When used by well-trained professionals, formal tests of process variables can identify personality dynamics related to the child's presenting problem, as well as problem-solving strengths and weaknesses (Stellern and Vasa, 1973). In addition, ability tests can serve to confirm or rule out the presence of mental deficiency, point out general areas of academic failure, and demonstrate modality strengths and weaknesses. Hammill (1971) cautions, however, that:

> At worst, the formal evaluation is instructionally useless and will (1) demonstrate the obvious, namely, dwell at length on what is already vividly apparent to the teacher, (2) stress excessively etiological factors, such as brain dysfunction, which are of no value to the teacher, or (3) dwell at length on the interpretation of minimal and dubious evidence (p. 343).

Other concerns, or limitations, surrounding the use of process tests center around the negative influence of anxiety on test performance and the risks involved in interpreting test results for types of children not represented in the instrument's standardization sample.

In spite of these criticisms, reports based on findings from formal testing of process variables *can* be useful *if,* and only if, the results are interpreted by the examiner into an educational framework, *and* accompanied by detailed information gained via informal methods. For some insightful approaches to the educational and clinical interpretation of standardized tests, the reader is encouraged to study part II of Stellern and Vasa's *Primer of Diagnostic-Prescriptive Teaching and Programming.* These authors emphasize that, "The only justification for testing is to acquire information that will assist

with the resolution of a presenting problem'' (p. 21), and that the interpretation of psycho-educational testing and assessment should be approached in
terms of the student's *strengths*. Stellern and Vasa, while clearly adhering to
the ability model and contending that prescription or remediation is a function
of etiology or cause, also stress the use of informal and task analysis methods.

Skill Testing

The testing of specific skills is generally designated, along with observation
and task analysis, as an "informal" assessment method, although standardized tests for academic areas may be included. Informal assessment is,
according to Hammill and Bartel (1975, p. 7), "undertaken by an educationally oriented person usually an educational diagnostician or teacher," in the
classroom, for the purpose of determining very specific "instructional and
behavioral needs" which will then define the student's program. The rationale
for skill testing is that we can measure performance directly, without inferring
process or ability strengths and weaknesses, thereby determining the student's
position on various skill continua and gaining information about what instruction the student needs in order to progress to the next skill level. Instructional
programs can then be designed to directly teach specific component skills
(e.g., naming letters) and their integration (e.g., spelling words), as opposed
to training general underlying abilities (e.g., perception). Both diagnostic
tests and criterion referenced measures are aspects of, or approaches to, skill
testing. Specific diagnostic tests and criterion referenced tests will be described in a later section which deals with assessing various academic behaviors. Criterion referenced measurement is discussed below in the context
of a "systems approach" to on-going educational assessment.

A Systems Approach to Assessment

As implied above, process testing and skill testing are based on two very
different theoretical models for diagnostic-prescriptive teaching—the ability
training model and the task analysis model (Ysseldyke and Salvia, 1974).
Though we are emphasizing skill testing in this chapter, the intent is not to
convey that there is no place in the assessment phase for process testing;
rather, our purpose is to present an argument for a "systems" approach,
which allows the instructional process itself—not psychometric tools—to be
the initial, and indeed primary, vehicle for assessment of the mildly or
moderately handicapped.

Support for a systems approach to assessment can be found in the literature;
Van Etten and Adamson's "Fail-Save" program described in Chapter One is a
"systems" model. You will recall that a significant feature of the "Fail-Save"
program (1972) is its capacity for providing handicapped students with a
continuum of services that meet their needs via an operational design, which

avoids the problem of students getting permanently trapped in any particular service plan. The amount of time a child can spend in any phase of the program is limited, thus forcing program accountability. Movement from phase to phase is determined by the student's progress. The five phases of the "Fail-Save" model are summarized below:

PHASE I: *Consultation*—student (and teacher) receive help of specialist while remaining in regular classroom.

    II: *Resource Room/Regular Class*

   III: *Special Class/Resource Room*

  IV: *Self-Contained Special Class—Full Time Placement*

  IV: (Alternate) *Special Residential or Day School*

Note that not until Phase IV is the student totally isolated from contact with students participating in the mainstream and a student cannot go directly from Phase I to Phase III or IV.

Now, how does all this relate to assessment? First, let's look more closely at Phase I. Here the assessment involves in-class observation of the referred student and the learning environment by the Materials and Methods Consultant/Teacher (analogous to the resource teacher) and the use of diagnostic procedures to determine:

1. if sensory channels are intact
2. child's best learning mode (visual, auditory, etc.)
3. what motivates, or reinforces, the child
4. specific academic and/or behavior problems
5. academic skill deficits—what *skills* are in the child's repertoire and which are lacking, thus preventing him/her from being successful with the regular curriculum? (Van Etten and Adamson, 1972, p. 160.)

Following the assessment, the teacher, principal, and consultant meet to review and discuss the results. The teacher and the consultant then work out an instructional plan for the student. For ten weeks the consultant continually assists the teacher to assess changes in the student's behavior, and to modify the instructional plan and teaching strategies. After the ten-week period, the child's rate of achievement is calculated and compared to his/her previous performance. If the child has *not* made sufficient progress (amount varies for individual students) s/he can go through Phase I for a second ten-week interval or be moved into Phase II, where process tests are used to study or assess behavior in depth. Notice the strong emphasis on "in situ" assessment in the "Fail-Save" program. Teachers and specialists look for subtle differences in learning style which may result in a student's success or failure in the regular class and, through successive trial-and-error approaches in the design of instructional strategies, attempt to bring about positive behavior changes. Underlying abilities are measured only when the first approach fails; all possible attempts to keep the student close to the regular program are made.

The Van Etten and Adamson "Fail-Save" model has, in our opinion, great relevance to the role and function of the local school assessment teams which operate in states providing comprehensive special education services. In California, for example, a pupil study is conducted by the local School Appraisal Team. This includes (in addition to school history): educational progress report; health screening; observation in the regular program; assessment of academic functioning; appraisal of cultural and language factors; and assessment of career and vocational aptitudes (for secondary pupils). If necessary, the pupil may be referred for further assessment in the areas of adaptive behavior and cognitive, affective, sensori-motor, and language functioning by the Educational Assessment Service or a specialist, such as a school psychologist, audiologist, or physician.

It would appear that skill testing in academic and vocational areas is clearly a major responsibility of local school assessment teams, and that process testing is to be conducted only when this approach fails to provide an adequate determination of the student's educational problem, or when the student, having been served by the local school team, fails to make significant progress. The systems approach to assessment facilitates effective educational planning.

Criterion-Referenced Measurement (CRM)

CRM is a method for testing skill development and student progress which is based on the principles of task analysis. Task analysis refers to the identification of the major sequential steps through which the learner must progress to get from his/her present, observed level to the desired terminal behavior. Terminal behaviors are *benchmarks* or *universals,* such as "Demonstrates self-care skills," or "Demonstrates ability to use checking and savings accounts," which might be goals for students at a particular age or grade level. Terminal behaviors are frequently attained by the student through accomplishing a number of specific instructional objectives. Task analysis is the process of breaking each of the objectives leading to the terminal behavior into component parts and sequencing the parts into a series of steps, or tasks, to be presented to the student. If the desired terminal behavior is "reads at grade level," we must consider all of the skills that the student must possess in order to be able to do this. Such skills are sometimes called "en route" or "enabling objectives," and in this example might include identifying basic sight vocabulary and using word attack skills effectively. We then need to look closely at what underlying skills are implied in these behaviors—recognizing and naming letters of the alphabet, for example. When we have identified all the skills, we list them sequentially. We then have a checklist of skills which we can use to assess where the student is in terms of being able to read at grade level—what skills are already in the student's repertoire.

Instruction begins at the student's present level in the skill hierarchy and proceeds step-wise until each major objective involved in reading at grade level is met. To summarize, task analysis enables us to identify a specific set of skills which should be assessed prior to instructional planning, and, thus, what tasks are appropriate for the student. Task analysis is used frequently, and often intuitively, by competent teachers.

Criterion-Referenced Measurement or Testing is simply a more formalized use of task analysis. CRM is any test which is purposely designed to provide measures which can be interpreted in terms of specified performance standards. Criterion-referenced testing requires a clearly defined and delimited domain of learning tasks and thus requires breaking the curriculum down into manageable units and sequences. The mastery of one set or subset of behaviors is prerequisite in order to progress to the next unit of instruction. Results of the criterion-referenced test can be used to gear the instructional sequence to the individual student's rate and style of learning, individual goals, and so forth. Use of criterion-referenced tests allows for recycling or follow-up instruction on missed or failed items.

Information from criterion-referenced tests can also assist the teacher in evaluating the effectiveness of the "match" between the student, the method, the material, the environment, so that any or all can be modified to insure success for the student. In addition, the teacher can evaluate the learning sequence itself. Because the test items on a CRM instrument are directly related to the objectives of instruction, if the student does not pass the test, the blame probably rests in the instruction itself.

Criterion-referenced measurement is part of the movement in education toward instructionally relevant testing for assessment, placement, and evaluation. In using CRM we are asking the question "What can the student do?" not "How does s/he compare with others?" "The meaningfulness of an individual score is not dependent on comparison with others" (Popham and Husek, 1969, p. 1), as it is with norm-referenced tests. Let's look at some examples:

> Steve, in looking over his test results found that . . . with his raw score of 92 . . . he ranked at the 79th percentile rank and at the seventh stanine. His raw score had been compared with those scores obtained by his classmates (Smith, 1973, p. 2).

> Mary's score is second from the top.
> Danny's score is lowest in the class.
> David's score is average.

These statements are examples of the use of traditional norm-referenced tests. The progress of these students has been assessed in relation to the performance of the others in their class by using the same instrument. The students are aware of how they rank with their classmates, or with the reference group on whom the test was standardized, but they have no feedback on the extent to which they met, or failed to meet, the objectives of instruction. Now, contrast the preceding statements with the following:

> Ted can add all combinations of single digit whole numbers from 1 to 9 without error.
> Helen can spell 90% of the words from the unit word list.
> Betty can type 40 words per minute with no more than 2 errors.

These statements are examples of the use of a criterion-referenced test. The student's performance on specific skills is described in behavioral terms without reference to the performance of other members of the class. Also, the criterion, or level of satisfactory performance, is built in: 100%, 90%, 40 wpm, and no errors. The following chart summarizes a few of the critical differences between norm-referenced and criterion-referenced testing.

Comparison of Norm-Referenced Testing and CRM

Norm-referenced	*Criterion-referenced*
Reference points are average, relative points.	Referenced points are fixed at specified, cut-off points.
Evaluates individual performance in comparison to a group of persons.	Evaluates individual performance in relation to a fixed standard.
Are used to evaluate a student as "below grade level," "at grade level," or "above grade level."	Not concerned with grade level descriptions.
Fails to indicate which individuals have mastered the spectrum of instructional objectives.	Identifies individuals who have mastered the spectrum of instructional objectives.
Generally poor aids in planning instruction.	Geared to provide information to be used in planning instruction.
Is vague in relation to the instructional content.	Is content-specific.
Is more summative than formative.	Is more formative than summative.
Does not operationally define mastery and/or success.	Operationally defines mastery and/or success.
Applies poorly to the individualization of instruction.	Applies directly to the individualization of instruction.
Is not concerned with task analysis.	Depends upon task analysis.
Does not lend itself to applied behavioral analysis.	Lends itself to applied behavioral analysis.
Standardized tests are classical examples.	Does not tend to be standardized.

Tests not sensitive to the effects of instruction.	Tests very sensitive to the effects of instruction.
Tests have a low degree of overlap with actual objectives of instruction.	Tests are directly referenced to the objectives of instruction.
Test items evaluated in reference to persons.	Test items evaluated in reference to instructional objectives.
Tests results interpreted in reference to a person's position in relation to the scores of others.	Tests results interpreted in reference to a person's position in relation to the curriculum. (Housden and LeGear, 1974, pp. 191–92).

The issue is not that one approach is good and the other bad; it is understanding and knowing how and when to use each. A major problem to date has been the lack of information on just what norm-referenced tests are designed to sample, as well as improper interpretations being made from the resulting data. We must remember that we cannot speak with precise certainty about norm-referenced data—this is a big danger. It is important to examine your purpose in testing and to understand which type of test is most appropriate to accomplish a particular purpose. If your purpose in testing is to select the top few students, and identify the average, or to survey the relative attainment of students in terms of generally accepted skills and knowledge outcomes, use a norm-referenced test. If your purpose is to assess what *specific content* and *objectives* have been *attained* and to *determine progress* students have made on sequential units of curricula, use CRM. Sample test materials are discussed in the next section of this chapter. In certain areas, criterion-referenced measurement may be irrelevant because no meaningful criterion applies—a social studies curriculum, for example.

Criterion-referenced testing is important to any subject where future academic success is dependent upon cumulative information or skills. It is most important and relevant in the more structured subjects such as reading and math. There are certain tasks that, by their very nature, must be performed at a specificable, high level in every situation, such as landing an airliner, compounding a prescription, and obeying safety signs. In these situations we do not care how one compares with others but how well he or she performs according to a set standard. Here criterion-referenced measurement is a necessity.

To sum up, then, the three major uses for CRM are for *placement, assessment* and *evaluation and instructional planning:*

Placement: a criterion-referenced test may be used as a pretest; use it to assess students' mastery for placement at appropriate instructional levels and/or placement in learning groups.

Assessment: criterion-referenced testing can be used to target behaviors that need to be shaped through instruction. Criterion-referenced testing can help identify specific skill deficiencies for remediation. Through CRM, a teacher can obtain samples of learning outcomes and identify and analyze common errors as instruction proceeds.

Evaluation: analysis of criterion-referenced test items aid in evaluating the effectiveness of instruction. Errors, or the failure to achieve objectives, may indicate that the instruction was inadequate, or that the objectives were beyond the reach of the learners. This information should be used for revising procedures, methods, materials, or objectives themselves, to insure learner success in the future.

Bloom (1971, pp. 91–92) provides additional comparative information on diagnostic, formative, and summative evaluation.

Assessing Specific Behavioral Areas

Assessments of mildly or moderately handicapped students conducted by school assessment teams typically involve the areas of academic, affective, language, sensori-motor, and social functioning and, for secondary students, career and vocational aptitude. The remainder of this chapter will present specific comments regarding assessment in these and other behavioral areas, as well as some representative tests and techniques. Behavioral assessment should, of course, be preceded by attempts to determine that there is nothing biologically wrong with the child—that nutrition, health, and sensory factors are not the bases of the child's problem.

The major intent throughout this chapter has been to provide ideas and suggestions and to promote the use of educationally relevant assessment tools. The information presented below is offered in the same spirit. It should not be interpreted as exhaustive, final, or sufficient; nor, should the tests mentioned be construed as comprising a standard battery, the consistent use of which we regard as often inefficient and sometimes unprofessional. We urge, instead, that assessment be relevant to the student in question and based on the requirements of the situation. The essence of competence as an educational diagnostician is the ability to devise one's own assessment procedures to determine the unique educational needs of students.

Assessing Academic Skills

In assessing the academic skills of mildly or moderately handicapped students it is very important to consider the curriculum of the mainstream education program. If the student is to succeed in a regular class, s/he must acquire the basic skills appropriate for his or her grade placement. We need to know what those skills are; how to determine the extent to which the student mastered them and how those skills are taught in the regular class. We must avoid concluding that, because a child has been referred for further assessment, s/he cannot learn and make academic progress in the regular classroom. Some suggestions for assessing reading and math competencies are listed below. Many of these suggestions are drawn from the works of Hammill and Bartel (1975), Smith (1969), and Lowenbraun and Affleck (1976), whose books are highly recommended as handbooks for resource teachers. Representative criterion-referenced materials are listed at the end of this chapter, along with other assessment resources.

1. *Reading.* Standardized tests can provide estimates of a child's reading ability but typically they yield little or no information on a child's reading process. Often the teacher will need to construct skill-specific tests, or probes, to determine what instruction the student needs. Boyd (1975), Brabner (1969), and Lowenbraun and Affleck (1976) offer extensive summaries of *informal* devices which can be used to determine level of instruction and specific reading difficulties. Only a sampling of these techniques is presented here. The reader is advised to consult primary sources.

1.1 *Checklists:* These can be teacher-constructed to reflect common reading problems such as "adds words," "omits words," or "makes guesses." The checklist can be designed to cover general reading problems as well as those related to oral reading and to comprehension. Boyd (1975) suggests that the teacher keep such a record on each student.

1.2 *Word Recognition Tests:* One example is the *San Diego Quick Assessment* (LaPray and Ross, 1969). A graded word list is constructed using words from basal readers and the Thorndike Word List. LaPray and Ross include lists up to the eleventh grade. The graded word list allows the teacher to determine reading level and to identify word analysis errors. Classroom teachers can also construct their own word recognition tests, based on the students' reading material (see Boyd, 1975, pp. 23–24).

1.3 *Comprehension Checks:* Boyd (1975, pp 24–26) gives detailed instructions for designing informal tests of comprehension skills. Brabner (1969) defines hearing comprehension as the "highest level at which a child can understand what is read to him" (pp. 73–74), stating that at least 70% should be comprehended. Informal assessment involves selecting paragraphs from basal readers and carefully constructing questions on the content. Silent reading comprehension level should also be checked; the 70% score also applies here. Brabner (1969) recommends a test involving sentence absurdities which has been found very useful with socially disadvantaged children and young adults:

Basic Test of Reading Comprehension
by S. A. Cohen & R. D. Cloward
Mobilization for Youth, Inc.
214 E. Second Street
New York, N.Y. 10009

1.4 *Informal Reading Inventory:* This is a diagnostic reading test based on a series of graded books or other types of reading materials, such as newspapers. The inventory can be used to detect reading difficulties and also to select appropriate reading materials for students.

1.5 *Checks for Verbal Concept Formation and Vocabulary:* Brabner suggests using subtests of standardized reading tests and asking the student questions on word meaning. "Book analysis" is another technique in which the teacher analyzes the vocabulary from the basal reader into lists of nouns, verbs, and so on, then finds a picture which corresponds to the word. The child reads the word and selects the correct pictorial representation (Brabner, 1969, pp. 75–76).

1.6 *Standardized Tests:* Both group and individual tests are available; some tests are primarily achievement measures, while others are diagnostic tools. Group standardized reading tests should be considered as screening instruments, rather than assessment devices. Boyd (1975, p. 29) includes a highly useful comparative summary (originally compiled by Farr and Anastasiow, 1969) of the more common reading tests.

Ward et al. (1973) summarize a comprehensive approach to assessing reading performance when they state:

> Evaluation of a learner's progress in reading needs to include criterion-referenced tests on his reading skills, some more general testing of his comprehension and application of reading (perhaps by teacher-pupil conferences), and teacher observation of his attitude toward reading to detect evidence of both independence and enjoyment in reading (p. 349).

In their book, *Teaching Children with Learning and Behavior Problems,* Hammill and Bartel include chapters on two additional academic areas: spelling and writing.

2.0 *Arithmetic:* Spencer and Smith (1969) cite two areas of potential weakness in arithmetic: "(1) those skills that are necessary for an adequate understanding of quantity, including the development of a minimum level of skill in computation; and (2) the application of quantitative concepts and computational skills in the solution of arithmetic reasoning problems" (p. 153). These authors list some simple techniques which classroom teachers may use to study the arithmetic performance of individual students. Included are:

2.1 *Observation:* List specific arithmetic operations where students are weak and systematically collect data on individuals (e.g., reverses digits; omits a column; fails to borrow). A diagnostic chart developed by Buswell and John (1925) is a useful resource; this chart is included in the Spencer and Smith chapter cited above (pp. 168–69).

2.2 *Examining Written Assignments:* Checking written work can provide valuable progress information. Spencer and Smith (1969, p. 157) suggest that a student whose error rate is greater than ten % should receive a more detailed assessment. Systematic procedures for analyzing students' written work are described in detail by White and Haring (1976).

2.3 *Oral Questioning:* Return to a level where the child has been successful and proceed to where the difficulty arises by asking the student to explain his/her reasoning methods aloud. This approach should be used with great care so as not to precipitate an emotional outburst from a child who is confused and upset about arithmetic performance. The teacher can also question the child about his/her feelings regarding arithmetic thereby discovering motivational or attitudinal problems.

Bartel (1975) lists both general and specific factors which may be involved in arithmetic difficulty. General factors include ineffective instruction, poor reading and/or memory ability, and problems in abstract thinking. Specific factors are disabilities that show up only in certain situations, such as failure to learn to tell time. Bartel points out that, compared to reading, a few formal or informal assessment techniques have been developed for arithmetic skills. Both Bartel (1975) and Spencer and Smith (1969) present summaries of the more widely used formal achievement and diagnostic tests in arithmetic, including the California, Stanford, and SRA Achievement Tests. Additional informal techniques described by Bartel (1975) are:

2.4 *Analysis of Survey Test Performance:* While the diagnostic value of standardized achievement tests is limited, their value can be increased when the teacher analyzes the types of errors the students make, for example, computation versus reasoning errors.

2.5 *Teacher-Made Tests and Records:* Teachers can create short written tests designed to measure specific skills and facts which have been taught. Again, through error analysis, the teacher can more precisely identify the student's problem and design remediation. Teacher-constructed check sheets listing basic math skills can be used as an ongoing progress summary on the student. Excellent examples of teacher-made tests and inventories can be found in Lowenbraun and Affleck (1976) and in White and Haring (1976), along with guidelines on how to construct skill tests.

Assessing Language and Speech

In assessing the language growth of young children, Ward et al. (1973) suggest making a general, impressionistic assessment to find out:

1. What level of verbal functioning a child is at (words only; phrases; simple, compound, or complex sentences).
2. Whether his receptive language command is adequate.

3. Whether the quality of his verbal output is comparable to other children's.
4. Whether he is intelligible relative to his age and amount of speaking.
5. Whether his expressive vocabulary is adequate (pp. 284–85).

These authors recommend the subsequent use of standardized tests if there are serious doubts about any of the above areas. Making and analyzing a tape recording of the child's speech provides a reliable check on overall impressions.

Assessment of language and speech should include all aspects of verbal behavior: imitation, comprehension (receptive), and production (expressive). When expressive language is at a higher level than receptive, suspect a hearing loss or emotional problems and refer the student to a speech and hearing specialist; this applies also to the child with voice disorders or stuttering problems.

Bartel (1975) emphasizes that if remediation of language deficits is to take place, language evaluation must be based on a viable instrument which is both theoretically sound and practical. The test must be based on an adequate language model, be developmental in nature, and recognize variations in dialect. "An examination of current tests of language clearly shows that no satisfactory test battery of language is extant today, although some tests of specific linguistic ability are available" (Bartel, 1975, p. 170). Among the formal measures available for use by resource specialists are: Goldman-Fristoe *Test of Articulation* (1969); *Slingerland Screening Tests for Identifying Children with Specific Language Disability* (Slingerland, 1970); the now familiar *ITPA* (Kirk et al., 1968); and the *Peabody Picture Vocabulary* Test (Dunn, 1965). The *Test of Language Development* (TOLD) by Newcomer and Hammill (1976) is probably the most recent formal technique, and is designed to measure receptive and expressive skills of children aged 4:0 to 8:11. The specific language skills measured are: word discrimination, word articulation, picture vocabulary, oral vocabulary, grammatic understanding, sentence initation, and grammatic completion.

Other formal approaches to language assessment are discussed in a volume on learning disabilities by Wiig and Semel (1976). Informal techniques for language assessment, as noted by Bartel (1975), include:

1. *Vocabulary Assessment:* By using objects or pictures the teacher attempts to elicit the correct verbal response from the child.
2. *Articulation Assessment:* Errors can be noted during vocabulary testing and remedial practice provided on-the-spot.
3. *Comprehension Assessment:* By reading a short paragraph to the student and then asking questions, comprehension can be checked. With

younger children, the teacher can give short verbal commands to perform certain behaviors, such as "Put the doll in the bed," "Put the pencil on the table," and so on.

4. *Syntax Assessment:* The teacher can keep records of deviations in verb tense, use of plural, possessive, and contractions, use of the negative, passive tense, the imperative, and so forth.

For more complete descriptions of these assessment procedures the reader should consult the work of Bartel (1975).

Assessing Perceptual-Motor Functioning

Included in this area are educational techniques to assess visual and auditory perception and gross motor skills. Medical evaluation is necessary to determine problems in sensory processing (vision, hearing). While there are a number of formal perceptual-motor tests available, including the Frostig, Bender, and Memory for Designs Test (Graham and Kendall, 1960), these are, in the opinion of Hammill (1975), more appropriate for screening groups of children than for studying individual performance. For a review of formal tests in this area the reader should consult Hammill (1975).

Both Smith (1969) and Hammill (1975) offer several informal procedures, useful to teachers and resource persons, which are based on interpreting the child's actual performance in teacher-directed activities. Many of the tasks used in perceptual *training* programs are themselves appropriate as assessment tasks. Subtests from formal assessment instruments can also be used diagnostically. Again, experience with children and a sound knowledge of developmental norms is necessary. Teacher observation is a primary source of information on the child's perceptual-motor functioning.

Smith (1969, p. 62) suggests some behaviors to watch for as we observe an individual student:

how s/he holds a pencil—draws, writes
how well s/he can copy, trace
techniques used to form numerals, letters
consistent pattern of reversals
moving about without tripping, bumping into things
identifying and separating foreground objects from background
discrimination of size, shape, color.

In attempting to isolate the perceptual-motor difficulty, the assessment activity chosen should emphasize only one process at a time (Smith, 1969).

Hammill (1975, p. 215) lists some steps the teacher can follow in determining the presence of auditory perception problems. These include:

repeating an auditory test or subtest (e.g., memory for digits) using reinforcers for correct responses to see if performance improves;

checking to see if the problem involves symbolic auditory memory skills, such as recalling words, phrases, following directions.

As mentioned earlier in this chapter, there is a growing controversy over the use and value of perceptual training programs. Larsen and Hammill (1975) reviewed over 60 correlational studies which focused on the relationship of visual perception and academic performance. These researchers reported that the relationship between these variables is not great enough to be of use to teachers and that reading improvement cannot be expected as a result of perceptual-motor training. Hammill (1975) takes a strong stand on this issue, stating that, "In general, perceptual-motor training is viewed as more acceptable for preschool than for kindergarten or school-aged children, and is never recommended as a substitute for teaching language, reading or arithmetic skills" (p. 230). This statement has definite implications for the extent to which assessment should focus on perceptual-motor behaviors.

Assessing Vocational and Career Needs*

Vocational and career education assessments monitor two discrete content areas: social-affective awareness, and academic skills or achievement. While most educators recognize the importance of both areas, assessments have, to date, tended to deal primarily with skill (job related) or achievement measures. In the assessment of mildly or moderately handicapped students, the importance of vocational maturity, as well as social and personal maturity, becomes more obvious and crucial.

Most assessment instruments for social-affective behaviors, as related to vocational and career needs, are directly reflective of the long-range goals implied in the particular program for which the assessment is done. There appears to be great commonality among the goals of vocational and career programs established by the various state and local education agencies across the country. The following are examples:

1. employability
   economic self-sufficiency
   family living
   personal habits
   communication ability (from Halpern et al., 1975a)
2. awareness of vocational education in context of personal capabilities, interests, etc.
   positive self-concept, motivation
   positive attitude toward work world

*The section on Assessing Vocational and Career Needs was researched and written by Linda Polin, California Regional Resource Center, 1976.

increased understanding of relationship of United States' economic system and work to own economic situation
achievement of necessary consumer awareness
increased responsibility (from California State Department of Education, 1974)
3. self-awareness; self-worth
confidence, increased self-concept
greater understanding of interpersonal relationships
discovering, developing, clarifying values system
decision-making competency
positive attitude toward world of work
awareness of job trends likely in future
appreciation of leisure time, cultivation of hobbies, recreation activities (from Lewis et al., 1974).

These social affective area goals can be reduced to four basic representative social roles and their prerequisite affective competencies: (1) parent and/or adult, (2) employee, (3) citizen, (4) consumer and/or head of household. All roles require an ability to communicate with others and a mature sense of responsibility. Accordingly, assessment instruments in the social-affective area of vocational and career education attempt to determine the student's present operating level of communication and interpersonal skills, as well as the student's level of social maturity and responsibility. Representative approaches to assessing vocational and career education needs are briefly described below.

1. *Rehabilitation Research and Training Center, University of Oregon, Eugene.* This center developed *The Social and Prevocational Information Battery* (Halpern et al., 1975b), which consists of nine tests measuring social, prevocational abilities in terms of the five long-range goals cited on p. 124. This battery was created from secondary curricula for educable mentally retarded students and was standardized against that population. An outstanding feature of these tests is their attempt to facilitate valid responses from handicapped students by avoiding reliance upon written presentation and response modes. Almost all of the items in the nine tests are exclusively oral in presentation, and often the response mode is simply placing a mark beside a pictorial representation, or indicating whether an item is true or false. Each test requires approximately fifteen to thirty minutes to administer, is simple to score, and may be administered to a small group.
2. *Rocky Mountain Educational Laboratory* (1969) developed a pupil test battery for the social-affective area which includes an adaptation of an existing scale which they renamed *Opinions About Work*. The second test in this battery is the *Manpower Attitudes* test, developed by the

Center for Economic Education, College of Business Administration, Ohio State University. Both tests use a Likert-type scale for responses. Note that these tests were *not* developed for use with handicapped students. Both would likely require further adaptation in readability, and perhaps intellectual levels, before they would be appropriate for mildly or moderately handicapped students. The final test in this battery is called *Work Cases* and was developed from responses received from fifty large firms or corporations. The test consists of ten case problems which involve values-related decisions.

3. *Yonkers Career Education Project* uses a diagnostic battery as the initial step in their program (Le Voci, nd.). In addition to two standardized tests which measure academic achievement and assess relationships at home, at school, and with peers, the battery includes an adaptation of a vocational interest scale. Renamed *Occupational Awareness*, this test is used to determine the student's general level of understanding about job tasks, titles, and environments. The last test in this battery is the *Occupational Preference* test, described as a timed drawing experience in which the student draws eight occupations s/he would possibly want to pursue, and a ninth picture—his or her preferred choice. Student responses to both of these instruments are assessed verbally via student-teacher discussion. In addition to the formal assessment described above, the Yonkers model utilizes a "Recommendation Sheet" as the next step in assessment toward planning. The educational planning team reviews the results of the battery and provides further recommendations or other assessment information related to program goals. The recommendation sheet stays with the student, providing a cumulative record of data from the battery and other (e.g., observational) assessments. The educational planning team then completes a Prescriptive Instructional Activities form where student progress on specific activities is continuously recorded.

The basic appeal of the Yonkers Career Education Project model is its openness to input and feedback related to short-term goals. Also, the diagnostic assessment battery does not rely exclusively on written presentation and response modes, and it allows for direct teacher input during prescription and planning.

The above noted program goals and test batteries offer some assessment ideas for the affective and social awareness domain of vocational and career education. The more readily assessable skills and achievement aptitudes area of vocational and career education has a wealth of instruments; so only two will be mentioned below.

1. The *Differential Aptitudes Tests* (1966 forms L and M) consist of the following tests: verbal reasoning, numerical ability, abstract reasoning,

clerical speed and accuracy, mechanical reasoning, space relations, and language usage.
2. *The Ohio Trade and Industrial Education Services* program (1972) includes achievement tests in twelve job areas (e.g., carpentry, cosmetology, dental assisting).

Note that these tests were not specifically designed for exceptional students, and may require adaptation. An excellent source of information on skill and achievement assessment instruments in the area of vocational education is:

The Center for Vocational and Technical Education
Ohio State University
1960 Kenny Road
Columbus, Ohio 43210

This center is developing career education programs at all grade levels, kindergarten through twelve.

Assessing Reward Preferences

An important, but often neglected, type of student entry behavior relates to the whole area of motivation. A child's willingness to perform a given task is related to variables such as fear of failure and interest in the task. Interest can often be stimulated by providing appropriate and meaningful reinforcement. Cartwright and Cartwright (1970) have developed a technique called *Modified Reward Preference Assessment.* Five reward categories are used: (a) adult approval, (b) competition, (c) consumables, (d) peer approval, and (e) independence. The teacher lists four appropriate sample rewards in each category and develops sets of test cards; each card depicts sample rewards 'from two different categories (e.g., Adult Approval/Independence: "Teacher gives you an A"/"Free time in the classroom.") The cards are then systematically presented to each student. The child makes one choice per card and the choices are tallied for each reward category. The category with the highest number of choices is then assumed to be the most preferred. Validity of the results can be tested in the classroom by providing various forms of the preferred type of reward for acceptable performance. Stellern and Vasa (1973) use a *Reinforcement Inventory* (pp. 187–88) to help identify what the learner regards as rewarding and aversive (unpleasant). The inventory contains questions such as "What do you like to read?" and "I will do almost anything to avoid. . . ." The information gained from the student can then be used to increase the success of planned intervention strategies. Less formalized approaches to determining what students find rewarding or reinforcing are discussed in the context of a total contingency management system by Langstaff and Volkmor (1975).

Assessing Social and Affective Behavior

In this area we are concerned with the student's ability to relate to other persons, to display a positive view of him/herself, and to profit from life experiences. Ward et al. (1973) point out that the two major sources for self-concept development are the student's direct experience with success and failure, and the feedback s/he receives from other people regarding personal strengths and weaknesses. For the mainstreamed mildly handicapped student, the development and protection of a positive self-view is of hightened importance and it is the responsibility of educators to assist the students in developing behaviors which will result in the attainment of peer assimilation and acceptance so that the social milieu of the regular class will be beneficial rather than damaging to the self-concept (Kaufman et al., 1975). Sociometric techniques are often a helpful starting point.

Generally, teachers and resource teachers are not qualified to administer or interpret personality tests or tests of social development. For this reason, this section will present only informal approaches. Situational observation and interviewing are the two main techniques which can assist the teacher to identify social-emotional problems. Actually, observation has some distinct advantages over interviewing and other self-report techniques in this behavioral realm since it is not so dependent upon the child's trust in the teacher (interviewer). Lister (1969, p. 181) offers a list of situations, where the student can be observed, which will provide a picture of his/her personal and social effectiveness:

1. informal discussion periods
2. self-directed activities
3. discussion of controversial issues
4. informal social activities outside the classroom
5. role-playing and drama
6. creative art activities
7. on the playground

Lister (1969) cites several behaviors, including dishonesty, withdrawal, fatigue, and over-identification with adults, which he describes as "external symptoms represent(ing) the coping efforts of children who view themselves as inadequate to meet the challenges and opportunities of their daily lives" (p. 184). Assessment techniques presented by Lister (1969) include the following:

1. *Expressive Methods,* such as drama, role-playing, or art productions, can provide clues as to how the student views him/herself and others. These approaches are extremely open to the problems of personal bias

on the part of the teacher and must be used with utmost caution. Selective data-gathering to support our own beliefs about a child's problems must be avoided. In addition, many of the expressive techniques are very powerful and should not be attempted by the inexperienced.

2. *Self-Report Techniques* include interviews, open-ended questions, questionnaire checklists, autobiographies, and diaries. Many of these methods are discussed thoroughly in a book on values by Raths, Harmin, and Simon (1966). Respect for the student's privacy is critical here.

2. *Leaderless Groups* in which students discuss a topic and report on the group consensus, or work out assigned problems, provide a vehicle for the study of leadership and cooperation.

In summary, the assessment process, as it relates to the social, personal, and affective behavior of mildly handicapped students, should focus on identifying those behaviors which will enable the student to function effectively and joyfully with normal agemates—behaviors which can be nurtured and strengthened in the classroom milieu by caring teachers. Clinical evaluations of personality dynamics should be left to other competent specialists (school psychologists and therapists), and these persons should be consulted immediately when significantly deviant emotional or social behaviors are noted. The essence here, as in all assessment, is to find out what students need educationally. As David Nyberg writes in his powerful book, *Tough and Tender Learning:*

> Feeling good about yourself is necessary for doing most things well . . ., and it is certainly necessary for sensing any joy in being conscious. It would therefore seem to me that all the motivation junk that teachers are supposed to learn and use on students means nothing more than learning how to notice what kids are telling you they need in order to feel good about themselves so they can get on with whatever mysteries are calling them (1971, p. 32).

Reporting Student Needs

The assessment phase culminates with a statement, or listing, of the student's educational needs. The needs statement then becomes the basis for instructional planning.

In order to make a precise determination of student needs, it will be necessary to analyze, summarize, and compare all the various pieces of information gathered through assessment. It requires a great deal of practice to effectively use assessment data to develop initial teaching hypotheses.

Cross-validating data across and within tests and comparing it with observation and interview information is a necessary step when a variety of assessment techniques have been used. Needs statements should be supported by at least two sources of evidence.

Sabatino (1972) suggests that a learning profile be prepared for each student which includes: a diagnostic summary, a graphic picture of academic achievement, and a statement on the student's preferred reinforcers. *An Individual Student Profile Form,* used by the South Carolina Region V Resource Room Project (1975), summarizes weaknesses, strengths and specifies the student's best sensory mode. This profile is shown at the end of this section, followed by the assessment summaries and student's needs statements for our two case studies, Leonard and Richard.

Various formats can be used to state, summarize, and prioritize student needs. Regardless of format, arranging need statements in priority order is critical for instructional planning and teaching. One need-area at a time should be the main focal point for instruction. Attempting to remediate several areas at once is frustrating for the teacher and failure-inducing for the child. Care should be taken to express the assessment findings in a way that they will not be detrimental to the child's progress after she/he returns to the regular program. This is best accomplished through emphasizing the student's positive aspects as well as in areas where change or improvement is needed.

In summary, the best guideline for determining student needs is the discrepancy between his/her level and manner of functioning and the instructional processes of the regular classroom. Once the student's needs have been defined and prioritized, it is time to consider his/her best educational placement and to involve both the present and the receiving teacher in the instructional planning phase. Reynolds and Davis (1971) make an important observation with regard to placement:

> . . . every teacher has a range of tolerance for behavioral and academic differences among her children. A crucial determiner of whether a given handicapped child will survive and succeed in a regular classroom is whether he falls within the individual range of tolerance of a particular teacher (p. 104).

Individual Profile Form*

INDIVIDUAL PROFILE FOR Jimmy (Case Study #1)

    I. *Weaknesses*
        1. Language—can't find right words for definitions (expressive)
        2. Would rather give up than struggle for word attack skills
        3.
        4.

*South Carolina Region V Educational Services Center, *The Resource Room : An Access to Excellence,* 1975, p. 27.

II. *Strengths*
1. Arithmetic
2. Factual information
3. Good understanding of directions and explanations
4. Sports—Is a good team member

III. *Best Sensory Mode*
Assumption: Visual, Kinesthetic
Best Reinforcer
Sport related activities

IV. *Academic Performance (current)*
Reading 1.9   Spelling 1.7   Math 6.1

V. *Areas of Needed Remediation (i.e., beginning blends digraph; carrying with 2 place addends)*
1. Verify vowel sound understanding
2. Sound blending
3. Syllabication rules—for sophisticated sound blending (5th grader needs to feel this blending is not "baby junk.")
4.

VI. *Materials Recommended for Specific Remediation*
1. Conquests—(1 to 1, then present on cassette)
2. *Linguistic Reader*
3. Language Master for reinforcing activity
4. Graflex for reinforcing activity

VII. *Anticipated Area of Highest Achievement*
Reading. Spelling level will always be lower than reading.

VIII. *Recommendations to Classroom Teacher*
Continue to support and praise his math achievement, schedule resource room so it does not interfere.

IX. *Method for Evaluation*
Oral review and test.

Assessment Summary for Case Study I: Leonard

Date: 12/15/75

Prepared by: T. Ramirez, Resource Teacher

School: Moore

1. Tests Administered:
   PIAT: Math   6.2
           Reading Rec.   3.6
           Reading Comp.   5.8
           Spelling   3.5
           General Info: 7.5
2. Informal Assessment
   a. System FORE: Reading
                     Decoding Level   10
                     Comprehension Level   11
                     Study Skills Level   8

Math
  Geometry Level   15
  Number Level   17
  Operations Level   16
  Language Level   12
Note: See attached student profile for specific objectives for this year.
  b. Teacher Estimates of Current Academic Functioning
        Reading   4.5
        Spelling   3.0
        Math   6.0
  c. Interviews: Interviews with Leonard, special ed teacher and counselor indicate Leonard should be integrated into regular classes with resource room support. Math teacher states Leonard is no problem and is eager to work.

  Science teacher states priority for Leonard is work on following directions and remembering a series of activities, writing skills and written direction comprehension.

  History teacher states priority for Leonard is reading comprehension and decoding.

Individual Student Profile

System FORE Assessment

Student:_____Leonard_____
  Reading
    Decoding
        6.10.2 reads aloud accurately
        6.10.3 root words
        6.10.4 decodes irregular plural forms (mice, mouse)
    Comprehension
        7.11.1 predicts outcome
        7.11.2 selects appropriate conclusion
        7.11.7 selects words omitted from sentence to complete analogy
        7.11.8 selects main idea
    Study Skills
        8.8.3   reads silently through short selection and answers two comprehension questions
        8.9.2   locates specific information in reading selection
        8.9.3   groups information under topical headings
  Math
    Geometry/Measurement
        9.14.4 estimates areas of irregular shapes drawn on graph paper
        9.15.2 converts inches, feet and yards
        9.16.4 converts measures both liquid and linear
        9.18.1 constructs bar graphs to record data
        9.18.3 converts scale distance on maps to real distances (scale $1'' = 1$ mile)

Number/Numeral

   10.17.1 identifies fractional parts of units $\frac{1}{5}$ to $\frac{1}{8}$

   10.17.4 reads and writes mixed numbers

Operations/Applications

   11.16.1 performs multiplications through products of 81 and related divisions

   11.16.2 solves word problems involving X or + to products of 81

   11.16.3 uses distributive property

Language

Phonology (Sound System)

   1.12.1 recognizes written digraphs—th, ch, sh

   1.12.4 substitutes medial vowel to change words: lick-lock

   1.12.6 writes words in alphabetical order using first and second letters

   1.12.7 copies a sentence correctly using correct punctuation

Morphology (Inflections and Derivational Forms)

   2.12.1 uses present and past tense of "be"

   2.12.2 uses possessives

Syntax (Sentence Structure)

   3.12.1 identifies complete sentences

   3.12.2 transforms questions

   3.12.3 recognizes and uses negatives

   3.12.4 uses plural nouns

Semantics (Meaning)

   4.12.1 writes very short stories (with support)

   4.12.2 makes inferences (how do you know?)

   4.12.3 uses details in description

   4.12.5 makes up simple riddles

   4.12.6 describes creatively through personification

   4.12.7 identifies question words

   4.12.8 tells a story about a picture answering "wh" questions

   4.12.9 recognizes homonyms

Case Study I: Leonard

SUMMARY OF STUDENT'S NEEDS*

Areas
of Need

The following areas were assessed:	Yes	No	
_X_BASIC SKILLS	X		Pupil: Leonard
__Readiness Skills			
_X_Reading	X		Birth Date: 11/7/61
Other Communication Skills			
_X_ Oral Language	X		Grade or Class: 8th
_X_ Nonoral Language	X		

*Form developed by Stanislaus County Department of Education, Modesto, California, 1975.

X Written Language	X_____	School or Residence:
including Spelling		Moore
X Computational Skills	X_____	_____
__ SELF-HELP SKILLS	_____	School of Attendance:
		Moore
__ BODY COORDINATION	_____	_____
X SELF-CONCEPT	X_____	SAT/EAS Recommended Placement:
__ COMMUNITY	_____	Regular Classes/Resource Room
ADJUSTMENT:		_____
__ School Adjustment	_____	Plan Written By: Date:
__ Outside-of-school	_____	T. Ramirez
Adjustment		_____
__ VOCATIONAL & CAREER	_____	Years in School:
DEVELOPMENT		8
__ HEALTH & HYGIENE	_____	School or Special Class Placement:
__ OTHER: _____		Resource Room

PRIORITY	STATEMENT OF NEEDS		DOCUMENTATION USED
1.	Reading		PIAT
	Comprehension		System FORE
	Decoding		
	Study Skills		
2.	Language		PIAT
	Written	improve writing skills	System FORE
	Oral	improve spelling skills	Student interview &
		improve vocabulary	observation/wk. sample
		skills	work samples
3.	Math		PIAT, System FORE
4.	Self-Concept	integration into regular	Student, teacher and
		math, science and history	counselor interviews
		classes with resource	
		room support.	

Assessment Summary for Case Study II: Richard

Date: 10/15/75   Prepared by: M. Patterson, Resource Teacher

1. *Tests Administered*

   Wide Range Achievement Test (10/7/75): Reading = 2.5; Spelling = 2.2; Arithmetic = 3.9 (note that Richard's present spelling and math scores are *lower* than those obtained on 5/27/75).

2. *Informal Assessment*
   a. Color encoding, Richard could track only three sounds with success.
   b. Precision Timings:
      Sounds—40/8 errors—1 minute
      Blends—35/10 errors—1 minute
      Vowels—20/8 errors—1 minute
      Words (CVC)—e.g., man, sat, fed, rug (first 20 words/10 errors)
      Dolch words—50 words/12 errors
   c. Reader Inventory. Richard read 85–90% up through 1st grade basal.
      Could not read 85% on 2nd grade basal.
   d. Distar Format. Richard could not do sequencing, rhyming and blending to criteria. Could do no spelling by sounds.

Case Study II: Richard

SUMMARY OF STUDENT'S NEEDS*

The following areas were assessed:	Areas of Need		Pupil:
	Yes	No	Richard A.
X̱BASIC SKILLS:			
X̱Reading	X		Date:
X̱Oral Language	X		10/15/75
__Non-oral Language			School:
X̱Written Language	X		
__Computation			Cordova
__Self-help			
__BODY COORDINATION			Grade:
__HEALTH & HYGIENE			5
X̱SELF-CONCEPT	X		Pupil No:
__VOCATIONAL & CAREER DEVELOPMENT			009
__OTHER:			

Prepared by:
M. Patterson,
Resource Teacher

PRIORITY	STATEMENT OF NEEDS	DOCUMENTATION USED
1.	*Reading:* 2½ years academically behind grade placement	WRAT; Teacher report Precision Timings
	a. word attack skills	Reader Inventory
	b. comprehension skills	Reader Inventory

*Form developed by Stanislaus County Department of Education, Modesto, California, 1975.

2.   *Language:*   Distar
       a. auditory skills   WRAT; Teacher report
       b. spelling
3.   *Self Concept:*   Home interview
                                     Classroom observation
                                     Parent interview
                                     Interview with Richard

Study Questions and Activities

1. How does a systems approach to assessment of the mildly handicapped differ from traditional approaches to assessment in special education? What additional variables are assessed in the former (especially where classroom observation is emphasized) that are often overlooked in the latter? (See Chapter One, the section on *The Influence of Professional Educators,* and Chapter Three, the section on *Testing.*)
2. Traditional psychometric approaches to assessment in special education have often been criticized for lacking relevance to the classroom (instructional planning). In what ways will the move to informal, educationally oriented assessment make instructional planning more effective? More efficient?
3. Indicate which observation recording procedure (a. anecdotal, b. event, c. duration, d. time-sampling, e. placheck) would be most appropriate for collecting data in each of the following school situations:

___The principal has asked for a description of all "incidents" created by Billy on the playground during the coming week.

___What percent of the nursery school class make use of the sand table during free activity time daily?

___The teacher can only record Sandra's behavior during one minute every half hour during the day.

___Rodger's mother wishes to know how many "cuss words" the teacher has observed him using during a typical school day.

___The teacher wishes to lengthen the amount of time Shy Sally and Withdrawn Willy engage in social interaction with their peers.

4. Mrs. Hammond, a new resource teacher, decided to obtain independent classroom observations of Howard Hazzard, a third grader reported to have behavior problems. Mrs. Hammond observed Howard during his reading circle and the aide observed him during his math seat work. When the aide and Mrs. Hammond compared their observations, they were

surprised to find no behavior problems observed during reading and a multitude of problems during math. Mrs. Hammond and the aide had both used identical recording systems (event recording) and both observed exactly one hour. Give at least two possible explanations for their disagreement. How could Mrs. Hammond and her aide resolve this disagreement?

5. Visit a classroom (nursery or elementary preferably) of a cooperating teacher and ask permission to observe (or interview the teacher regarding) the most hyperactive pupils in the room. If observed, the pupils should be seen during at least two different periods of the day. Conduct an informal behavior analysis to determine the environmental correlates of the behavior problems. This can be done by listing in columns side-by-side (see the "is-plan" format used by Precision Teachers): (1) the behaviors of greatest concern to the teacher; (2) the setting(s) in which these problem behaviors occur; (3) the teaching methods, materials, and instructions presented the pupil during the high problem periods; (4) the consequences provided the pupil (by teachers and/or peers) for appropriate and inappropriate behaviors during the high problem periods. On the basis of the correlations between problem behaviors and environmental variables observed, generate hypotheses regarding possible environmental causes (e.g., teaching methods, expectations, instructions, consequences, feedback, peer attention, etc.) Suggest possible strategies for remediating the problem behaviors on the basis of the hypotheses generated.

6. Review the issue of process versus skill testing presented in Chapter Three. How does a systems approach to assessment resolve this issue?

7. Brainstorm the minimal survival skills (preacademic, academic, and social) for succeeding in an elementary or secondary school (e.g., can orally read class texts at 80 words correct per minute; can answer literal, interpretive and critical comprehension questions on material read; can work cooperatively with classmates on class projects; completes written assignments accurately and on time; can assert own rights; etc.). Divide into teams of two or three and task analyze each terminal objective into subskills. Use the hierarchy of subskills generated to develop a placement test or rating scale to informally assess a pupil's baseline for the purpose of planning remediation and evaluating pupil progress. (See Chapters Three and Four regarding task analysis of long-range objectives.)

8. Given the following list of referral problems, describe at least two informal techniques for assessing baseline behaviors or entry skills for each of the following referral problems (all from different 6th-grade boys):
   a. "Does not understand instructions or appropriately follow directions (English spoken at home)."
   b. "Neither his classmates nor I can understand his speech when reciting in class (English spoken at home)."

c. "Lacks motivation to complete assignments. Never turns in work on time. Always doing other things (talking, reading comics, etc.)."
d. "Reads like molasses. I hate to call on him to read because it takes him five minutes per paragraph. It's embarrassing."
e. "He complains that his math assignments are too difficult. He works at grade level in social studies and reading."
f. "Poor peer relations. I am unaware of any friends and do not know how to group him for class projects or field trips."
g. "Never raises his hand or waits his turn. Blurts out, interrupts, and disrupts class discussions interminably. Gets in fights for 'taking cuts' in lunch line."
h. "Can read aloud, but does not understand what he has read. Recites some facts, but these are often unrelated to the story read."
i. "Recently moved here from Mexico. He does not follow directions, nor express himself in class. If he does not improve, he should be considered for the EMR class."

References

Almy, M. *Ways of studying children: A manual for teachers.* New York: Teachers College Press, Columbia University, 1959.

Bartel, N. Assessing and remediating problems in language development. In D. D. Hammill & N. R. Bartel (Eds), *Teaching children with learning and behavior problems.* Boston: Allyn and Bacon, 1975.

Bartel, N. R. Problems in arithmetic achievement. In D. D. Hammill & N. R. Bartel (Eds), *Teaching children with learning and behavior problems.* Boston: Allyn and Bacon, 1975.

Bender, L. *The Bender Visual Motor Gestalt Test for Children.* Los Angeles: Western Psychological Services, 1962.

Bennett, G. K., Seashore, H. G., & Wesman, A. G. *The Differential Aptitude Tests.* New York: The Psychological Corporation, 1966.

Bloom, B. S., Hastings, J. T., & Madaus, G. F. *Handbook on formative and summative evaluation of student learning.* New York: McGraw-Hill, 1971.

Boyd, J. E. Teaching children with reading problems. In D. D. Hammill & N. R. Bartel (Eds), *Teaching children with learning and behavior problems.* Boston: Allyn and Bacon, 1975.

Brabner, G. Reading skills. In R. M. Smith (Ed.), *Teacher diagnosis of educational difficulties.* Columbus, Ohio: Charles E. Merrill, 1969.

Buswell, G. T., & John, L. *Diagnostic chart for fundamental processes in arithmetic.* Indianapolis, Ind.: Bobbs-Merrill, 1925.

California State Department of Education. *Career education: A position paper on career development and preparation in California.* Sacramento, Ca.: Author, 1974.

Cartwright C. A., & Cartwright, G. P. Determining the motivational systems of individual children. *Teaching Exceptional Children,* 1970, *2*(6), 143–149.

Cartwright C. A., & Cartwright G. P. *Developing observation skills.* New York: McGraw-Hill, 1974.

Cartwright G. P. & Cartwright C. A. Gilding the lily: Comments on the training based model. *Exceptional Children,* 1972, *39* (3), 231–234.

Cohen, S. A. Studies in visual perception and reading in disadvantaged children. *Journal of Learning Disabilities,* 1969, *2* (10), 498–507.

Cromwell, R. L., Blashfield, R. K. & Strauss, J. S. Criteria for classification systems. In Nicholas Hobbs (Ed.), *Issues in the classification of children:* (Vol. I). San Francisco, Ca.: Jossey Bass, 1975.

Deno, S., & Gross, J. The Seward-University project: A cooperative effort to improve school services and university training. In E. N. Deno (Ed.), *Instructional alternatives for exceptional children.* Arlington, Va.: The Council for Exceptional Children, 1972.

Dunn, L. M. *Peabody Picture Vocabulary Test.* Circle Pines, Minn.: American Guidance Service, 1965.

Dunn, L. M. Special education for the mildly retarded—Is much of it justifiable? *Exceptional Children,* 1968, *35* (1), 5–22.

Farr, R., & Anastasiow, N. *Tests of reading readiness and achievements: A review and evaluation.* Newark, Dela.: International Reading Association, 1969.

Frostig, M., Maslow, P., Lefever, D. W., & Whittlesey, J.R.B. *The Marianne Frostig Developmental Test of Visual Perception.* Palo Alto, Calif.: Consulting Psychologists Press, 1964.

Goldman, R., & Fristoe, M. *Goldman-Fristoe Test of Articulation.* Circle Pines, Minn.: American Guidance Service, 1969.

Graham, F. K., & Kendall, B. S. Memory for Designs Test: Revised General Manual. *Perceptual and Motor Skills,* 1960, *11* (2), 147–190.

Hall, R. V. *Behavior modification: The measurement of behavior.* Lawrence, Kan.: H and H Enterprises, 1971.

Hall, R. V., Hawkins, R. P., & Axelrod, S. Measuring and recording student behavior: A behavior analysis approach. In R. A. Weinberg & F. H. Wood (Eds), *Observation of pupils and teachers in mainstream and special education settings: Alternative strategies.* Minneapolis: University of Minnesota Press, 1975.

Halpern, A. S., Raffeld, P., Irwin, L., & Fink, R. Measuring social and prevocational awareness in mildly retarded adolescents. *American Journal of Mental Deficiency,* 1975, *80* (1), 81–89. (a)

Halpern, A. S., Raffeld, P., Irwin, L., & Fink R. *The Social and Prevocational Information Battery.* Rehabilitation Research and Training Center in Mental Retardation, Eugene, Oregon: University of Oregon Press, 1975. (b)

Hammill, D. Evaluating children for instructional purposes. *Academic Therapy Quarterly,* 1971, *6* (4), 341–353.

Hammill, D. D. Assessing and training perceptual-motor processes. In D. D. Hammill & N. R. Bartel (Eds), *Teaching children with learning and behavior problems.* Boston: Allyn and Bacon, 1975.

Hammill, D., Goodman, L., & Wiederholt, J. L. Visual-motor processes: Can we train them? *The Reading Teacher,* 1974, *27* (5), 469–477.

Hammill, D. D., & Larsen, S. C. The relationship of selected auditory perceptual skills and reading ability. *Journal of Learning Disabilities,* 1974, *7* (7) 429–435. (a)

Hammill, D. D., & Larsen, S. C. The effectiveness of psycholinguistic training. *Exceptional Children,* 1974, *7* (7), 429–435. (b)

Hammill, D. D., & Bartel, N. R. (Eds). *Teaching children with learning and behavior problems.* Boston: Allyn and Bacon, 1975.

Harms, T. Evaluating settings for learning, In B. C. Mills & R. A. Mills (Eds), *Designing instructional strategies for young children.* Dubuque, Iowa: William C. Brown, 1972.

Housden, J. L., & LeGear, L. An emerging model: Criterion-referenced evaluation. In William Georgiades & D. C. Clark (Eds), *Models for individualized instruction.* New York: MSS Information Corporation, 1974.

Kanfer, F. H., & Phillips, J. S. *Learning foundations of behavior therapy.* New York: Wiley, 1970.

Kanfer, F. H. & Saslow, G. Behavioral diagnosis. In C. M. Franks (Ed), *The behavior therapies: Appraisal and status.* New York: McGraw-Hill, 1969.

Kaufman, M. J., Gottlieb, J., Agard, J. A., & Kukic, M. B. Mainstreaming: Toward an explication of the construct. *Focus on Exceptional Children,* 1975, *7* (3), 1–12.

Kirk, S. A., McCarthy, J. J., & Kirk, W. *Illinois Test of Psycholinguistic Abilities.* Urbana, Ill.: University of Illinois Press, 1968.

Langstaff, A. L., & Volkmor, C. B. *Contingency management.* Columbus, Ohio: Charles E. Merrill, 1975.

LaPray, M., & Ross, R. The graded word list: Quick gauge of reading ability. *Journal of Reading,* 1969, *12* (4), 305–307.

Larsen, S., & Hammill, D. D. The relationship of selected visual perceptual skills to academic abilities. *Journal of Special Education,* 1975, *9* (3), 281–291.

LeVoci, J. P. Career education: Implication for special education. Career Education Monograph Series Vol. 4 Yonkers, N. Y.: Yonkers Career Education Model Project, n.d.

Lewis, J., Simpson, D., & Miles, D. *Student needs assessment guide* (A Component of the Community Experience Based Career Exploratory Program for Vale Middle School and a Sixco Project). Vale, Ore.: School District 15, and Salem, Ore.: Oregon State Department of Education, Division of Community Colleges and Career Education, 1974.

Lister, J. L. Personal-emotional-social skills. In R. M. Smith (Ed.), *Teacher diagnosis of educational difficulties.* Columbus, Ohio: Charles E. Merrill, 1969.

Los Angeles Unified School District, Special Education Division, *System FORE—An approach to individualizing instruction.* Los Angeles, 1972.

Lowenbraun, S., & Affleck, J. Q. (Eds). *Teaching mildly handicapped children.* Columbus, Ohio: Charles E. Merrill, 1976.

Mercer, J. R. Psychological assessment and the rights of children. In Hobbs (Ed.), *Issues in the classification of children.* (Vol. I), San Francisco: Jossey Bass, 1975.

Meyen, E. L. *Developing units of instruction for the mentally retarded and other children with learning problems.* Dubuque, Iowa: William C. Brown, 1972.

Newcomer, P. & Hammill, D. *Test of Language Development.* Columbus, Ohio: Charles E. Merrill, 1976.

Northway, M. L., & Weld, L. *Sociometric testing: A guide for teachers.* Toronto: University of Toronto Press, 1957.

Nyberg, D. *Tough and tender learning.* Palo Alto, Calif.: National Press, 1971.

O'Leary, K. D., Kent, R. N., & Kanowitz, J. Shaping data collection congruent with experimental hypothesis. *Journal of Applied Behavior Analysis,* 1975, *8* (1), 43–52.

Phillips, J. S., & Ray, R. S. Basic interviewing skills manual. Unpublished manuscript, 1972.

Popham, W. J., & Husek, T. R. Implications of criterion referenced measurement. *Journal of Educational Measurement,* 1969, *6* (1), 1–9.

Raths, L. E., Harmin, M., & Simon, S. B. *Values and teaching: Working with values in the classroom.* Columbus, Ohio: Charles E. Merrill, 1966.

Reynolds, M. C. & Davis, M. D. (Eds.). *Exceptional children in regular classrooms.* Leadership Training Institute for Special Education, 1971. Distributed by Audio-Visual Extension, University of Minnesota, Minneapolis, Minnesota.

Risley, T. R. Spontaneous language in the preschool environment. In J. Stanley (Ed.), *Research on curriculums for preschools.* Baltimore: Johns Hopkins, 1971.

Rocky Mountain Education Laboratories. Image of the world of work (Volume II). *Development of Instruments and Evaluation.* Greeley, Colo.: Author, 1969.

Sabatino, D. Resource rooms: The renaissance in special education. *Journal of Special Education,* 1972, *6* (4), 335–347. (a)

Sabatino, D. School psychology—Special education: To acknowledge a relationship. *Journal of School Psychology,* 1972, *10* (2), 99–105. (b)

Semmel, M. I. Application of systematic classroom observation to the study and modification of pupil-teacher interactions in special education. In R. A. Weinberg & F. H. Wood (Eds.), *Observation of pupils and teachers in mainstream and special education settings: alternative strategies.* Minneapolis: University of Minnesota Press, 1975.

Slingerland, B. H. *Slingerland Screening Tests for Identifying Children with Specific Language Disability.* (2nd ed.). Cambridge, Mass.: Educators Publishing Service, 1970.

Smith, C. W. *Criterion-referenced assessment.* The Hague, Netherlands. A Paper Presented at the International Symposium on Educational Testing, July 1973.

Smith, R. M. (Ed.). Perceptual-motor skills. In R. N. Smith (Ed.), *Teacher diagnosis of educational difficulties.* Columbus, Ohio: Charles E. Merrill, 1969.

Smith, R. M. (Ed.). *Teacher diagnosis of educational difficulties.* Columbus, Ohio: Charles E. Merrill, 1969.

South Carolina Region V Educational Services Center. *The resource room: An access to excellence.* Lancaster, S.C.: Author, 1975.

Spencer, E. F., & Smith, R. M. Arithmetic skills. In R. M. Smith (Ed.), *Teacher diagnosis of educational difficulties.* Columbus, Ohio: Charles E. Merrill, 1969.

Stellern, J., & Vasa, S. F. *A primer of diagnostic-prescriptive teaching and programming.* Laramie, Wyo.: Center for Research, Service and Publication, College of Education, University of Wyoming, 1973.

Thorndike, R. L., & Hagen, E. *Measurement and evaluation in psychology and education.* New York: Wiley, 1955.

Tubesing, D. A., & Tubesing, N. L. *Tune in: Empathy training workshop.* Milwaukee: Listening Group, 1973.

United States Public Law P.L. 94–142, *The Education for All Handicapped Children Act, 1975.*

Van Etten, G., & Adamson, G. The fail-save program: A special education service continuum. In E. N. Deno (Ed.), *Instructional alternatives for exceptional children.* Arlington, Va.: The Council for Exceptional Children, 1972.

Ward, M. E., Cartwright, G. P., Cartwright, C. A., Campbell, J., & Spinazola, C. *Diagnostic teaching of preschool and primary children.* The Pennsylvania State University: Computer Assisted Instruction Laboratory, College of Education, 1973.

White, O. R., & Haring, N. G. *Exceptional teaching: A multimedia training package.* Columbus, Ohio: Charles E. Merrill, 1976.

Wiig, E. H., & Semel, E. M. *Language disabilities in children and adolescents.* Columbus, Ohio: Charles E. Merrill, 1976.

Willems, E. P. & Rausch, H. L. (Eds.). *Naturalistic viewpoints in psychological research.* New York: Holt, Rinehart and Winston, 1969.

Yarrow, M. R., Campbell, J. D., & Burton, R. V. *Child rearing: An inquiry into research and methods.* San Francisco: Jossey Bass, 1968.

Ysseldyke, J. Diagnostic-prescriptive teaching: The search for aptitude-treatment interactions. In L. Mann & D. A. Sabatino (Eds). *The first review of special education.* Philadelphia, Pa.: Journal of Special Education Press, 1973.

Ysseldyke, J. E., & Salvia, J. Diagnostic-prescriptive teaching: Two models. *Exceptional Children,* 1974, *41* (3), 181–185.

Resources

Observation

Allen, K. E. et al. Early warning: Observation as a tool for recognizing potential handicaps in young children. *Educational Horizons,* 1971–72, *50* (2), 43–55.

Boehm, A. E., & Weinberg, R. A. *The classroom observer: A guide for developing observational skills.* New York: Teachers College Press, Columbia University, 1975.

Simon, A., & Boyer, E. G. (Eds). *Mirrors for behavior: An anthology of classroom observation instruments.* Philadelphia, Pa.: Research for Better Schools, 1970.

Interviewing

Psychosituational interview. Edwardsville, Ill.: Southern Illinois University, 1974.
This is one in a series of 38 Microteaching Modules; it is a half-inch videotape (15 minutes) with a manual. The module is designed to train teachers in how to conduct

a parent interview. Direct inquiries to Emmet G. Beetner, Special Education Microteaching Clinic, Southern Illinois University, Edwardsville, Ill. 62025.

Precision Teaching

Haughton, E. Great gains from small starts. *Teaching Exceptional Children,* 1971, *3* (3), 141–146.

Kunzelmann, H. P. (Ed.), Cohen, M. A., Hulten, W. J., Martin, C. L., & Mingo, A. R. *Precision teaching: An initial training sequence.* Seattle, Wash.: Special Child Publications, 1970.

Starlin, C. Peers and precision. *Teaching Exceptional Children,* 1971, *3* (3), 129–139.

White, O. R., & Haring, N. G. *Exceptional teaching: A multimedia training package.* Columbus, Ohio: Charles E. Merrill, 1976.

Tests and Techniques

Babikan, E., & Buchanan, A. *Developing a system of criterion referenced assessment: Reteaching cycles in textbook supported mathematics instruction.* Los Angeles: Southwest Regional Laboratory. The system described in this paper may be applied to any math text. Describes how to establish desired instructional outcomes and create criterion exercises.

Baxter, I., Barber, L., & Thurber, G. *Development and implementation of secondary special education programs.* Lansing, Mich.: Michigan State Department of Education, 1975.

Clymer, T. (Ed.). *Reading 360.* Boston: Ginn and Company, 1969. Criterion-referenced reading assessment and materials for elementary through junior high school levels.

Connolly, A. J., Natchman, W., & Pritchett, E. M. *Key Math: Diagnostic Arithmetic Test.* Circle Pines, Minn.: American Guidance Services, 1971. A criterion-referenced test providing four levels of diagnostic information for students in grades kindergarten through nine.

Diagnosis: Level A. Chicago: Science Research Associates, 1973. This package contains 34 criterion-referenced tests of reading skills (grades 1–4). Also included are: *Survey Test; Prescription Guide; Class Progress Wall Chart;* and *Teacher's Handbook.*

Gooden, B. L. *Career development guides: Special education.* Jefferson City: Missouri State Department of Education, Research Coordinating Unit, and Montgomery County K–2 Public Schools, Montgomery, Mo., n.d.

Individual Pupil Monitoring System. Boston: Houghton-Mifflin. A series of criterion-referenced tests to measure pupil performance on specific math objectives. Objectives are cross-referenced to the most widely used mathematics programs (elementary).

Language Arts Skill Center. New York: Random House. A criterion-referenced system for assessing and remediating vocabulary, spelling and punctuation skills at the regular junior high school level.

Mann, P. H., & Suiter, P. *Handbook in diagnostic teaching: A learning disabilities approach.* Boston: Allyn and Bacon, 1974. A practical handbook for teachers, containing techniques and ideas for assessing learning skills and for individualizing instruction. Directions on how to develop assessment inventories and criterion-referenced tests are given. Spelling and reading inventories are provided.

Mercer, J. R. et al. *System of Multi Pluralistic Assessment (SOMPA).* New York: Psychological Corporation, forthcoming. A culturally specific assessment model consisting of a structured Family Interview, an Adaptive Behavior Inventory, a Health History Inventory, and pluralistic norms for use with the WISC–R.

Meyers, E. S., Ball, H. H., & Crutchfield, M. *The kindergarten teacher's handbook.* Los Angeles: Gramercy, 1974. This book contains informal assessment procedures to be used by the kindergarten teacher in cooperation with the school psychologist. Techniques for planning individualized instruction are discussed; also included are charts and record forms.

Ohio State Center for Vocational and Technical Education. Ohio State University, 1900 Kenny Rd., Columbus, Ohio. Thelma Turner, Publications Department, (614) 486-3655.

Santa Clara Inventory of Developmental Tasks. Huntington Beach, Calif.: Richard L. Zweig Associates, 1974. An indexed notebook of assessment tasks and materials for children from birth through seven years.

four

Instructional Planning and Evaluation

Introduction

Within the past few years, legislation has been enacted, at the federal level and in many states, which is aimed at remedying the problems of exclusion, inappropriate programming, and misclassification. *The Education for All Handicapped Children Act* (Public Law 94–142) was signed into law by President Ford in November 1975. This law mandates provision of an individualized program for all handicapped children by the states if they are to receive federal funds for education of the handicapped. Specifically, an individualized educational program means a written statement for each handicapped child, developed by local education agency personnel, the teacher, parents, and the child when appropriate. The written plan must include the following information:

1. The child's present level of performance
2. Annual goals
3. Short-term objectives

146

4. A statement of specific educational services to be provided
5. The extent to which the child will be able to participate in regular education programs
6. Anticipated date for initiation and duration of services
7. Appropriate objective criteria
8. Evaluation criteria and a schedule for determining, at least on an annual basis, whether instructional objectives are being met.

In addition, states are required, under this law, to provide assurance that each handicapped child will be educated, in the least restrictive alternative and with nonhandicapped children, to the maximum extent appropriate.

Public Law 94–142, as it is implemented, will have a profound effect on the educational system. The demand for increased skill and effort in the area of instructional planning will be felt by both the regular and special education teacher. These new requirements will enable all educators to move toward achieving what has really been a long-time goal—providing individualized instruction for all students.

The Educational Planning Process

The Educational Planning and Programming process, as defined by Kaufman (1975), is "an ongoing cyclical process consisting of two elements—planning and programming" (p. 7). The *planning* phase is related to the assessment of a child's educational needs and the resulting goals and objectives. The *programming* phase involves the identification and selection of regular and special education resources available to provide the educational services required by the child.

Kaufman suggests six steps in the planning and programming process. These are:

1. Assessment of educational needs.
2. Formulation of goals and objectives.
3. Identification and selection of resources (human, fiscal, and material) for delivery of needed educational services. This step includes selecting instructional strategies to insure accomplishment of objectives and selecting appropriate materials related to the teaching strategies.
4. Development of the educational plan.
5. Establishment of the educational program (*implementation* and commitment of needed services and resources).
6. Evaluation of both the educational plan and the program.

Notice that the development of the actual instructional plan appears fourth in the above list. The written instructional plan is a "synthesis of the planning elements (educational needs assessment, determination of educational goals and objectives) with the programming elements (identification and selection of resource allocation alternatives)" (Kaufman, 1975, p. 8).

Assessment and instructional planning are intimately related as shown in Figure 6. Assessment information is meaningless if instructional programming doesn't follow immediately. The assessment information should pinpoint the exact skill levels at which the child is performing. These skill levels are then translated into meaningful classroom activities to meet the child's particular needs. Assessment is an ongoing process *and* occurs continuously as the instructional plan is being implemented.

The instructional plan itself is a written commitment of intent describing the most appropriate objectives, teaching strategies and services, interventions, and materials to meet an individual child's needs. Instructional plans may be short-term plans or long-term plans, or both. A short-term plan involves specific sets of objectives and teaching strategies designed to be accomplished

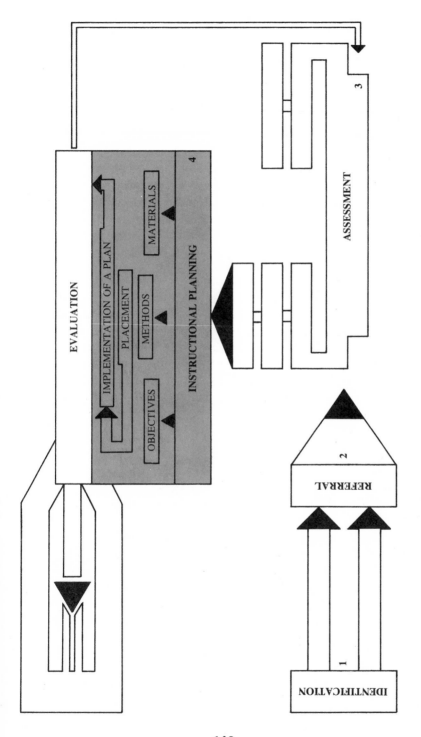

Figure 6. Instructional programming process.

149

in a specific period of days, weeks, or months. A long-term plan encompasses the detail of a short-term plan, but may outline a total program for a few months or a year and describe the total educational program.

Instructional plans with objectives written for six months or longer to satisfy state and local requirements are necessary, but can quickly become meaningless unless the plan is looked upon by its implementors as a continuing worksheet. Changes in teaching methods and materials must occur on a day-to-day or weekly basis as specific tasks are mastered or not mastered. The plan must be updated at regular intervals. Instructional planning is a process which not only involves the child, but also input and participation from a variety of professionals at various points along the way, including resource teachers, principals, regular teachers, psychologists, parents, and auxiliary services personnel.

It is critical that classroom teachers be involved in the assessment and instructional planning process. We cannot emphasize this enough! Too often, it seems, the assessment and educational plan are conducted and developed by "outside" personnel who have not been dealing directly with the child in the classroom. The classroom teacher has already been assessing that student daily and knows best what individual children can or cannot do. The classroom teacher is most often better able to relate assessment information to instructional procedures.

It is essential, too, that the personnel involved and functions performed at both the planning phase and the programming phase be carefully articulated and integrated. The same assessment team members (including the child's teacher) must be involved throughout the assessment, instructional planning, implementation, and evaluation phases for maximum efficiency and most effective results.

In summary, the educational planning process is dynamic, not static. It is an ongoing process, involving *all* those responsible for insuring that the child receives the best possible education at the least distance from the "mainstream." The process requires ongoing evaluation of the appropriateness and effectiveness of both the written plan and the program itself.

Planning Considerations

Before the instructional program is completely formulated and the plan is written, there are some planning considerations and concurrent decisions that must be made. These decisions involve temporal, environmental, and social considerations.

When planning an instructional program we need to consider the amount of *time* that the child will spend in the regular classroom with nonhandicapped peers. We need to consider the amount and intensity of any special services he or she will need and build this into the plan. This relates directly to scheduling remedial tutoring in the resource room and any other special services that the child will need to facilitate his successful functioning in the regular classroom.

Next we must carefully examine the *instructional environment* of the child's potential placement—to what extent will the child share in the instructional environment of the regular classroom? Kaufman et al. (1975) make some important points, related to instructional integration, that must be considered.

1. The child's learning characteristics and educational needs must be compatible with the learning opportunities provided to non-handicapped peers in the regular classroom. (p. 6)

An educational plan for a student must be directed toward helping the child secure the information he needs to remain in the regular classroom. The curricular materials in use in the regular classroom must be considered when developing objectives and related teaching strategies for the child.

2. Compatibility must exist between a . . . child's learning characteristics and educational needs and the regular classroom teacher's ability and willingness to modify his instructional practices. (p. 6)

A comfortable match between teacher/student and teaching style/learning style is critical. If a child functions most successfully in a rather structured environment, placement in an open classroom would not be appropriate. If a teacher's most comfortable teaching mode is via lecture, the child who learns best visually or kinesthetically would not fit there.

The instructional plan is written for both the child and the teacher. Any program designed for an individual child must also involve the teacher in its formulation and fit the teacher's modus operandi in order to be successfully implemented.

3. The special education services provided to a . . . child (such as resource room help) must be compatible with and supportive to the regular classroom teacher's instructional goals for the child. (p. 6)

The inability of special education and regular education to complement each other results in an ineffective, segmented program.

Finally we must consider the question of *social integration:* the relationship between the handicapped child and his normal peers and his inclusion in the ongoing social milieu of the peer group. What problems are likely to occur here and what can we do about insuring that the child will be accepted? What can we do to help change attitudes?

How To Design an Instructional Plan

What Does the Plan Include?

As we have mentioned before, a written instructional plan for an individual child is a synthesis of all the elements (assessment information, prioritized needs, stated goals and objectives, and appropriate resources) of the total instructional planning process. The focus is on academic and behavioral skills to be taught, as well as on strategies for instruction. Educational goals and objectives provide the basis for development of the child's educational plan.

An instructional plan includes educational goals and objectives based on the student's educational needs, as determined by the assessment. Furthermore, the objectives should be stated in terms of pupil performance, be time-referenced, and indicate the methods of measurement or data used to determine whether or not anticipated levels of attainment have been reached.

Some specific areas in which objectives may be developed are as follows:

1. Basic Skill Areas, including pre-academic and readiness skills.
   A. Self-Help Skills
   B. Reading
   C. Other Communication Skills:
      1. Oral Language
      2. Non-Oral Language
      3. Written Language
   D. Computational Skills
2. Body Coordination
3. Health and Hygiene
4. Self-Concept
5. Community Adjustment:
   A. School Adjustment
   B. Outside-of-School Adjustment
6. Vocational and Career Development.

The above are general areas upon which an instructional plan may focus. Within one or more of the given areas an instructional plan more specifically includes:

1. instructional objectives directly related to the child's need areas,
2. learning tasks sequentially arranged and designed to enable the student to master each objective,
3. descriptions of methods and techniques for presenting the learning tasks to the student,

4. descriptions of appropriate instructional materials, and
5. recommendations of environmental conditions which will maximize achievement of the learner objectives.

There are a variety of forms and formats used for writing instructional plans and some examples are presented on the following pages.

General Guidelines

No matter what format is used for developing the written plan, some general guidelines for its design hold true for all plans.

1. An instructional plan must be realistic, well organized, and easily understood. It must communicate clearly to all who use it.
2. Writing good learning/teaching recommendations is difficult, if not impossible (for one person), to do in isolation. Therefore, a team effort is most effective. Include the teacher who will be implementing the plan. The plan is written for both the teacher and the student.
3. The plan should clearly state the student's major strengths and learning preferences and indicate how to use these in instruction.
4. Objectives and teaching methods should be appropriate to the teacher and classroom where the plan will be implemented.
5. Curriculum and materials recommended should be available and, if possible, familiar to the implementing teacher.
6. Teaching methods and strategies should include a clear statement of where to begin and what level of performance indicates mastery (criterion).
7. Support services needed should be described (including materials and methods demonstrations).
8. Utilize as much as possible the curricula and materials of the regular classroom. Develop remedial sequences based on these materials. The student will be more likely to generalize the learning and maintain dignity. Some techniques using regular classroom curricula include:
   a. utilizing existing teacher's manuals; the many ideas included here for expanding and reinforcing lessons are often overlooked;
   b. narrowing the scope of lessons;
   c. supplementing with concrete materials, special equipment (e.g., tape recorders), and so on;
   d. using peer tutoring.

Instructional Plan*

Student's Name _____ Birthday _/_/_ Teacher _____ Date Prepared _____

Page _____ of _____

Integration Time _____ (average minutes per day)

Total Time Integrated _____

Total School Time _____

Instructional _____
Recreation _____
Nutrition _____
Transportation _____

Prepared By: _____
_____
_____

Review Dates

1. Mo.___ 2. Mo.___
   Da.___   Da.___
   Yr.___   Yr.___

Pre Assessment	Target	Strategies/Materials	Evaluation 1	Evaluation 2	Post Assessment
	Objective:				
	Objective:				
	Objective:				

*Adapted from a form developed by Sacramento City Schools, Sacramento, California.

154

Instructional Plan*

Student Name _____ School _____

Teacher _____ Plan Date _____

Resource Teacher _____ Approval _____

Parent Approval _____

Plan Reviewed _____

Student's Strengths and Deficits (including affective-cognitive-sensori-motor) _____

Educational Goals

	Regular Education	Special Services
Performance Objectives	Evaluation	Methods/Strategies/Materials

*Adapted from a form developed and used in Santa Monica Unified School District, California.

155

Instructional Plan*

Pupil Name _____ Date: _____ Teacher _____

Objectives: 1. _____
2. _____
3. _____

Learning Activities (specific curriculum; time on task; instructions; materials)	Student Behavior (pinpointed behavior desired to meet each objective)	Feedback (from teacher; schedule of reinforcement)	Reinforcer (eg. free time, etc.)

*Adapted from a form developed for use in the Houston Independent School District, Houston, Texas.

Instructional Plan*

Pupil: _____ Prepared by: _____

Date: _____

Grade: _____ Pupil No: _____ Approved by: _____

School: _____

SAT/EAS Signature

GOAL: _____

EXIT PERFORMANCE OBJECTIVE (for 1 year or less)	MODE(S) OF INSTRUCTION			ACHIEVEMENT—% or Pass/Fail & DISPOSITION			STRATEGIES, METHODS AND MATERIALS
	Type of Program	Instructor	Time/Duration	Date	% or P/F	Disposition	

*Developed by Stanislaus County Department of Education, Modesto, California.

Pupil: _____

GOAL: _____

EXIT PERFORMANCE OBJECTIVE (for 1 year or less)	MODE(S) OF INSTRUCTION			ACHIEVEMENT—% or Pass/Fail & DISPOSITION			STRATEGIES, METHODS AND MATERIALS
	Type of Program	Instructor	Time/Duration	Date	% or P/F	Disposition	

Writing the Plan

Specifying Objectives

Once the child's needs are prioritized, specific objectives can be written for each need area. Objectives are usually apparent in the need statements. It may be wise to concentrate on the one or two needs of highest priority at first to increase the likelihood of implementation of the plan. When an educational prescription is attempted for all areas of need, "the results are usually frustrating for the teacher and demoralizing for the student, as both fail to see the needed progress, and the child's inability to learn is reinforced" (Van Etten and Adamson, 1973, p. 161). Objectives are based on the pinpointed need areas and must tailor the task to the individual child.

Objectives are written behaviorally, are time-referenced, and include a criteria for success and/or an evaluation process and technique. The objectives must tell:

1. the terminal behavior: what the student will *do*
2. the conditions: what materials the student will use; how the student will perform the behavior
3. the criteria: to what extent (a minimum standard of achievement)

Criteria are the minimal acceptable performance standards for the behavior. Criteria statements can focus on the *number* of behaviors, the *time* a behavior takes, characteristics of the *process* of performing a behavior, and characteristics of the *product* of a behavior.

Here is an example of an objective which contains all three of the above components—the behavior, the conditions, and the criteria:

Terminal behavior: writes answers to arithmetic problems

Conditions: given an addition fact sheet sums 0–18

Criteria: at a rate of 60 digits per minute with 2 or less errors

There is a wealth of information available on how to write objectives, so we will not go into detail on the subject in this book. Some references on behavioral objectives are listed at the end of this chapter.

Below are some sample objectives taken from actual instructional plans which have been written for individual students. Objectives are included for some of the specific need areas listed on page 152. Some are short-term objectives and some are written for the course of a year's instruction.

READING:

(S) will be able to decode 80% of the words on a teacher-made list consisting of sight and phonic words found in a 4th grade reader after the year of instruction.

By June 1975, (S) will be able to recognize, within two attempts, 85% of the words which have been taught to him through the Sullivan Programmed Reading Program.

WRITTEN LANGUAGE:

(S) will be able to reproduce drawing and cursive writing equal to his age-mates as measured by a teacher-made test, at end of school year.

COMPUTATIONAL SKILLS:

(S) will know his times tables through 10 at 80% accuracy on teacher-made test by end of school year.

(S) will count to 20 by rote with 100% accuracy.

BODY COORDINATION:

(S) will be able to indicate left or right hand, eye, arm, leg, foot, etc. with 100 % accuracy at the end of a two-month period of instruction and *emphasis*.

SELF CONCEPT:

(S) will be able to go into a "K" or 1st grade class on a regular basis as a tutor and teacher helper 45 minutes per day.

SCHOOL ADJUSTMENT:

To establish a demeanor and attitude w/peers that is absent from: impulsive pushing, shoving, or hitting no more than 10 times a day or 30% of time.

VOCATIONAL AND CAREER DEVELOPMENT:

(S) will be able to define and list common labor union terminology with 80% accuracy.
(S) will be able to list 3 benefits associated with labor unions.
(S) is able to describe one particular future job and how he/she would prepare for it; i.e., education he/she thinks it would require, special skills, etc.

(S) is able to list two fields or clusters of jobs that do not yet exist.

Objectives are developed for each need area *in order of priority* for the individual student. Next, specific learning tasks are developed and written for each objective. Learning tasks are the steps the child must take to master each objective.

Developing Learning Tasks

Task analysis is the process of isolating, describing, and sequencing all the essential subtasks which, when the child has mastered them, will enable him to perform the objective. Defined a little differently by Worell and Nelson (1974), a "task analysis consists of breaking down a task or skill into sequential component parts for teaching" (p. 120).

Though the words *task analysis* may carry a negative emotional loading, just like the term *behavioral objective,* the process is actually simple. It can be said to resemble a road map, a description of how to get from one place to another as efficiently as possible. Success is the key to task analysis; we aim at making learning as errorless as possible.

The number of components or subtasks included in a task analysis depends on the child and the nature of the task. It is only necessary to break the task down finely enough so that the child can succeed at each step. A task analysis results in an instructional sequence. Task analyses tell *what* to teach not *how* to teach. The focus is *only* on that skill which we are trying to teach. To perform a task analysis, begin with the instructional objective and consider all the things the learner will have to do before he/she can perform the task to the criteria and conditions stated in the objective. Break the objective down carefully into subskills by working through the task itself. It is often helpful to work backwards from the terminal behavior, identifying all prerequisite en route behaviors. Ask the question, "What skills must the child have in order to perform this task?" When identifying sequential components keep in mind that it is necessary to move from concrete to abstract and from simple to complex. The resulting substeps are then arranged in a logical order or sequence. The sequence does not have to be perfect; it can be rearranged during the teaching process if it is not correct. A sample task analysis is shown in Figure 7.

When all the subskills and steps are listed for a behavioral objective, an instructional sequence has been formulated. Siegel and Siegel (1975) outline some important points to keep in mind when writing instructional sequences. Some of these are:

1. Avoid extraneous material—stick to the specific objective.
2. Don't spend too much time teaching the prerequisite. If a specific objective has been set for a child, the assessment process should have determined he has the prerequisite skills.
3. Use what the child knows—and this includes the prerequisites—to help him learn the new.

Terminal Objective:	Child demonstrates ability to write digits 0–10
	Correctly (legibly) at rate of 50/minute, 0 errors in 2 weeks.
Skills necessary:	Symbol formation
Entry:	1. Hold pencil
	2. Make a circle
	3. Make straight line

Given a digit series on paper, child can trace digits at a rate of 50/minute, 2 errors, in 14 days.

1 2 3 4

Given a set of digits with faded cues, child will trace digit at 50/minute, 0 errors, in 14 days.

1 2 3 4

Given the beginning cues, and a model, child will write the digits at 50/minute, 1 error, in 14 days.

1 2 3 4

Given a model, the child will write digits at the rate of 50/minute, 2 errors, in 14 days.

1   2   3   4

Given the direction to "write the numerals as I say them" and a model, child will write numerals at 55 digits/minute, 2 errors, in 14 days.

Teacher says:	1. "Write 5." (demonstrates 5, then erases her 5.)
	2. "Your turn, write 5."
Child does it,	
Teacher says:	"Write a 6." (Writes it as she says it, erases it.)
	"Write a 3", and so on.

Given the direction "Write the numerals I tell you," child will write numerals at 50 digits/minute, 0 errors, in 14 days. Free operant rate.

Figure 7. Task Analysis: Writing numerals.*

4. Assume motivation—often too much time is spent on developing activities to "motivate" instead of concentrating on the task at hand.
5. Identifying sequential components (task analysis), keep in mind moving from concrete to abstract, simple to complex, and so on.
6. Avoid scientific jargon—use language that communicates to all who are involved with the child.

---

*Towle, M. *Resource Specialist Training Program, Volume V: Instructional Strategies,* (Eugene: University of Oregon, n.d.).

7. Don't just present, teach—require the child to *do* something to show he is learning (pp. 16–19).

Teaching Strategies and Instructional Materials

To individualize means to find the best match between the instructional strategy and the characteristics of the child (Ward et al. 1973, p. 115).

The assessment information should reveal child characteristics which have implications for planning teaching methods and techniques. Some relevant child characteristics to attend to include energy level, attention span, and sensory limitations, which may demand special materials or modes of instruction.

The next step in developing an instructional plan is to specify and describe the instructional methods and techniques which are most likely to promote learning success for the student. Worell and Nelson (1974) suggest three steps for developing intervention strategies for accomplishing objectives:

1. specifying materials and techniques
2. matching these techniques to the learning needs of the child
3. designing an appropriate behavioral management and/or motivational system.

Here are some suggestions to keep in mind when developing instructional strategies for the teacher and the student:

1. Methods and techniques should be described in detail for both academic and management or social behaviors (e.g., use of tape recorder, typewriter, Fernald method, precision teaching, peer tutoring).
2. Activities should be specified for both the teacher and the student. Include activities the teacher must perform as well as those the student performs. Three types of activities should be considered and incorporated:
   a. *presentation of lesson*—mode of presentation (e.g., tape, one-to-one with teacher or aide, worksheet or filmstrip, lecture)
   b. *practice for the student*—a variety of ways to practice skills
   c. *evaluation procedure* to determine success of strategies
3. Review instructional materials and make recommendations for several alternate materials which are matched to each task sequence. When choosing materials, consider the task and how it is taught as well as the child's characteristics and the type of materials, i.e., concrete, pictorial, or abstract (words and symbols). Include ideas for creating teacher-made materials. Where possible, indicate availability sources for instructional materials.

4. Keep in mind the materials already in use in the regular classroom. Suggest adaptations and modifications to these materials.
5. Suggest environmental conditions which would be optimal for the child, such as open vs. structured classroom; group vs. tutorial instruction, and so forth.
6. Determine through direct contact with the child and his/her teacher such things as reward preferences of the child and behavior management systems already operating within the classroom. Some of this information is obtained during the assessment process.

Samples of instructional strategies, again taken from actual instructional plans, are described below. These strategies were developed to accompany objectives presented earlier in this chapter. (Our thanks to California Regional Resource Center consultants Carol Kennedy, Alan Jensen, Gene Russ, Florence Schaefer, and Paula Sullivan for the examples of objectives, teaching strategies, and materials from the plans they developed.)

Reading

Objective:

By June, (S) will be able to recognize, within two attempts, 85% of the words which have been taught to him through the Sullivan Programmed Reading Program.

Strategies:

1. Sullivan Programmed Reading Series. Time spent on this segment should not be less than 30 minutes per day. The half an hour period may, if desired, be divided into 2–15 minute periods, but the total 30 minutes is only the time spent working on the reading and is not meant to include getting the book, settling in, dawdling, chatting, etc.
2. At the end of the school year, (S) should be given an informal reading inventory to formulate the reading instructional plan for the next year.
3. Several small books from the Follett Co. have been ordered and (S) should be encouraged to look through these, check them out for home reading, etc.
4. Some reading activity sources (e.g., "The Reading Box") for games and activities have also been ordered and should be used for spare time activities.

Reading

Objective:

(S) will be able to decode 80% of the words on a teacher-made list consisting of sight and phonetic words found in a 4th grade reader after a year of instruction.

Strategies:

Instruct 30 minutes per day using a structured auditory-visual approach: a sequenced phonetic reading program that retains a structured sequence of sounds within words and a consistent sequence of sentence structure, like Distar Reading Program, or Corrective Reading Program.

Long Vowel Sounds:

Given a word orally (S) will be able to identify the long vowel sound. Vowel lotto game may help.

Ride	Cope			
Rode	Cub	Circle the word I say in each box		
Read	Cube			
Red	Cape	(1) ride	(2) cube	

Final Blends:

When given a group of words orally ending with the same blend, (S) should be able to supply another word having the same final blend. Example—give me a word that ends the same way that stick, thick and trick do. Do the same for nt, nd, and nk. Possible materials are Webster Word Wheels and Ideal Phonic Tapes.

Present Word Families:

From the word *man* show him how he can change the initial consonant to form other words (pan, fan, ran). Final consonants also should be varied to form other words (rag, rat, ran). The letters should be observable so that he can see how the words are alike; then he must go through the physical operation of changing the initial or final consonant. Hence anagrams, or cut out letters, should be used.

Short Vowel Sounds:

Given a word orally (S) should be able to identify the short vowel sound. Example:

Sed	Hat			
Sod	Hot	Circle the word I say in each box		
Sid	Hit			
Sad	Hut	(1) sad	(2) hot	

Common Syllables:

Given a common syllable, (S) should be able to give the sound the letters represent. This is one of his weak areas. Example:

Give list of syllables.

ail	ate	ick	
op	ite	ock	Have him pronounce each syllable and then
tion	aim	ide	give a word using that syllable.
ter	ake	ile	
all	ight		
est	ile		

Written Language

Objective:

(S) will be able to reproduce drawing and cursive writing equal to his grade level as measured by a teacher-made test at the end of the year.

Strategies:

Tasks emphasizing finger manipulations, i.e., cutting out and along curved lines, tracing pictures, copying.

Exercises to improve fine motor control would include cutting out geometric shapes along curved lines and circles. Tracing pictures and alphabet. Copying geometric shapes, letters, and cursive letters. Materials that can help are: (1) Frostig Program of the Development of Visual Perception, p. 26, (2) Valett-Perceptual-Motor Skills #29–33g, (3) Visual Materials, Inc. *Cursive Writing,* WL 093, grade 1–3 (dittos and transparency).

Computational Skills

Objective:

Count to 20 by rote with 100% accuracy

Strategies:

Use manipulative objects from Structural Arithmetic by Stern; count objects; instruct 20 minutes daily.

Objective:

(S) will know his times tables through 10 at 80% accuracy on a teacher-made test by the end of the school year.

Strategy:

Emphasize flash cards, math games, and rote practice. Time: 20 minutes per day.

Body Coordination

Objective:

(S) will be able to indicate left or right hand, eye, arm, leg, foot, etc., with 100% accuracy at the end of a two-month period of instruction.

Strategies:

Type of Program:
a. During all sports and physical activities
b. Use of special training materials in activities and math centers
c. While following directions in art and handcraft center

Time/Duration:
At least 30 minutes three times a week/8 weeks

1. Attach different decals to (S)'s left and right hands to help him remember which is which. Be sure he has a chance to choose motivating symbols himself and wants to use them.
2. As (S) participates in sports activities, be sure to have him verbalize which hand and/or foot he is using and in which direction he is moving. (Do this as often as possible without artificially limiting or inhibiting his participation.)
3. Take opportunities to emphasize left and right positioning as (S) participates in art and woodworking projects. Color cue correct guidelines and positions at first and/or use the symbols that match the ones on his hands.
4. Schedule regular use of Dubnoff School Program (directional-spatial pattern board) Teaching Resources, cat. #20–210, pp. 18 and 19. The set of cards provide not only laterality training, but other basic directionality concepts that (S) needs badly.
5. Schedule use of the Directional Mat, Teaching Resources, cat. #16–100, p. 25. This combines laterality training with auditory memory (digit span) which is another important objective for (S). (Math games can be incorporated too.)

Self-Concept

Objective:

(S) will be able to go into a K or first grade class on a regular basis as a tutor and teacher helper, 45 minutes per day.

Strategy:

Student's teacher and receiving teacher must determine those areas in which (S) can help the younger students. Teacher must prepare and do some inservice with (S), i.e., his behavior with younger kids.

School Adjustment

Objective:

To establish a demeanor and attitude w/peers that is without impulsive pushing, shoving or hitting no more than 10 times a day or 30% of time.

Strategies:

Employ reinforcement system.

The desired act is to be rewarded, but *never* punish student. If there is a need for punishment, then admonish the act, but do not reject student.

Reinforcement should be 100% administered within ½ second of desired performance for 30 trials and then changed to a random or intermittent schedule.

Reinforcers should be as kinesthetic and social as possible:

A. Smiles, frowns, laughter
B. Praise, reassurance
C. Attention and recognition, affection
D. Gentle touch on shoulder or head; physical contact
E. Hugs
F. Positive/Negative voice inflections
G. Food
   1. Basic: small candies (preferably natural foods), dried fruits, nuts, etc.
   2. Occasional small meals
H. Art modes
   1. Finger paints, water colors, crayons, etc.
   2. Drawing, sketching, etc.
   3. Crafts
I. Tokens earned for later purchase of desirable goods.

Vocational and Career Development

Objective:

(S) will be able to define and list common labor union terminology with 80% accuracy.

(S) will be able to list 3 benefits associated with labor unions.

Strategies:

Filmstrip "Labor Unions" (Eye Gate series); small group discussion; teacher-prepared sheet on "Labor Unions" and "Terminology of Workers"; question and answer sheets on both.

Objective:

(S) is able to list two fields or clusters with future job possibilities that do not yet exist.

(S) is able to describe one particular future job and how he/she would prepare for it, i.e., education he/she thinks it requires, special skills, etc.

Strategies:

    a. Discussion of jobs today that didn't exist before (may select particular time period from social studies curriculum)
    b. Discussion of new possibilities, e.g., space, housing
    c. Filmstrips
       1. *Job Outlook Series,* U.S. Government Printing; 20 slides re: employment trends
       2. *Career Planning in a Changing World,* Popular Science Audio Visuals, Inc.
       3. *New Career Opportunities,* Popular Science Audio Visuals, Inc.
       4. *Preparing for the Jobs of the 70s,* Guidance Associates
    d. Student writes job description of a job s/he thinks may exist in the future.

Setting Criteria

In an individualized remedial program, the emphasis is not on evaluating the student's performance for grading purposes. The purposes of evaluation are:
    1. to obtain information which will be useful for modifying the program and
    2. to provide feedback to the child and teacher on his/her progress.

When establishing criteria (minimum standards of achievement) for objectives in an instructional plan, we are also interested in ways of obtaining continuous and daily evaluative data to aid us in determining progress and making necessary revisions. The data we collect depends on the objective; the behavioral objective guides us in determining an evaluative procedure for each skill. There are two basic types of criteria which may be applied to objectives to measure success:
    1. Rate: a combination of time and accuracy, e.g., 30 words read in one minute.

2. Accuracy: percent or number correct, e.g., 80% correct on daily math, (most common on paper/pencil tasks in math, reading, and spelling).

Refer to the objectives on the preceding pages and note the criteria built into each objective.

Content for Instructional Plans

In this section we will present some representative but not definitive methods, techniques, approaches, and related materials for the major subject areas which may be considered when developing instructional plans. There are several excellent texts which provide more comprehensive descriptions and these are mentioned in the bibliography for this chapter. Hammill and Bartel's *Teaching Children with Learning and Behavior Problems* is a particularly good reference.

Reading

There are a wide variety of reading methods and approaches. Included are phonics methods, linguistic approaches, modified alphabets, language experience approach, multisensory approach, programmed reading, and individualized reading (paperback books). Some of these methods move in and out of vogue, but it is necessary to be familiar with a wide variety of methods in order to be able to select the most appropriate method, or combination of methods, for a particular child.

Basal Reading Series. The most widely used reading approach involves use of the basal reading series. The series in use in the regular classroom must be considered when developing a reading plan for a child ready to be mainstreamed. The teacher's manuals are full of suggested methods and activities, often overlooked, which can be used to extend and intensify the regular reading program. Try to build some interesting remedial activities around the basal reading program already in use. It is necessary to keep good records of specific skills that individual children have mastered or need help on.

Individualized Reading. This approach involves teaching word recognition and comprehension skills as each child needs them. The child reads materials of his own choice at his own rate, and needs close monitoring by teachers. This can be a particularly relevant approach at secondary level.

Language Experience Approach. This method is based on the experience and language of the child. Writing, reading, speaking, and spelling are all incorporated. It may be used with both beginning readers and older students.

Programmed Reading (Sullivan and so on). While providing immediate feedback to the student's response, small and carefully sequenced learning units are presented.

Fernald. This method uses a multisensory approach which involves four modalities simultaneously (visual, auditory, kinesthetic, and tactile). It is a word-learning technique based on perception of the word as a whole and on child initiation of words to be learned.

Gillingham Phonics. This is an "alphabetic system" which stresses auditory discrimination abilities, with supplementary emphasis on kinesthetic and tactile modalities. It provides a systematic approach to reading, spelling, and writing adapted to all levels through high school.

Spalding Phonics Approach. This is based on auditory phonograms representing basic sounds in the English language.

Math

The following are some selected approaches that may be used, or adapted for use, with children who have difficulty in arithmetic.

Structural Arithmetic (Stern, 1963). This approach utilizes concrete materials for self-discovery of number facts. It presents carefully sequenced experiments from simple number concepts to mastery of arithmetical computation and problem solving.

Montessori Materials. These are designed to be self-teaching, concrete materials.

Cuisenaire Rods. This program uses wooden rods of varying lengths and color. It is based on a definition of mathematics as a process of observation and a discovery of relationships.

The Greater Cleveland Mathematics Program. One criticism of this program is that it moves too fast from skill to skill with insufficient practice provided.

Programmed Math (Sullivan). The stress is on computational skills, while providing immediate feedback to the student. The child must already have a conceptual foundation in mathematics.

Social/Affective

How a child feels is more important than what he knows (Ward et al., 1974, p. 391).

The amount and kind of learning that occurs is greatly influenced by the way a child feels about himself, his peers, and his classroom environment. The child with a positive self-concept generally has a fairly realistic opinion of his strengths and weaknesses, and is generally accepted by his peers. The child with a negative self-concept generally has an unrealistic opinion of his strengths and weaknesses because of his direct experiences with failure and the feedback he gets from those around him in relation to his strengths and weaknesses. Children with damaged self-concepts may or may not possess the skills or competence that they themselves are certain they do not have. A low self-concept is characterized by chronic self-criticism and low self-evaluation. Problems in self-concept are critical in the education of exceptional children. A child must feel good about himself in order to maximally profit from instruction.

The teacher is in a key position to influence the social-emotional behavior, feelings, and attitudes of the learner. The expressed attitude of teachers toward exceptional children can greatly affect acceptance of that exceptional child by his peers. Teachers can create an environmental climate that ensures that the learner will:

a. feel his ideas have personal value and significance;
b. become more honest and open (this is encouraged by a teacher who is real, open, and honest with his own feelings); and
c. know that the teacher is sensitively understanding.

Figure 8 is taken from the CARE handbook, *Diagnostic Teaching of Preschool and Primary Children* (p. 392), and outlines some ways the teacher can promote positive social-emotional development among students.

Procedures widely promoted for improving self-concept include use of puppets, dramatic play, sociodrama, and role-playing. Worell and Nelson (1974) suggest the following techniques for use with children with low self-esteem:

Set beginning achievement goals low to insure success.

Reward early and often at first.

Reinforce successful trials after failure. Never leave a child until he has produced a response that is correct enough to earn reinforcement.

Avoid overpraise. Children with a history of failure are suspicious of social reinforcement and may not believe that your enthusiasm is real.

Try providing nonsocial reinforcement initially for a suspicious child; tokens or points may be less threatening than your early enthusiasm.

Focus on working hard and trying. Reward the child for "getting a good start," or "trying hard," or "not giving up."

Select specific products and provide reinforcement for observable achievement.

Consider using programmed materials at first so as to provide small steps and frequent reinforcement.

Encourage overlearning of material so that correct responses can be repeated a number of times. This will avert terminal errors and may prevent backsliding and discouragement. Have the child test himself out in a number of situations, including role play, self-rehearsal, etc. (p. 171).

TEACHER	ENVIRONMENT	LEARNER
1. Makes the subject matter *relevant* to the learner.	Subject matter is *relevant* to the learner.	Perceives subject matter as *relevant to him.*
2. Perceives children and environment as *nonthreatening* to self.	Is *nonthreatening* to the learner.	Perceives teacher, environment, and peers as *nonthreatening* to his self.
3. Creates an environment which encourages the learner to be *active* and *doing* in the teaching-learning process.	Encourages learner to be *active* and *doing.*	Is *active* and *doing* in the teaching-learning process.
4. Is *honest* and *open.*	Conducive to *honest* and *open* interaction.	Is *honest* and *open.*
5. Interacts within the teaching-learning process both at the *intellectual* and *feeling* levels.	Encourages *intellectual* and *feeling* levels.	Interacts within the teaching-learning process both at the *intellectual* and *feeling* levels.
6. Feels *accepted,* involved, comfortable, respected, and competent within the teaching-learning process.	Promotes *acceptance.*	Feels *accepted,* involved, comfortable, respected, and competent within the teaching-learning process.
7. Enters into *positive* and *cooperative* relationships with children.	Encourages *cooperative, positive* relationships.	Enters into *positive, cooperative* relationships with teacher and peers.
8. *Evaluates* himself and his own work.	Encourages *self-evaluation.*	*Evaluates* himself and his work.
9. Is accepting and *trusting* of children.	Creates atmosphere of *trust.*	
10. Is *sensitively understanding* of children.	Encourages *sensitive understanding.*	
11. Is *flexible.*	Promotes *flexibility.*	
12. *Plans* activities with children.	Encourages planning of activities with children and teacher.	
13. Accepts his own limitations.		

The characteristics of the learner, the teacher, and the environment are all related to each other, and they are all interacting with each other in the teaching-learning process.

Figure 8. Characteristics of the Teacher, Environment, and Learner Which Facilitate the Teaching-Learning Process*

*Spinazola, C. Application of the Diagnostic Teaching Model to Social Emotional Development. In Ward et al., *Diagnostic Teaching of Preschool and Primary Children,* 1973, pp. 392–93.

There are more and more books and materials commercially available aimed at the area called *affective education*. The following list names a few.

Anderson, J. et al. *Focus on Self-Development,* Chicago: Science Research Associates, 1973. Three developmental programs—Awareness, Responding, and Involvement—focused on developing the child's understanding of self, others, and environment. Includes filmstrips, cassettes, photoboards, activity books, and manuals.

Bessell, H. and Palomares, U. *Human Development Program,* San Diego: Human Development Training Program, 1972. Curriculum of methods and materials designed to give students the opportunity to understand and deal with their attitudes, values, and emotions. (Magic circle technique.)

Dinkmeyer, D. *Developing Understanding of Self and Others* (DUSO), Circle Pines, Minn.: American Guidance Association, 1970. Kits of activities and materials designed to facilitate the social and emotional development of children.

Glasser, W. *Schools Without Failure,* New York: Harper and Row, 1969.

Behavior Management

There is a wealth in information available, both printed and mediated, on behavior management techniques and principles of reinforcement. Some resources for further information are provided in the bibliography for this chapter. It is important to remember that unless a child's behavior is under control, learning cannot take place. An essential part of the instructional planning process involves determining the child's reward preferences. Just what does this child prefer, both academically and recreationally? Important clues to the child's preferences and to what is most likely to work can be obtained during the assessment phase, from information on the classroom environment and observations of the child and teacher. This information is then incorporated in the instructional plan.

Ward, et al. (1974) suggest several consequences that can be tested as possible reinforcers. These are:

1. *attention and social reinforcers*—includes praise, touch, eye contact. Compliments, when genuinely merited, are often forgotten or left unsaid. Use them to reward *learning* instead of teaching or directing, as in, "That's a neat paper, if only you'd spelled those words right." A compliment is often a reinforcer.
2. *food reinforcers*—should be paired with social reinforcers and gradually phased out.
3. *knowledge of results*—letting children know criteria against which they may evaluate their own learning, and teaching them to count and chart their own behavior so that they can watch their own change and growth.

(See the *Precision Teaching* entry in the resources section at the end of chapter.)

4. *activities as reinforcers*—a choice of a favorite activity for free time following performance of a specified task behavior. Also known as contingency contracting. (See contingency contracting in the resources section at the end of the chapter.)

5. *token economies as reinforcers*—use of a token, point, or checkmark system (pp. 122–24).

Vocational and Career Education

The area of career/vocational education ranges from career awareness activities beginning at the elementary level and continuing through the secondary level, to actual on-the-job work experience programs. There is a need for increased effort toward integrating career education into the regular curriculum, especially for the mildly handicapped at the secondary level. There is a need for more utilization of community resources (people and facilities), teacher awareness, and information of what is available in the field in order to strengthen the career education components of the school program.

Many states have curricula and guides already prepared and there are increasing numbers of media and materials on career and vocational education available on the commercial market. The following is a sampling of materials available commercially.

Career Awareness Materials (primary level). Individual activities including career identity cards and occupation match-up game. Developmental Learning Materials, Niles, Illinois.

Why Work Series. Designed for use with the Job Corps. Includes 21 graded reading selections, some cassettes, a teacher's manual, and an objective test for each selection. Behavioral Research Lab, Palo Alto, California.

World of Work Kit and Human Relations Kit. Stories about work situations and simulation exercises for developing work habits published by Webster-McGraw Hill.

SRA Materials Grades K–12. Some of the many titles available are:
   Work: Widening Occupational Roles Kit
   Job Experience Kits
   Occupational Awareness Kit (Grades 8–12)
   Science Research Associates, Chicago, Illinois.

Additional resources may be found in the resources section at the end of this chapter.

Case Studies

The instructional plans which appear on the following pages were developed for Case Studies I and II, which were presented in Chapters Two and Three.

Case Study I: Leonard T.

Leonard T.
Grade 8
BD 11/7/61
Special Teacher D. Walker

School: Moore Junior High

Date: 12/15/75

Educational Goals	
Regular Education	*Special Education*
Leonard will be integrated into regular program with no more than one period per day in the Resource Room.	Resource Room for one period per day for help in oral reading, comprehension, spelling and language. Continuous consultation with regular teachers.

Performance Objectives	Methods/Strategies/Materials
Reading	Resource Room and Reading Lab:
1. Given reading material at the 4th grade level, Leonard will read orally with 80% accuracy (word omissions and changes counted as errors)	Leonard reads orally twice a week and Resource Teacher or aide will note errors and grade level of oral story. Comparison of accuracy will be charted to show progress. Two hours per week Resource Room. Can move toward having students time each other's oral reading rate and accuracy and self-chart progress. Materials: SRA materials
2. Given 4th grade reading materials, Leonard will be able to answer with 80% accuracy, main idea, detail and inference questions orally and written, as judged by the Resource Teacher and Reading Lab Teacher	*Reading Lab:* SRA Practice Readers Clues Reading, Reading and Thinking Skills One hour per week = Resource Room and Reading Lab

Math	
By June, Leonard will be able to do three-digit division problems, fractions, decimals, and measurement at the 5th grade level as measured by the Math Lab Tests.	Resource Teacher in consultation with Math Teacher and use of *Math Lab Program, Working Makes Sense, Time and Measurement* materials in Regular Classroom.
Following Directions	
Within three months will demonstrate ability to attend to and follow directions as evidenced by earning 80% of available checkmarks each day in RS program. Carry over into regular classes—take card with him.	1. Resource Room and regular math, science, history and reading classes consistent with checkmarks and verbal praise. 2. Individually adapted tasks to ensure understanding and lead to completion. 3. Leonard repeats directions back to Resource Teacher.
Spelling	
Leonard will spell 80% of the words at the 4th grade level correctly by the end of the school year—success will be measured by a paper and pencil test.	Resource Room tutoring. Multisensory spelling approach; use of tape recorder language master, continuous progress in spelling, peer tutoring; two hours per week.

Instructional Plan for Case Study II: Richard* (pp. 178–187)

Pupil: Richard A.
Date: 10/20/75
Grade: 5   Pupil No: 009
School: Cordova

Prepared by: M. Patterson — Resource Teacher
J. Bates — Teacher

Approved by: Parent   Cecelia A.
Assessment Team: Chas. Rowe

GOAL:

EXIT PERFORMANCE OBJECTIVE (for 1 year or less)	MODE(S) OF INSTRUCTION			EVALUATION: Achievement % or Pass/Fail & Decision			STRATEGIES, METHODS AND MATERIALS
	Type of Program	Instructor	Time/ Duration	Date	% or P/F	Decision	
Priority: *Learn Basic Word Attack Skills* Objectives (one year or less):	Resource Room	Patterson					1. Resource Teacher uses the following approaches or may train aide to use them.
1. Richard will decode with 90% accuracy the words of CVC (Consonant-Short Vowel-Consonant) pattern on a teacher-made list							A. Tasks from Distar Reading I—spelling track and spelling by sound format.
2. Richard will perform as follows: Given the appropriate type precision chart, he will say the corresponding sound to following criteria: A. Consonant only 40/per min.,							B. Distar Reading II— fast cycle and continuing with one 30 minute lesson daily thereafter.

*Form developed by Stanislaus County

178

C. Precision teaching projects (charting) in the following order.
  1. Single consonants
  2. Initial consonants (in words)
  3. Final consonants (in words)
  4. Consonant blends
  5. Regular digraphs and blends
  6. Initial digraphs and blends (in words)
  7. Final digraphs and blends (in words)
  8. Vowels long and short with diacritical marks
  9. Vowels and consonants
  10. CVC word (medial short vowel)
  11. Diphthongs (oi, oy, ow, ou)
  12. Vowel digraphs (ei, ee, ie, ai, oa, ey, ay, ow)

B. Consonants and digraphs 40/per minute,
C. Consonant blends 37/per minute,
D. Consonants and vowels (with diacritical marks) 40/per minute,
E. Vowels (long and short) 35/per minute.
Maximum errors: One.
3. Richard will read orally from a second grade basal reader with a minimum of 50 wpm with two or less errors

179

GOAL:

EXIT PERFORMANCE OBJECTIVE (for 1 year or less)	MODE(S) OF INSTRUCTION			EVALUATION: Achievement % or Pass/Fail & Decision			STRATEGIES, METHODS AND MATERIALS
	Type of Program	Instructor	Time/ Duration	Date	% or P/F	Decision	
							13. 11 and 12 together
							14. "R" controlled vowels
							15. Words per minute from reader (Richard reads two minutes for timing)
							16. Vocabulary list words from basal reader
							17. Dolch words
							18. 15, 16, & 17 can be done concurrently with the sound project
							D. PDI (Performance Determined Instruction). Use word lists daily and a reader from a linguistic series.

E. Other supportive materials:
   1. Linguistic readers—Stanchfield, Merrill and Lippincott series;
   2. STAR supportive materials and worksheets (Title II);
   3. Program coordinator handbook (Fresno City Title VI), interventions and activities which are appropriate for Richard;
   4. Continue using Sullivan, SRA word games and other materials which are individualized for Richard.

GOAL:							
EXIT PERFORMANCE OBJECTIVE (for 1 year or less)	**MODE(S) OF INSTRUCTION**			**EVALUATION:** Achievement % or Pass/Fail & Decision			**STRATEGIES, METHODS AND MATERIALS**
	Type of Program	Instructor	Time/ Duration	Date	% or P/F	Decision	

Priority: *Improve Comprehension Skills*

Objectives (one year or less):
1. Richard will demonstrate improved comprehension skills by scoring 90% or above on Distar II Mastery Test.

2. A contingency management program would be helpful for Richard. Contracting could be utilized in resource center and possibly also in the regular classroom.

3. Cross-age tutoring program with Richard timing other students on projects he has successfully completed. He can also listen to youngsters read daily.

Improve Comprehension Skills

1. Following activities can be done in the resource center or by regular teacher if appropriate:

182

2. Richard will score 90% or above on written questions from teacher-designed stories which last a number of days and require Richard to remember what he has read.

Priority: Improve Auditory Skills
1. Given a set of different colored blocks, Richard will track four sounds in a nonsense word (e.g. flam) by laying out four different blocks. Criteria = 90%, ten examples.
2. Given the set of blocks Richard will track four sounds with two the same (e.g., akas, flal, cric) by laying out four blocks with the first and the last being the same color. Criteria 90%, ten examples.

A. Distar II stories and take-homes.
B. Other teacher-designed stories which require Richard to read critically and remember details.
C. Teacher asks many comprehension questions whenever Richard reads any material. Some demand simple recall; others require logic and deduction.
E. Distar Language II (taught quickly) and III.

Improve Auditory Skills
1. Resource specialist or classroom teacher if appropriate can do following activities:
   A. Auditory Discrimination in Depth kit (ADD)—color encoding portion.

183

GOAL:

EXIT PERFORMANCE OBJECTIVE (for 1 year or less)	MODE(S) OF INSTRUCTION			EVALUATION: Achievement % or Pass/Fail & Decision			STRATEGIES, METHODS AND MATERIALS
	Type of Program	Instructor	Time/ Duration	Date	% or P/F	Decision	
3. Given printed sound tiles Richard will "spell" four-letter nonsense words by laying out the correct tiles. Criteria 90%, ten examples.							B. Precision projects in color encoding. C. Spelling by sounds format, Distar I reading. D. Auditory sequencing tasks: imitating sound patterns, following complex set of direction repeating letter, words or digits in a series. 2. Cross-age tutoring in which Richard works with youngers in sound tracking. 3. Consider further assessment and possible *Michigan Language Program* if Richard fails to progress.

Priority: *Improve Richard's Spelling Skills*

1. Given CVC pattern phonetic words, Richard will spell them (ten examples) with 90% accuracy.
2. Richard will gain a minimum of eight months on the WRAT.
3. Richard will write five word sentences from basal second grade speller using initial capital letter, period and 90% spelling accuracy.

Resource specialist, paraprofessional or regular teacher use following activities and strategies:

A. Distar Spelling Tracks—initially give Richard words with Distar orthography until he is firm on vowels and digraphs.
B. Provide daily practice, correction and reinforcement of success.
C. Precision projects in spelling.
D. Use spelling tasks of word families.
E. Allow Richard to choose one word (minimum) a day he wishes to spell.
F. Cross-age tutoring— Richard may be the tutor or the tutee.

185

GOAL:

EXIT PERFORMANCE OBJECTIVE (for 1 year or less)	MODE(S) OF INSTRUCTION			EVALUATION: Achievement % or •Pass/Fail & Decision			STRATEGIES, METHODS AND MATERIALS
	Type of Program	Instructor	Time/ Duration	Date	% or P/F	Decision	
							G. Language Master—dictation sentences—Sullivan, Basal speller or teacher designed.
							H. Tasks where Richard must choose correctly-spelled words in a list.
							I. Proofreading exercises and emphasize proofreading own written work.
Improve Richard's Self-Concept							*Improve Richard's Self-Concept*
1. Richard will show a change in the positive direction on a teacher-designed inventory for self-concept.							1. Cross-age tutoring. Richard can tutor younger in controlled reader (he monitors). Precision projects (his proficiencies). Giving
2. Recorded information by teacher will show positive remarks by Richard about cross-age tutoring experience.							

186

spelling words. Checking word cards athletic skills.

2. Contingency management system might be helpful for Richard working on a contract. Lots of reinforcement for having realistic expectations of himself.

3. Placement decision must be carefully made to enter Richard into an instructional sequence which will lead to mastery. Although he wishes to appear like other students, it is ultimately self-defeating for him to use the same materials in spelling and reading. Resource specialist may choose Richard's materials in reading and spelling, give Richard feedback about reasons for certain materials and methods, and allow him some input on scheduling.

Some Principles of Good Instruction

Teacher Behaviors

We all have been exposed, at sometime in education courses, to those principles, concepts, and techniques which come under the umbrella of "Good Teaching Principles." These are such things as direct instruction, motivational techniques, providing "follow-up" or appropriate practice, reinforcing appropriate behaviors and approximations, and sequencing tasks—easy to more difficult. Commercially available and teacher-made instructional materials are important in the teaching/learning process, but so are teacher behaviors. The ability to relate to children and youth in a positive way comes up again and again in studies of effective teachers.

Studies conducted at the Exemplary Center for Reading Instruction in Salt Lake City, Utah, have identified some teacher behaviors which are important to, and correlate with, reading achievement of low ability students. The focus in these studies is on reading achievement, but it seems that some of the teacher behaviors effective in promoting gains in reading can also be generalized to other areas of instruction. According to the studies' results, the more effective teacher:

1. deviates more from prescribed materials, e.g., basal textbooks, teacher's guides, and so on
2. spends more time in *direct* instruction
3. uses rewards such as social praise, and/or reward systems such as contingency management
4. elicits oral responses from students [it was found that use of oral *group*-responding techniques (where all children in a group respond in unison to every teacher stimulus) increases retention, comprehension, and accuracy in reading.]
5. moves from prompted to unprompted learning as she/he teaches
6. teaches parents to teach their children
7. expects high levels of mastery, with rate as a criterion. (This means the more effective teacher was more concerned with mastery of material than with number of books read or "covering" a predetermined amount of material. More time was spent on drill and review to insure mastery.)

Before the instructional process can begin, the teacher must carefully select and prepare materials and tasks, select appropriate methods and materials, and plan for arrangement of the necessary space and time.

Selecting and Preparing Materials

When selecting materials for individual children, we must consider whether the material fits the objective we are working on and whether the child has the prerequisite skills necessary to use the material. It has been suggested that materials fall into three categories of difficulty:

1. The *frustration level*—the child is making too many errors and, there-fore, little or no progress toward mastery. If this is the case, we probably need to "slice back" or break the existing task down into smaller steps, or "step back" and use a different material altogether to get at a prerequisite skill the child has not yet mastered.
2. The *instructional level*—the child can use the materials and is making some errors but also is making progress.
3. The *independent level*—the child can use the material with ease, with very few errors, and is very close to proficiency (White and Haring, 1976, pp. 181–82).

Use commercial skill sequences and materials whenever possible. Always examine the task sequence to determine if it moves from simple to complex, if it includes subtasks which lead to the terminal objective, and if it avoids "large jumps" from concept to concept.

If a commercial sequence or material is not appropriate, try to *adapt* it. Consider adding extra practice sheets for each concept, drill cards, or games to reinforce concepts, or combine the existing materials with alternative ways for the student to learn the concept. Some possibilities for alternative ways of learning a particular skill or task include utilizing

1. the language master
2. a tape recorder
3. another student as a tutor
4. a different book
5. concrete materials
6. a different response from the one called for originally, e.g., tracing or matching *before* writing.

If adapting existing materials is not the answer, *make* your own sequences. It seems as though many teachers are always looking for the "magic" material or program—the one where it's all there for us and one that will fit every student. We must come to grips with the hard fact that there are no "magic" procedures; there is no all-encompassing material. In order to individualize and meet every student's educational needs, we will always have to make our own materials, and adapt or develop new skill sequences.

Selecting Methods and Procedures

Lowenbraun and Affleck (1976) suggest that a child passes through three stages of acquisition in learning a new skill or concept. The first stage is *initial acquisition,* during which the child receives input on how to perform the behavior and gains some knowledge and minimal usage of the skill. Next comes the *proficiency* stage, during which the child is improving his accuracy and rate of performance. The last stage is the *maintenance* stage. This stage occurs when the child has reached the level of proficiency desired and now engages in some ongoing practice in order to maintain the skill. These three stages of skill acquisition determine the kind of instructional methods and techniques the teacher must select for teaching the desired skill or concept. Lowenbraun and Affleck outline two basic types of teaching activities that occur in classrooms: *direct teacher activities* and *independent child activities*.

Direct Teacher Activities

These methods are used during the initial acquisition stage of learning. During this stage, the teacher must provide instructional input to students, explain, or demonstrate a skill or concept. Techniques such as molding (actually guiding a child's response physically as in tracing letters of the alphabet), demonstrating, explaining, using audio-visual aids, and providing closely supervised practice are appropriate during direct-teacher instruction. These methods allow for immediate feedback to students to assist them in making correct responses initially and to prevent practicing errors.

Lowenbraun and Affleck (1976) list the following guidelines for providing instructional input and supervised practice during teacher-directed instruction.

1. Focus on skills at the level of initial acquisition.
2. Provide instructional input on how to perform the skill.
   a. Be sure the child is attentive.
   b. Actively include the child in instruction.
   c. Use visual stimuli in addition to verbal instruction.
   d. Use consistent, simple vocabulary.
   e. Present information in a logical, organized fashion.
   f. Demonstrate the desired behavior.
3. Provide supervised practice of the new skills.
   a. Provide prompts or partial prompts when needed.
   b. Provide physical guidance when needed and appropriate.
   c. Fade out use of cues and prompts.
   d. Provide corrective feedback on performance (p. 58).

Independent-Child Activities

Once the child has an initial understanding of the task, he needs practice and drill to increase his proficiency. During this proficiency stage, the teacher can provide opportunities for practice which the child can do with a minimum of teacher direction. The teacher *must* plan for and utilize independent child activities in order to allow time to instruct other individual children.

Independent child activities can include using analogous tasks for drill, extended tasks, learning center activities, peer tutoring, aides, and parents. Activities at this level must still insure success, and feedback is still important for growth and reduction of errors. Feedback at this stage can involve use of self-correcting exercises, correction keys, peers checking each other, and written comments or smiling faces on teacher-corrected papers. Lowenbraun and Affleck list some guidelines for independent child activities:

1. Focus on skills at the level of proficiency or maintenance.
2. Provide equivalent or analogous exercises for a specific objective.
3. Insure independence of task completion.
   a. Use simple directions.
   b. Use one task per page or assignment.
   c. Use standard formats that the child can recognize.
   d. Insure that the child knows the exact demands of the task and when she has completed the task.
   e. Use responses that can later be corrected by the teacher.
4. Insure success on the child-directed tasks.
   a. Use visual prompts.
   b. Use verbal prompts.
5. Provide feedback on responses made (p. 63).

Maintaining proficiency in a skill (maintenance stage) also involves the use of independent-type activities. Some skills (e.g., math skills) are maintained through performance at higher levels, but others are not. Spelling words, for example, often need much review and can be reviewed without the teacher's direct supervision. Don't forget the use of learning centers and games for review purposes.

Arranging Space and Time

The traditional ways of scheduling a class—dividing the day up into discrete time periods for each subject—do not always meet the needs of individual children. We must work on ways of creating flexible scheduling so that *routines* are familiar and regular to children, but time periods are more flexible. Flexible scheduling allows children opportunities to work at their own rate and allows the teacher the opportunity to work with individuals and small groups.

The physical set-up of the room is also crucial when implementing a system of individualized instruction. Activity centers, small group areas, and individual areas are necessary. Flexible scheduling and individualization can be enhanced through the clever and creative use of aides, parents, peer, and cross-age tutors. Take the time to develop a specific set of procedures for peer tutors and paraprofessionals to follow and then inservice them in what you expect. Your program will run much more smoothly. Some resources to aid you in setting up a classroom geared to individualized instruction are provided in the resources section at the end of the chapter.

Implementing the Plan and Evaluating Student Outcomes

Under P.L. 94–142 and the various state regulations, the local education agency is responsible for conducting an annual, and often a semiannual, review of each child's progress as related to the objectives stated in his/her instructional plan. This is one level of evaluation. The other level of evaluation involves the continuous progress checks, which provide feedback to the child and teacher, as the plan is being implemented on a day-to-day basis.

In individualized remedial programs the idea is not to assess the student's ability for grading purposes, but to:
1. obtain information which is useful for modifying the instructional plan for continued success and
2. obtain feedback for the child himself.

As the plan is being implemented in the classroom, we are continually assessing the student's performance, and in so doing, testing out the efficacy of the instructional plan itself. Gaps in instructional sequences may appear and be modified and corrected, or instructional materials may be changed. The plan is continually being updated as feedback from student performance dictates.

Educational evaluation is an ongoing monitoring of pupil progress. Methods of evaluating pupil progress are specified within the instructional plan so that teaching/learning procedures can be evaluated continuously. Precisely stated criteria within each objective should communicate clearly to the user (teacher) so that she/he can readily determine when the child has mastered each objective. Instruction and evaluation are intermeshed. If the child's performance matches the level of performance stated in the objective, a new objective is specified and a new set of instructional strategies and materials is selected to reach the new objective. This type of evaluation is called criterion-referenced measurement, as the focus is on a comparison of the individual's performance to a criterion or performance standard. Criterion-referenced measurement was discussed in more detail in Chapter Three.

If the child is not successful in mastering the objective to criterion, we need to ask the following questions: Was the objective appropriate? Did the child have the prerequisite skills? Are the steps too large? Are the methods,

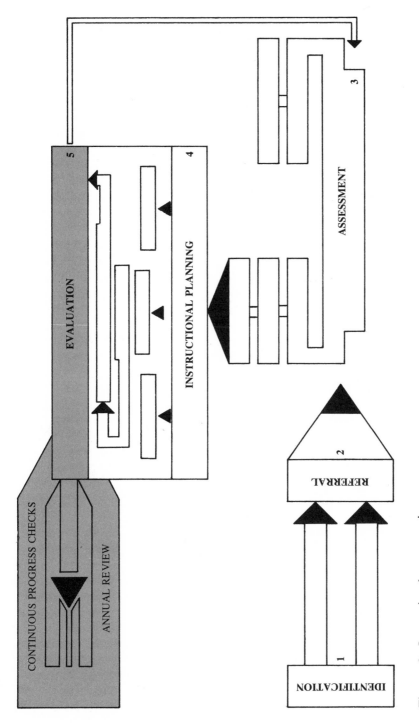

Figure 9. Instructional programming process.

193

procedures, and materials effective? After examining these areas, the faulty parts of the instructional plan are revised immediately and the new components are applied.

According to Ward et al. (1974, pp. 71–78), educational evaluation consists of four components:

1. *Establishing a criterion* which specifies the *amount* and *type* of pupil behavior required to satisfy the objective—a well-stated, complete objective supplies this information.
2. *Selecting an evaluation procedure.* The procedure is specified in the objective as the "conditions under which the behavior will be demonstrated."
3. *Collecting evaluative information or data.* There are many ways to collect data on student progress. The procedure and method for collecting data is dependent on the type of objective. Some objectives may require that the child demonstrate a behavior and the teacher observe and record. Other objectives may be measured by use of a multiple choice or true/false pre- and posttest. Many criterion-referenced curriculum programs and materials are now available which include pre/posttests and progress checks. Other behaviors may be measured via verbal explanations or written statements by the child. Graphs or charts are another means of collecting evaluative data. Data may be collected during the teaching process, while the student is practicing, during the student's free time, or in a formal test situation. Data may be collected daily, weekly, or monthly, depending on the objective. If the objective involves reading rates, data should be collected and charted or recorded daily. It is important, in any case, that the evaluation techniques utilized yield *immediate* information about learning performance.

   Examples for scheduling data collection to fit individual objectives could be:
   a. Percent correct on math *daily*
   b. Number of new words mastered *weekly*
   c. Evaluation of child's attitudes toward school *monthly*
   Self-charting or recording of data by the student himself simplifies the data collection task for the teacher and can serve to motivate the student. (See *Exceptional Teaching* and *Precision Teaching* in the resources section.)
4. *Making decisions based on the data obtained.* Once data are collected, they are compared with the criterion stated within the objective. If the performance is adequate, move to a new objective and update the instructional plan. If the performance does not meet criterion, the plan is revised. Criterion-referenced measurement techniques provide a listing

of specific skills mastered and those not yet mastered. The results allow us to pinpoint errors, analyze them, and use this information to plan alternate instructional methods and procedures. Implementing the instructional plan and evaluating student outcomes occur simultaneously. Through adequate evaluation and systematic progress checks, we are continually assessing student needs. Ongoing assessment and good teaching go hand-in-hand.

Suggestions for Determining Adequacy of Instructional Plans*

1. Are specific academic strengths identified?
2. Are learning strengths identified?
3. Are learning weaknesses identified?
4. Are student interests identified and incorporated?
5. Are the best probable reinforcers identified?
6. Is there a choice of instructional materials appropriate to student's
   age
   sex
   learning problem
   learning style?
7. Is there a choice of instructional materials suited to student's regular classroom instructional program?
8. Are objectives clearly stated and do they include evaluative criteria?
9. Are teaching procedures detailed and clearly understandable?

Evaluation of the Instructional Program

It is not a child's performance on a standardized test which renders him eligible for special education services, but rather the discrepancy between his rate of acquiring skills and the minimum rate required of all children to achieve essential education within the usual 12 or 13 years of public schooling (Christie and McKenzie, 1974, p. 16).

An established continuum of the essential minimum objectives that each child must demonstrate to criterion at the elementary level, the junior high school level, and the high school level is critical. Within each span of grades, minimum objectives for all children at each grade level or subject area must be clear. It is only when objectives are clear for all children that we are alerted to

*Adapted from Region V Educational Services Center, *The Resource Room: An Access to Excellence.*

those children for whom special services are warranted; and it is only when minimum objectives for all children are clearly specified that we can determine when it is time to *phase out* special services for those children with special needs.

There are no handicapped children under this criterion-referenced system. There are only children who are eligible for some level of specialized service because the "levels of their current behavior are less than the levels of the minimum objectives applicable to the child with his years of schooling" (Christie and McKenzie, 1974, p. 5). A child is eligible for special services when he or she is not acquiring essential skills at a minimum rate. He is ready for total integration into the regular classroom when he is acquiring essential skills at a minimum rate.

Evaluating the Effectiveness of the Services

One of the biggest dangers of special education is that once a child has been identified and placed, he tends to stay there indefinitely. Inadequate provision for "phase out" is a severe weakness in the system. When a child receives specialized services designed to accelerate his mastery of minimum objectives established for all children within the school, evaluation of those special services is essential. If a child's achievement rate is not accelerated by those services, the child has not been served and the services have not been effective.

The special educator shares accountability with the regular classroom teacher in a mainstreaming situation. When the child meets minimum objectives set for all children in his grade level, he is ready to be phased out of the special service program. Establishing minimum objectives for students at each grade level and relating remedial objectives to the objectives of the regular curriculum provide a means for determining an exit point for the child from special service support to maintenance by the regular classroom teacher.

The efficacy of special support services is determined by examining the results produced. The most important result is growth in student achievement. Other results are more difficult to assess. The following pages represent some sample forms for generating feedback on the effectiveness of resource services for handicapped students.

Regular Faculty Evaluation of Resource Model*

1. How many of your students have you referred to the resource teacher?
   a. _____ (1–3)   b. _____ (4–5)   c. _____ (6–10)   d. _____ more than 10
   e. _____ none
   (If *none* (e), respond only to questions #16 thru #19.)

---

*Taken from South Carolina Region V Educational Services Center, *The Resource Room: An Access to Excellence,* 1975, pp. 177–83.

Rate the quality of service you have received from the resource room teacher for the following eight questions (thru #9). The questions will be answered on your separate answer sheet using the following rating scale:

    a—excellent
    b—good
    c—fair
    d—poor
    e—no help at all

2. Testing students
3. Offering suggestions and ideas
4. Preparing materials for your use
5. Tutoring your student in the resource room
6. Tutoring your student in your classroom
7. Observing students in your classroom
8. How would you rank the overall service the resource unit has been to your school?
9. How would you rank the overall service the resource unit has been to yourself?

Instructions:

Use this scale to rate the next 6 questions (10 thru 15):
Though all situations may not be precisely described by *one* of the three possible responses, please select the *one* most closely approximating your situation.

    a. I needed much more assistance
    b. I needed more assistance
    c. Assistance has been adequate

The resource room teacher could have provided more assistance in the following areas:

10. Tutoring students in resource room
11. Tutoring students in my room
12. Preparing materials for students to use in my room
13. Offering ideas and techniques that were of assistance to me
14. Demonstrating materials for specific remedial needs
15. Testing students
16. Have you participated in a placement committee meeting?
    a. yes _____   b. no _____
17. Have you participated in meetings with the resource teacher and two or more teachers to discuss the needs of specific students? (A diagnostic team meeting)?
    a. yes _____   b. no _____
18. How many years have you been teaching?
    a. 0–1 yr. _____   b. 2–3 yr. _____   c. 4 yrs. _____
    d. 5 or more yrs. _____
19. If you have knowledge of other ways that the resource unit has been of service to you, please use the green sheet to state your opinions.

Principal's Evaluation of Resource Units*

I. General

1. What is the basic organization of your school?
    _____a. Primary
    _____b. Elementary
    _____c. Middle
    _____d. Junior High
    _____e. Senior High
2. How long have resource rooms been a part of your school's organization?
    _____a. 1 year
    _____b. 2 years
    _____c. 3 years
    _____d. 4 years
    _____e. 5 or more

If you do *not* have a resource room serving learning disabled children, stop at this point. Otherwise continue with the remaining questions.

3. What is the administrative organization pattern of the school?
    _____a. Traditional self-contained
    _____b. Departmentalization
    _____c. Team teaching
    _____d. Unit Teacher
    _____e. Other

Which of the following curriculum organization patterns are being used in your school?

4. Wisconsin Design Materials   _____a. yes   _____b. no
5. Individually Guided Education   _____a. yes   _____b. no
6. Fountain Valley Testing   _____a. yes   _____b. no
7. IMS Math   _____a. yes   _____b. no
8. Basals and adopted texts   _____a. yes   _____b. no
9. Others _____   _____a. yes   _____b. no

II. Student Instruction in L. D. Resource Rooms

10. What is the total number of children seen by the resource teacher on an average weekly basis?
    _____a. 26–28   _____b. 29–33   _____c. 34–38
    _____d. 39–43   _____e. 44 or more
11. What is the fewest number of children with whom the resource teacher works during any given period in the daily schedule?
    _____a. 1
    _____b. 2 to 4
    _____c. 5 to 6
    _____d. 7 to 10
    _____e. more than 10

---

*Taken from South Carolina Region V Educational Services Center, *The Resource Room: An Access to Excellence,* 1975, pp. 177–83.

12. What is the largest number of children with whom the resource teacher works during any given period in the daily schedule?
    ____a. 2 to 4
    ____b. 5 to 6
    ____c. 7 to 10
    ____d. 11 to 15
    ____e. 16 or more
13. Are the children willing to work with the resource teacher?
    ____a. yes ____b. no ____c. sometimes
15. How frequently have you observed in the resource room for a period of 10 or more minutes?
    ____a. 0
    ____b. 1–2
    ____c. 3–5
    ____d. 6 or more

III. Faculty Rapport

16. Is the resource teacher willing to share her skills, knowledge and materials with others?
    ____a. yes ____b. no ____c. sometimes
17. Is the resource teacher accepted as a peer?
    ____a. yes ____b. no ____c. sometimes
18. Is the assistance of the resource teacher sought by others?
    ____a. yes ____b. no ____c. sometimes

IV. Records

Is the following data concerning each child being served in the resource unit available in an organized manner to the appropriate persons?

19. Reason for referral	____a. yes	____b. no
20. Psychological evaluations	____a. yes	____b. no
21. Academic problems	____a. yes	____b. no
22. Behavioral problems	____a. yes	____b. no
23. Academic progress	____a. yes	____b. no
24. Behavioral progress	____a. yes	____b. no

Are reports of student progress made regularly to:

25. child?	____a. yes	____b. no
26. parent?	____a. yes	____b. no
27. regular teacher?	____a. yes	____b. no
28. placement committee?	____a. yes	____b. no

V. Scheduling

29. Are the children being seen for periods of at least 30 minutes?
    ____a. yes ____b. no
30. Are the children being seen for periods of more than 30 minutes?
    ____a. yes ____b. no
31. Does the resource teacher have some time (30–45 minutes) during the day for planning?   ____a. yes ____b. no

32. Does the resource teacher have some time (3 hours) during the week for student observations and instruction in the regular classroom? ____a. yes ____b. no

33. Does the scheduling permit the pupil in the resource room program maximum opportunities to participate with his peers in as many non-academic areas as possible? ____a. yes ____b. no

34. Is there enough flexibility of scheduling so that scheduling is in the best interest of individual pupils? ____a. yes ____b. no

35. Is scheduling frequently reassessed to determine if changes need to be made either for individual pupils or for groups? ____a. yes ____b. no

36. Are there *regularly scheduled* weekly meetings held between resource and regular class teachers? ____a. yes ____b. no

37. Are there *regularly scheduled* monthly meetings held between resource and regular class teachers? ____a. yes ____b. no

VI.   General Evaluation of the Resource Model for L. D.

38. Can the supplemental instruction and support offered in a resource setting meet the needs of L. D. students in your school?
    ____a. All of the students
    ____b. Most of the students
    ____c. Few of the students

39. Have the regular classroom teachers expanded or modified the curriculum of the regular classroom so that it is also appropriate for these handicapped pupils?
    ____a. yes ____b. no

40. Is there a need for additional resource units? ____a. yes ____b. no

41. Is there a need for self-contained classroom units- in your school?
    ____a. yes ____b. no

Rank each of the following using the following scale:
    a—excellent
    b—good
    c—average
    d—poor
    e—no assistance

42. ____Resource teacher as tutor
43. ____Resource teacher as organizer
44. ____Resource teacher as consultant
45. ____Resource teacher as school asset
46. ____Resource room service to the school
47. ____Regular teacher as a source of referrals
48. ____Resource room's capability of meeting needs of exceptional children
49. ____Regular teacher willingness to work with others for benefit of exceptional child

VII.   Strengths

The resource room has been effective in:

50. ____a. yes ____b. no Relieving the regular teacher of troublesome students.
51. ____a. yes ____b. no Tutoring students who are having trouble
52. ____a. yes ____b. no Providing expertise in the areas of classroom management

53. ____a. yes   ____b. no Providing expertise in the area of remediation

Structured Observation*

Person Observed   Observer

N = No basis for evaluation (can't observe)
1 = Attempting skill, but inadequate
2 = Adequate (minimum acceptable skill)
3 = Outstanding
____1. Arrangement of class
       3 = Areas for individual work, small groups, and private discussion
       2 = Areas for individual work and small groups
       1 = No variety
____2. Is the process up-to-date and complete?
       3 = Process checklist and supporting documents within time frame.
       2 = Following required documents present and noted within time frames:

	Folder #	Folder #	Folder #
a. notification of due process			
b. release of information			
c. permission to test			
d. certification			
e. instructional plan			

       1 = Required documents missing
       Ask RST to select two folders at random:
       3 = Both folders consistently complete
       2 = Both folders have required documents
       1 = Some or all have missing required documents
       Make comments if necessary.
____3. Documentation to indicate assessment
       3 = Documentation of all of the following areas:

	Folder #	Folder #	Folder #
a. classroom observation			
b. educational history			
c. academic skills			
d. cultural or language factors			
e. health			

       2 = Assessment documentation in folder to support all objectives
       1 = No evidence to support objective in educational plan
       Look at two folders. Comment if child is overly-assessed with no meaningful plan.

---

*This form was developed for use in the Humboldt-Del Norte Master Plan Project, Eureka, California, 1976.

_____4. Are appropriate signatures on educational plan?
    2 = Signatures of principal or designee, resource teacher, program specialist, parent, or other if needed
    1 = Less than required signatures
_____5. The child's activities are tied to the educational plan.
    3 = Activities are directly related to the child's objectives
    2 = Some activities tie into objectives
    1 = No relationship
_____6. Indications that class activities are individualized.
    3 = Evidence of where child started, where he is now, where he is going on majority of objectives and activities that provide for varied learning rates
    2 = Same as above for only one objective
    1 = No such evidence
_____7. Evidence of a variety of materials and/or approaches.
    3 = Variety of learning alternatives listed in plan and readily available materials reflect variety of learning styles on majority of objectives
    2 = Same as above with one objective
    1 = Only one or few things for all children
_____8. Observe each student's behavior over two five-minute periods. Note on and off task behavior at the end of each thirty-second interval.

Circumstances of observation (do not observe during transition period)

3 = Over 75% on task
2 = 65%–75% on task
1 = Below 65% on task

____9. What classroom management techniques are in evidence?

Yes   No

__   __ Individual children rewarded for academic behaviors
__   __ Individual children rewarded for social behaviors
__   __ Teacher rewards appropriate group behavior

Types of rewards (Check all rewards available, two checks if observed)

( ) Checkmarks   ( ) Praise, smile
( ) Activities privileges   ( ) Tangibles
( ) Touch, pat   ( ) Stars
( ) Free time   ( ) Tokens

Yes   No
( )   ( ) Kids have opportunity to choose type of reward.

Study Questions and Activities

1. How does the written instructional plan described in Chapter Four differ from the traditional lesson plan often required of teachers?

2. Does the federal legislation (P.L. 94–142), which requires written instructional plans, guarantee individualized, effective, coordinated instruction for all handicapped pupils? How does the preparation and implementation of these written plans assure the achievement of any or all of these laudable goals?

3. Why is it wise to establish priorities for the achievement of the objectives included in a written instructional plan? (See the section, *Writing the Plan.*)

4. Why is coordination of instructional planning, with the minimum performance standards, for the mildly handicapped pupil's regular class placement essential to both the planning and evaluation of the pupil's special instruction? (See the section on Planning Considerations and Evaluation of the Instructional Program in the text.)

5. Obtain examples of written instructional plans from cooperating resource/consulting teachers in a neighboring school district (or use the sample plans from the text). Critique these plans according to the following criteria: (a) Are the pupil's problem areas listed (from referral information)? (b) Have appropriate techniques been used to assess

baseline or entry skills in each of the problem areas? (c) Are learning strengths as well as weaknesses indicated or implied? (d) Are objectives directly related to pupil's areas of need? (e) Are priorities for areas of greatest need indicated? (f) Are at least two learning alternatives correlated to each of the high priority objectives to ensure the pupil a choice and increase the possibility of success? (g) Are environmental conditions for maximizing learning suggested (instructional grouping, preferred reinforcers, teaching styles, etc.)? (h) Is the responsibility for implementation clearly indicated (e.g., resource teacher, regular teacher, parent, or principal)? (i) Are appropriate procedures for evaluation of pupil progress planned? (j) Is space provided for indicating pupil's progress during evaluation? (k) Is there a clear correlation between referral problems, assessment techniques, written objectives, learning alternatives, and evaluation techniques throughout the plan? If the planning format used is unsatisfactory relative to these criteria, develop your own format for writing instructional plans which you feel is both workable and satisfactory.

6. Select approximately four compatible referral problems listed in Chapter Three, Activity 8, to describe Harold Hazzard, a mythical but typical sixth-grade referral to an elementary resource teacher. Write a complete (hypothetical) instructional plan covering communication, reading, computational skills, and school adjustment which meets the criteria in activity five above. Review Harold's instructional plan to ensure that there is a clear correlation between referral problems, assessment techniques, written objective, learning alternatives, and evaluation techniques. (This exercise may be done individually or as a group project. Either present individual written plans to your classmates and/or instructor for review, or select four members of the class to role play a school appraisal team meeting to plan Harold's instruction for the school year. If you choose to role play, use the roles of principal, resource teacher, school nurse, and referring regular teacher as in Chapter Two, Activity 5.)

References

Bateman, B. D. *The essentials of teaching*. San Rafael, Calif.: Dimensions, 1971.
California State Department of Education. *California Administrative Code, Title 5, Education*. Regulations for implementation of AB 4040 (Master Plan for Special Education) (Mimeo). Sacramento: 1975
California State Department of Education. *California master plan for special education*. Sacramento: Office of State Printing, 1974.

Champagne, D. W., & Goldman, R. M. *Handbook for managing individualized learning in the classroom*. Englewood Cliffs, N.J.: Educational Technology Publications, 1975.

Christie, L. S., & McKenzie, H. S. *Minimum objectives: A measurement system to provide evaluation of special education in regular classrooms* (Mimeo). Burlington, Vt.: University of Vermont, College of Education and Social Services, Spring 1974.

Deno, E. (Ed.). *Instructional alternatives for exceptional children*. Reston, Va.: The Council for Exceptional Children, 1973.

Hammill, D. D., & Bartel, N. R. (Eds). *Teaching children with learning and behavior problems*. Boston: Allyn and Bacon, 1975.

Kaufman, M. J., Gottlieb, J., Agard, J. A., & Kubic, M. B. Mainstreaming: Toward an explication of the construct. *Focus on exceptional children*, 1975, 7(3), 1–12.

Lowenbraun, S., & Affleck, J. Q. *Teaching mildly handicapped children in regular classes*. Columbus, Ohio: Charles E. Merrill, 1976.

Lerner, J. W. *Children with learning disabilities: Theories, diagnosis and teaching strategies*. Boston: Houghton-Mifflin, 1971.

Meyen, E. L. *Developing units of instruction: For the mentally retarded and other children with learning problems*. Dubuque, Iowa: William C. Brown, 1972.

Mills, B. C., & Mills, R. A. *Designing instructional strategies for young children*. Dubuque, Iowa: William C. Brown, 1972.

South Carolina Region V Educational Services Center. *The resource room: An access to excellence*. Lancaster, S.C.: Region V Educational Services Center, 1975.

Reid, E. Seven years of research in reading (Mimeo). Salt Lake City, Utah: Exemplary Center For Reading Instruction, n.d.

Reid, E. Teacher behaviors for reading instruction (Mimeo). Salt Lake City, Utah: Exemplary Center For Reading Instruction, May 1974.

Siegel, E., & Siegel, R. Ten guidelines for writing instructional sequences. *Journal of Learning Disabilities*, 1975, 8(4), 15–21.

Spinazola, C. Application of the diagnostic teaching model to social emotional development. In Ward, M.E., Cartwright, G. P., Cartwright, C. A., Campbell, J., and Spinazola, C. *Diagnostic teaching of preschool and primary children*. University Park: The Computer Assisted Instruction Laboratory, College of Education, Pennsylvania State University, 1973.

Towle, M. *Resource specialist training program, (Vol. V)*. Instructional Strategies (Part 1). Eugene, Ore.: Regional Resource Center, University of Oregon, n.d.

Van Etten, G., & Adamson, G. The fail-save program: A special educational service continuum. In E. Deno, *Instructional alternatives for exceptional children*. Reston, Va.: The Council for Exceptional Children, 1973.

Ward, M. E., Cartwright, G. P., Cartwright, C. A., Campbell, J., & Spinazola, C. *Diagnostic teaching of preschool and primary children*. University Park, Pa.: The Computer Assisted Instruction Laboratory, College of Education, The Pennsylvania State University, 1973.

Worell, J., & Nelson, C. M. *Managing instructional problems: A case study workbook*. New York: McGraw-Hill, 1974.

Resources

General Resources

Hammill, D. D., & Bartel, N. R. *Teaching children with learning and behavior problems*. Boston: Allyn and Bacon, 1975.

Haring, N. G., & Schiefelbusch, R. L. *Teaching special children*. New York: McGraw-Hill, 1976.

Lowenbraun, S., & Affleck, J. *Teaching mildly handicapped children*. Columbus, Ohio: Charles E. Merrill, 1976. Presents the components of a systematic instructional model for mainstreaming the mildly handicapped, from identification and assessment to selection of instructional activities and ongoing assessment (evaluation) of performance. Includes a section on techniques and resources for modifying behaviors. Examples of assessment and instructional materials are presented.

Mills, B. C., & Mills, D. D. *Designing instructional strategies for young children*. Dubuque, Iowa: William C. Brown, 1972.

Myers, P. I., & Hammill, D. D. *Methods for learning disorders*. New York: John Wiley, 1969.

Smith, R. M. *Clinical teaching: Methods of instruction for the retarded*. New York: McGraw-Hill, 1974.

Behavioral Objectives and Task Analysis

Baker, E. *Analyzing learning outcomes*. Los Angeles, Calif.: Vimcet Associates. In this program, techniques of task analysis are applied to learning objectives. Practice is provided so that an operational objective can be analyzed into subtasks (designated as either entry or en route skills). Filmstrip, tape, and manual ($12.50).

Gronlund, N. E. *Stating behavioral objectives for classroom instruction*. New York: Macmillan, 1970. *What it is:* This short paperback book ($1.95) is a detailed and very helpful guide to the writing of appropriate instructional objectives. It helps to define objectives as expected learning outcomes and a terminal behavior that will show that a particular objective has been obtained. Dr. Gronlund shows how the Taxonomies of the Affective and Cognitive Domain may be used to provide important, but difficult to define, concepts. The book contains examples of instructional objectives, teaching methods, and evaluation techniques. *Contents:* This fifty-seven page paperback contains eight chapters on stating, using, and selecting appropriate instructional objectives. The chapters on constructing test items and how to use them in marking and reporting are very concise and informative. *Strengths:* This has become a standard reference for teachers needing a basis for writing good instructional objectives. The chapter on selecting objectives gives the teacher an overview of the considerations that are relevant. It is like a good cookbook with recipes for writing, implementing, and evaluating instructional goals. The appendix on illustrative verbs gives the teacher vocabulary suggestions for stating goals and determining behavior that will demonstrate what level of cognition the student is achieving. It is particularly appropriate for junior or senior high school teachers.

Kibler, R. J., Cegala, D. J., Miles, D. T., & Barker, L. L. *Objectives for instruction and evaluation.* Boston: Allyn and Bacon, 1974.

Mager, R. F. *Preparing instructional objectives.* Palo Alto, Calif.: Fearon, 1962.

Behavior Management

Managing behavior (Parts 1–8), in numerical order, are:

Hall, R. Vance. *Managing behavior* (Part 1). Behavior modification: The measurement of behavior. Lawrence, Kan.: H and H Enterprises, 1974. ($2.25)

Hall, R. Vance. *Managing behavior* (Part 2). Behavior modification: Basic principles. Lawrence, Kan.: H and H Enterprises, 1975. ($2.25)

Hall, R. Vance. *Managing behavior* (Part 3). Behavior modification: Applications in school and home. Lawrence, Kan.: H and H Enterprises, 1974. ($2.25)

Panyan, M. C. *Managing behavior* (Part 4). New ways to teach new skills. Lawrence, Kan.: H and H Enterprises, 1975. ($3.25)

Wheeler, A. H., & Fox, W. L. *Managing behavior* (Part 5). A teacher's guide to writing instructional objectives, Lawrence, Kan.: H and H Enterprises, 1972. ($3.25)

Breyer, N. L., & Axelrod, S. *Managing behavior* (Part 6). Summaries of selected behavior modification studies. Lawrence, Kan.: H and H Enterprises, 1973. ($4.95)

Streifel, S. *Managing behavior* (Part 7). Teaching a child to imitate, Lawrence, Kan.: H and H Enterprises, 1976. ($3.50)

Harris, S. *Managing behavior* (Part 8). Teaching a non-verbal. Lawrence, Kan.: H and H Enterprises, 1976. ($3.95)

Homme, L., Canyi, A. P., Gonzales, M. A., & Rechs, J. R. *How to use contingency contracting in the classroom.* Champagne, Ill.: Research Press, 1970.

Criterion-Referenced Instruction—General

Drew, C. J., Freston, C. W., & Logan, D. R. Criteria and reference in evaluation: An evaluation model for the special education teacher. *Focus on Exceptional Children,* 1972, *4*(1), 1–10.

Fremer, J. *Handbook for conducting task analyses and developing criterion-referenced tests of language skills.* (P.R. 74–12) Princeton, N.J.: Educational Testing Services, 1974.

Gronlund, N. E. *Preparing criterion-referenced tests for classroom instruction.* New York: Macmillan, 1973.

Housden, J. L., & LeGear, L. An emerging model: Criterion-referenced evaluation. In Georgiades, W., & Clark, D. C. (Eds), *Models for individualized instruction.* New York: MSS Information Corporation, 1974.

Klein, S., & Kosekoff, J. P. *Determining how well a test measures your objectives.* Report No. 94, Center for the Study of Evaluation, Los Angeles, Calif.: U.C.L.A., 1975.

Criterion-Referenced Instruction—Systems

Prescriptive Math Inventory, New York: CTB/McGraw-Hill. P.M.I. is a criterion-referenced test system for measuring mastery of math objectives for grades 4–8. It is intended as a diagnostic and prescriptive tool providing a student profile of strengths and weaknesses with suggestions for learning activities to facilitate mastery at each objective. Also included are: individual study guide for the student, activity guide for the teacher, and interim evaluation tests for ongoing assessment.

Prescriptive Reading Inventory, New York: CTB/McGraw-Hill. P.R.I. is a criterion-referenced test system for measuring reading ability per behavioral objectives for grades 1.5–6.5. It is intended as a diagnostic-prescriptive tool for individualizing reading. Individual student profiles describe strengths and weaknesses in terms of behavior objectives for each of the process objectives, e.g., recognition of sound and symbol, phonic analysis, and structural analysis.

System FORE, Los Angeles: Foreworks, n.d. This is a developmentally oriented, criterion-referenced system, to be used as a diagnostic-prescriptive tool for obtaining a student-abilities profile in language, reading, and mathematics skills. The teacher is provided with an extensive listing of companion or reference materials and tests. *Kit 2* offers The Complete System FORE package of sequences, materials, inventories, a resource teacher guide, and a learning center guide. *Kit 1* is identical, but less expensive by excluding the introductory materials for those already familiar with System FORE material. The *Extension Kit* is just that, expanding upon resource and material listings, and including the new "age-equivalent pupil profile."

Peer Tutoring

Christopolos, F. Keeping exceptional children in the regular class. *Exceptional Children,* 1973, *40*(6), 569–572. This article provides a summary of teacher education priorities from a project in Baltimore elementary schools designed to help teachers develop approaches for teaching learning disabled students in regular classes. Peer tutoring is discussed as an integration technique; record keeping and task analysis are presented in the context of tutoring procedures.

Gartner, A., Kohler, M., & Reissman, F. *Children teach children.* New York: Harper and Row, 1971.

Gibbons, B. *Hosts: Help one student to succeed—Training volunteer tutors in your reading program, A complete guide.* New York: Random House, n.d.

Lippitt, P., Eiseman, J. W., & Lippitt, R. *Cross-age helping packet.* Center for Research on the Utilization of Scientific Knowledge. University of Michigan, 450 City Center Building, Ann Arbor, Michigan 48108.

Melaragno, R. J. *Tutoring with students.* Englewood Cliffs, N.J.: Educational Technology Publications, 1976.

Precision Teaching

Council for Exceptional Children. *Let's try doing something else kind of thing— Behavioral principles and the exceptional child.* Reston, Va.: The Council for Exceptional Children, 1972.

Haughton, E. Great gains from small starts. *Teaching Exceptional Children,* 1971, *3*(3), 141–146.

Kunzelmann, H. P. (Ed.), Cohen, M. A., Hulten, W. J., Martin, G. L., & Mingo, A. R. *Precision teaching: An initial training sequence.* Seattle, Wash.: Special Child Publications, 1970.

Starlin, C. Peers and precision. *Teaching Exceptional Children,* 1971, *3*(3), 129–139.

Reading

Exemplary Center For Reading Instruction. Ogden City and Granite School Districts, 4905 South 4300 West, Salt Lake City, Utah 84118. Director: Dr. Ethna Reid. The Center offers inservice training in reading instruction and instructional packages which can be purchased. The topical range of these packages is broad and includes "Teaching Letter Names and Sounds;" "Teaching Creative Writing;" "Teaching Critical Comprehension." Write to the Center's Director for further information.

Social/Affective

Gordon, T. *P.E.T.: Parent effectiveness training.* New York: Peter H. Wyden, 1970.

Gordon, T., with Burch, N. *T.E.T.: Teacher effectiveness training.* New York: Peter H. Wyden, 1974.

Palomares, U., & Ball, G. *The human development program* (Magic Circle). Human Development Training Institute, 7574 University Avenue, La Mesa, Calif. 92041, *or* 200 West 79th St., Penthouse F, New York, New York 10024.

Raths, L. E., Harmin, M., & Simon, S. *Values and teaching: Working with values in the classroom.* Columbus, Ohio: Charles E. Merrill, 1966.

Simon, S. B., Howe, L. W., & Kirschenbaum, H. *Values clarification: A handbook of practical strategies for teachers and students.* New York: Hart, 1972.

Volkmor, C. B., Pasanella, A. L., & Raths, L. E. *Values in the classroom: A multi-media program.* Columbus, Ohio: Charles E. Merrill, 1977.

Vocational/Career Education

California State Department of Education (Wilson Riles). *Junior high–high school group instruction for work experience education.* Sacramento, Calif.: California State Department of Education, 1973. Could be used in a learning center or other small grouping. Offers overall goals, unit goals, and lesson objectives. Includes original resources/materials, such as crossword puzzle games, interview sheets, values appraisal sheets, and so on. Also, estimated time for lesson.

Drier, H. Jr., & Associates. *K-12 guide for integrating career development into local curriculum.* Worthington, Ohio: Charles A. Jones, 1972. An exquisite volume of resources and objectives and suggestions for integration into subject curriculum. Worth having for the resource listings alone.

General Learning Corporation—Career Programs. *Career education resource guide.* Morriston, N. J.: General Learning Corporation, 1972. Excellent activity resource book for primary, middle and secondary levels. Also contains publishers' addresses and resource people in each state. Each activity includes listings for: concepts, performance objective, materials, capsulization of lesson procedure, and general comments.

Hoyt, K. B., Pinson, N. M., Laramore, D., & Mangum, G. L. *Career education and the elementary school teacher.* Salt Lake City, Utah: Olympus, 1973. General book for beginning career education. Offers K–6 activities by: major concepts, objectives, and strategies. Offers suggestions for pre- and inservice training for teachers. Includes parent and community activities and potential resources.

Ohio State Center for Vocational and Technical Education. *Comprehensive career education model (CCEM).* Columbus, Ohio: Center for Vocational and Technical Education, Ohio State University. CCEM is a developmental approach to the integration of career education into regular curriculum. A 104-cell matrix has been developed, combining twelve social/affectives and vocations related themes across grades K–12. Behavioral objectives within each cell consider cognitive and affective and psychomotor domains.

five

Support Strategies for Children and Teachers

People, young and old alike, succeed to the same degree that: (A) They control their own destinies and (B) Share responsibility with others, including responsibility for mutual growth and support. (Beery, *The Guts to Grow*, p. 6.)

This chapter deals primarily with *change* and various strategies and techniques to consider which will help precipitate and support the changes that must take place in order for mainstreaming handicapped children to be most effective and successful. Beery (1974) says that if a school or system wants to create needed change, a "growth environment" must be provided for all people who have a part in its life—teachers, children, principals, and parents. Instead of isolating ourselves from one another with walls, special classes, schedules, authoritarian hierarchies, and so forth, we need to create a climate of support, acceptance, stimulation, exchange, exploration, and communication with all adults and children in the school.

Mainstreaming requires that counselors, psychologists, special educators, and administrators develop some new skills to add to those they already possess. These personnel must be able to combine knowledge of assessment,

212

counseling, and special teaching with the instructional skills of the classroom teacher who provides most of the direct instruction. This means a new emphasis on indirectly working with students—with and through regular teachers; in other words, we need more emphasis on consultation.

In addition to the consultation role, some other roles must be assumed by professionals within a school building. We need child advocates, change agents, instructional specialists, and trainers—all contributing an important part to the goal of providing the best possible educational experience for all children and teachers.

The Role of the Resource Teacher

Although all professionals working with children (and the children themselves) need support, those mildly handicapped children being returned to the regular class, or already in regular classes, require some special support. This specialized support is usually the responsibility of a team of people within the school (an *Assessment Team*) and, in particular, the resource teacher. The

213

resource teacher is most often a credentialed special education teacher with prior full-time teaching experience, whose major skills are in the area of educational and behavioral assessment, individualized remediation, and development of educational plans. In addition, the resource teacher must be adept at establishing rapport and stimulating cooperation among other professionals. Some responsibilities of the resource teacher include:

1. The provision of assessment and instructional planning services to handicapped children in the regular classes.
2. Conducting remedial instruction of handicapped children for regularly scheduled periods of time.
3. Providing consultative services to regular teachers and parents.
4. Participating with the school-based assessment team to coordinate services to exceptional students.

A part of the resource teacher's function consists of *direct service* to identified children via actual remedial instruction for specified time periods. Another portion of the role involves *indirect* service via teacher consultation, inservice, and coordination of educational services. It is our bias that the provision of indirect services is the more expedient and effective method of bringing about change in the quality of education for all children. The more that the resource teacher role is designed to offer *real* support to the classroom teacher, the more change is likely to occur.

Some teachers lack the necessary information and skills to enable them to cope with difficult-to-teach children. Teacher training programs often fail to provide sufficient expertise in basic assessment procedures, diagnostic/prescriptive techniques, and remedial materials and methods. Resource teachers must have expertise in these areas and help and encourage other teachers to acquire them. The end goal must be for regular teachers to take over responsibility for a great deal of the assessment and planning process for both normal and mildly handicapped children. This goal cannot be accomplished with the resource teacher spending a majority of his/her time in an isolated room working with children who have been "pulled-out" of the regular classroom, even for short periods of time. Only a teacher can make and maintain changes in the classroom; others may help but cannot do so unless the teacher himself/herself desires a change. A teacher-initiated referral is, in itself, an indication that the teacher desires help and may be open to change. Emphasis then must be placed upon establishing an open, honest communication with teachers who are ultimately responsible for implementing the individual child's program.

Regular classroom teachers must become actively involved in providing special education since educational change can take place only if teachers implement effective programs. They also must become child advocates to ensure that these programs result in expanded opportunities for children to live more meaningful and purposeful lives. (Egner and Paolucci, 1974)

Professional Skills and Characteristics

Some general competencies widely accepted as being necessary for successful performance as resource teachers include:

1. Expertise in informal assessment procedures and techniques including observation.
2. Knowledge and understanding of the dynamics of learning and remediation of specific school problems.
3. Expertise in design and implementation of instructional plans.
4. Knowledge of a wide variety of remedial and developmental instructional approaches.
5. Acquaintance with a wide variety of instructional materials.
6. Knowledge of application of behavior management techniques.

More specific skills include:

1. Writing objectives.
2. Developing criterion-referenced tests.
3. Task analysis.
4. Pinpointing target behaviors.
5. Developing behavior-change programs.
6. Selection and application of observation procedures.
7. Adaptation of instructional programs and materials.

There are some critically important personality characteristics and attitudes which enable one to function successfully in the role of a resource teacher. A resource teacher:

1. Must accept and value handicapped children as people. This is crucial in dealing with regular teachers' (and others') stereotypes and feelings and in making efforts toward achieving empathy.
2. Must possess the interpersonal skills which facilitate joint problem solving and stimulate sharing of skills and resources.
3. Must respect the confidentiality of records and use good judgment in handling information related to individual child cases.
4. Should be "hungry for change."
5. Should have a high energy level.
6. Must be able to face problems directly.

7. Must be politically sensitive; aware of formal and informal power structures.
8. Must possess a strong personal and professional commitment to the needs of children.
9. Must have a self-directed attitude, including acceptance of the necessity for record keeping and accountability requirements.
10. Must possess an understanding of some basic techniques which can be used in successful inservice training.

Communication Skills

A major part of the resource teacher's role involves consultation and communication with regular teachers and other professionals directly involved with planning and implementing programs for children. Good consulting depends on effective communication, and there are some important points to consider in order to sharpen skills in communicating with others. As a consultant, trainer, and teacher, it is important to work on increasing our ability to send clear messages that cannot be misinterpreted by the receiver, and increasing our ability to listen carefully so that further communication will occur.

Worell and Nelson (1974) suggest three steps and include some tips for increasing effective communication with children. Their points apply equally as well to adults.

1. *Establish trust*—try to convey an attitude of acceptance and respect; let others know that you will not talk about them to others or betray confidences; don't be a phony; make sure your words match your actions—don't say one thing, and do another; be real, admit your mistakes and that you don't have all the answers.
2. *Send clear messages*—be specific; make sure your non-verbal behavior matches your verbal—e.g., giving a compliment while staring out the window transmits two different messages.
3. *Listen actively*—active listening means:
   a. Giving undivided attention.
   b. Waiting until the speaker's thought is completed before you begin talking.
   c. Thinking about what the speaker's message really means (decoding).
   d. Indicating when you understand what the speaker is saying via eye contact, nods, verbal statements of agreement, and questions to clarify meaning. (p. 36)

Jung et al. (1972) outline some additional techniques and tips for facilitating interpersonal communications:

Paraphrasing is any means of showing the other person what his statement means to you and can be used to make sure you understand what another person is trying to communicate. Repeat in your own words what the speaker has said to you. Do not assume you understand what the speaker intended.

Behavior description is "reporting specific, observable actions of others without placing a value on them as right or wrong, bad or good, and without making accusations or generalizations about the other's motives, attitudes or personality traits" (Jung et al., p. 49). Not "Jim, you are rude," but "Jim, you've talked more than others on this topic."

Feelings—communicate your feelings to others accurately—that way non-verbal and verbal expressions will not be misinterpreted. We need to let others understand how we feel and try to understand other people's emotional reactions. One way to do this is to practice identifying or naming feelings. Try making statements, such as "I feel embarrassed," instead of blushing or "I feel pleased," instead of saying nothing, or "I am worried about this," instead of becoming suddenly silent.

Perception check is a check to see if you understand another's feelings accurately. It conveys that you *want* to understand what another is feeling. This involves attempting to describe another's feelings by saying, "I get the impression you are angry with me?" Always describe feelings, never express disapproval or approval, such as "Why are you so angry?"

In summary, a resource teacher must successfully combine two major sets of skills; skill in assessment and instructional planning for handicapped students and communication/consultation skills. The resource teacher needs skills to work directly with students but, at the same time, needs skill in broader indirect helping processes. A resource teacher must combine direct and indirect service skills in order to meet the needs of students and to respond to the abilities and personalities of each teacher. A resource teacher must manage a greater variety of relationships—child, teacher, and total staff.

Methods of Providing Support

Be flexible and be a problem-solver. There will never be a *single* process that solves all problems, although we are forever searching for one. Expect change and a wide variety of skills and interests and adapt! (Hammill and Bartel, 1975)

"Support" can be many things, from demonstration of a particular technique or material for an individual teacher, to providing inservice for a group of teachers. In this section we will concentrate on tips and techniques for use as a consultant in a one-to-one situation and in an inservice situation.

Some General Tips to Establish Rapport

1. Be aware of the key people in the system and look for allies or potential allies; first seek out those teachers who are most open to change and new ideas.

2. Practice "good politics"—this includes an attitude of friendliness by making eye contact. Make it a habit to look for something positive about the teacher, the room, and so on, and say so.

3. Do something early that will be perceived as helpful or useful, such as distributing a useful article, pamphlet, lesson plan, or technique.

4. Be a good listener. Demonstrate this by nodding if you understand, and asking questions if you don't.

5. Establish realistic expectations—don't set yourself up as a "miracle worker"—don't oversell yourself.

6. Don't set expectations too low. Build your own knowledge and help teachers to see and *experience* the benefits of change.

7. Do all you can to minimize the perception of threat. Build an open relationship based on two-way communication and sharing of ideas and solutions. Admit you don't know all the answers.

As a Consultant

Consulting is the procedure through which teachers, parents, principals, and other adults significant in the life of the child communicate. Consultation involves sharing information and ideas, coordinating, comparing observations, providing a sounding board, and developing tentative hypotheses for action. In contrast to the superior-inferior relationship involved in some consultation with specialists, emphasis is placed on joint planning and collaboration. The purpose is to develop tentative recommendations which fit the uniqueness of the child, the teacher, and the setting (Dinkmeyer, 1968).

Savage (1959) has identified three types of consultants:

1. *The Expert*—Directs his efforts at arriving at the right answer for a particular problem in a particular situation.

2. *The Resource*—Directs his efforts toward providing an abundance of information so that the persons can have a choice of a wide range of alternative *pragmatic* solutions to the problem.

3. *The Process Person*—Directs efforts toward developing a method of working with all persons concerned which will bring about behavioral changes and these changes will enable them to solve their own problems and become competent in handling similar problems in the future. A consultant who leans toward being "the process person" probably has a better chance of actually facilitating some lasting change.

As a resource teacher/consultant your major functions will be to help teachers to:

a. Recognize and define needs,

b. Diagnose problems and set objectives,

   c. Acquire relevant resources,

   d. Design solutions,

   e. Implement solutions,

   f. Evaluate solutions.

Most people have trouble both in asking for and in giving help. Success in this area demands special skills in communicating and building relationships. Two-way communication must occur before "helping" can be relevant. As a consultant you must actively listen to the teacher's problem and hear what has already been tried. Without open-knowledge sharing, you will never know just how much help you can be. If you appear to be evaluating or judging, you will generate defensiveness. Don't give the teacher a feeling of inadequacy.

Consultation often begins with receipt of a referral. It continues with observation of the child in the classroom after referral. It may be necessary to help the teacher articulate and pinpoint needs more clearly. Spend some time identifying strengths and areas of greatest potential change in both the child and the teacher. Be certain to involve the teacher in diagnosing her own problems and solutions—this cannot be overemphasized. The level of teacher participation in the decision making and planning is directly related to level of adoption later on!

The following hints have been suggested as being helpful to one in a consultative role:

1. Listen, hear, and understand what is being said by the regular classroom teacher.
2. Acknowledge openly the skills held by the regular classroom teacher.
3. Be cognizant of the problems faced by the regular classroom teacher.
4. Adjust and modify suggestions you may have to the atmosphere of this particular regular classroom.
5. Be honest.
6. Seek the exchange of ideas and suggestions (Region V Educational Services Center, 1975, p.9).

There are some pitfalls to avoid in consultative situations:

1. Don't over-diagnose. Select one or two things to begin changing.
2. Be objective. Do not impose your own specialty on the teacher. Be sensitive to your client's personality and teaching style. Take off your blinders and widen your perspective. There is no cure-all method or material that can be applied to all teachers and students across the board.
3. Generate several alternate solutions—and examine how practical each is, how it fits into this particular classroom and how much time is involved to implement.
4. Don't overlook reinforcement for the teacher's knowledge and efforts.

As an Inservice Trainer

In the process of affecting change in the education of handicapped children, common needs for group inservice may arise. Awareness level inservice will be needed for parents and community agencies. Teachers may need inservice in such areas as identification and assessment, observation and screening, instructional planning, classroom environment, behavior management techniques, and curriculum modification. Resource suggestions for inservice content are presented at the end of this chapter. Here, we will concentrate on the process and methods for presenting the content, including some tips on making inservice successful.

There are a variety of methods for conveying information, knowledge, and skills to others. Some of these methods include demonstrations, consultation, and workshops. It is important, as a trainer, to be aware of each and of their advantages and limitations. The following methods are adapted from Havelock, pp. 124–28.

1. *Lecture.* Overused; mainly awareness level and interest creators; a one-way medium; presentor sends message—receives no counter message.
2. *Film or Slides.* Can be "lectures on celluloid"; used for awareness, interest, and introductory purposes.
3. *Demonstrations.* Build interest, awareness, and "pretrial" evaluation.
4. *Consultation or Person to Person.* Forces teacher to think about change immediately; two-way approach; increases reality; allows expression of feelings of doubt, difficulty.
5. *Group Discussions.* Increase feeling of safety and willingness to take risks; enable feelings to be discussed; provide opportunity to move toward concensus; allow cooperative involvement.
6. *Conferences or Workshops.* Can incorporate all methods one through five above and, in addition, can include use of tasks to allow participants to practice new skills; can include commitment to implement new skills in classrooms with resource teacher support.

Types of Training Experiences

The first type of training is informational in nature, where the objective is for the trainee to gain a greater *awareness* of a product, an idea, or a new approach. An example of this would be an "Introduction to Mainstreaming" meeting for parents. The second type of training has as its objective greater *skill* or *knowledge* on the part of the trainee. Most workshops are of this second type. Participants leave knowing more than when they came, but often lack a systematic approach or plan to enable them to actually implement the newly acquired ideas or skills back in their classrooms. The third type of training has as its objective, *visible, observable change* in the classroom of the trainee. The major thrust of this training is implementation by trainees in classrooms with children. In the following sections of this chapter, we are primarily addressing ourselves to the second and third types of training.

Designing Training Experiences

Content Preparation

The boundaries of any concept or content are broad. If you are after awareness-type training, provide a survey and be inclusive, if that is your objective. If your objective is implementation, you must be willing to simmer a large body of information down into several major actions which the participants can actually perform. This increases the chances that participants will experience initial success and increases the probability that participants will expand their knowledge later.

To develop content with *implementation* as the objective, first attempt a small sequence of concepts or substeps. Then take it, debug it, and polish it. Elicit responses and criticism from experienced experts—include those who may already be implementing the ideas. Once you have a draft of the content sequence, substeps, and skills to be learned, try dividing content up into *presentation* chunks and *task* chunks. Keep in mind that the sequence must be carefully paced, provide appropriate amounts of practice for learners, and work in ways of providing immediate feedback and knowledge of results. Delete anything that is irrelevant or extraneous, or anything that would be nice to teach but is not critical at this stage of training.

Task Design

The next step is to develop tasks for participants so they can practice what they learn. Tasks should be fairly short and focus on one, maybe two, small pieces of the total content. The most effective tasks actively involve the participants in responses and provide feedback on adequate performance. Tasks can be written and involve recall or application of information, or they can be directed toward implementation (actual live practice of skills learned). Tasks A through F which follow are samples taken from a variety of workshops.

Task A

Note: This task is an example which calls for simple recall of information
presented during a large group presentation.

List at least five steps, which you feel are important, from the initial referral of
a child to placement of that child in a Resource Program.

Task B

Note: Another example of a task which involves simple recall of information.

A. In the spaces below, list the four basic steps involved in Precision
Teaching:
1. _____
2. _____
3. _____
4. _____

B. Now list the three criteria for pinpointing a behavior. A pinpointed
behavior must be:
1. _____
2. _____
3. _____

Task C: Part 1

Note: This example illustrates a method for involving participants in *applying*
information received to themselves and their situations. This task was
used at a principal's workshop.

Problem: You are back in your own school situation. Your Appraisal Team is
operational. You have a Resource Teacher and an aide.
1. Fifteen students from five classrooms have been placed by the
Appraisal Team in the Resource Program.

2. Four of the above 15 students are also assigned for auxiliary services.
3. Six other students have been referred and are waiting to be processed.
4. Two Appraisal Team meetings have been scheduled for one week.

Based on the above information and the list of required Resource Teacher job activities (part 3), design a hypothetical schedule for a week of Resource Teacher time in your school.

Note: If you are in a rural school, assume that your Resource Teacher is assigned to three schools.

Task C: Part 2

RESOURCE TEACHER
HYPOTHETICAL WEEKLY SCHEDULE

	MON.	TUE.	WED.	THUR.	FRI.
A.M.					
P.M.					

Check the list in part 3 to be sure you have included all job activities.

Task C: Part 3

RESOURCE TEACHER JOB ACTIVITIES

- ☐ Attendance at Appraisal Team Meetings
- ☐ Consultation with Parents
- ☐ Consultation with Regular Teachers
- ☐ Observing in Regular Classrooms
- ☐ Conducting Assessments
- ☐ Coordination of Auxiliary Services for Referred Children

☐ Coordination of Referral and Assessment Information and Findings
☐ Professional Growth (Including Visits to IMC, Reading Literature)
☐ Remediation (Direct Service)
☐ Demonstrations
☐ Supervision of Resource Teacher Aide
☐ Assist in Writing Individual Instructional Plans

Task D

Note: This activity illustrates the use of hypothetical situations. The task was used in a workshop for parents on Parent Rights and Responsibilities.

Directions

Read the three "situations" below and respond to the questions. Work *independently* or in pairs. Refer to your handouts. Add to your responses following the group discussion.

Situation A

Mrs. Burns, the principal of the elementary school where Michael, a handicapped 10-year-old, is in a special class, says to Michael's mother, "Mrs. Green, we've tried everything and your son does not progress. We feel that you should place him in a private institution for the physically handicapped. Really, it would be the best for you *and* Michael. Public school is just not the place for a child like Michael."

1. Are Michael's rights being violated? __ Yes   __ No
2. What are Michael's (and his parents') rights in this situation?

3. What court cases(s) and/or legislation supports your response to question 2 above?

Situation B

A school superintendent says to Mr. Palmer, the father of a school-aged retarded daughter, "I understand your point. You want us to serve all handicapped children. I too think this is a fine goal, but we simply can't afford to open another special class. We don't have the money. Why, the last time we added a class for 'trainable' kids over there in Orchard District, we had to let an art teacher and a P.E. teacher go. I'm truly sorry, Mr. Palmer, but that's just the way it is right now.''

1. On what legal grounds might Mr. Palmer challenge the statement of the superintendent?_____

_____

2. What court decisions support your responses to the above question?

_____

_____

Situation C

Mr. and Mrs. Avila, following a conference with the school principal and psychologist, reluctantly agree to the placement of their son, Jose, in an EMR class. They are puzzled by what the school officials have told them about their son's performance on certain tests of mental ability, but conclude that the school knows best. In the Chicano community where they live, Jose has always appeared normal and well adjusted.

1. On what basis does it appear that the EMR placement decision has been made?

_____

_____

2. What court decisions have been handed down in California which address the problem faced by the Avilas? _____

_____

_____

_____

3. How do the provisions of P.L. 94–142 relate to this problem?

_____

_____

_____

Task E

Note: This task focuses on actual implementation with students. The work-shop content here was Precision Teaching.

Implementation

By now you will have gathered sufficient *baseline data* for your first project. The next step is to discuss the project with the student. Complete and check off the following steps with the behaver.

☐ 1. Discuss the project with the student. Show him the baseline data and together decide whether the pinpointed behavior should be *accelerated* or *decelerated*.

☐ 2. With the student, decide on a realistic aim and a target date for reaching that aim. Mark the *aim* on the chart.

☐ 3. Draw a *Phase Change Line* to indicate the end of the *before* Phase on the chart.

☐ 4. Discuss possibilities for the first *Intervention* with the child.

☐ 5. Begin the first *Intervention Phase* of the project as soon as possible and continue it for at least one week. Chart the data.

Remember . . .

. . . that behavior changes slowly; small steps are more easily and comfortably accomplished by the learner than are giant leaps. Sometimes it is necessary to establish subgoals or aims so that the final target will not seem impossible to the child.

. . . to try the Intervention for at least a week. If the Intervention does not bring about a change in the first day or two, don't give up!

Developing a Schedule

A carefully designed and well-thought-out schedule is a necessity for a smooth running workshop. Particularly in that part of the workshop or conference where the content or idea is being presented, we like to use a large group/ small group cycling process that goes something like this:

1. The presenter (ideally someone who is presently using the ideas or skill being presented) presents one major point to the total group being trained. This presentation is limited to 15 minutes.

2. The group goes immediately to pre-announced small groups where they are given a brief written task to do which relates directly to the presentation they have just heard in the large group.

3. After most of the people in the small group have completed this task, their responses are discussed. Since the written task is intended to be a learning device, as contrasted to a test, participants are encouraged to make any changes or additions to their task sheets that they wish.

4. At the completion of this discussion, at the time indicated on their schedule, the participants return to the large group setting for another chunk of input. The large/small group cycles take about one hour to complete 15 minutes for presentation, 35 minutes for task and discussion, and 10 minutes to move from large to small group and back.

This large group/small group format and the time segments alloted to each accomplishes several things.

First, it forces the presenter to plan his presentations carefully and get to the point almost immediately. Second, it provides for physical movement on the part of the participants. It requires the participants to become actively involved (through the task sheets) rather than just passively involved (listening). It provides a setting (the small groups) which is more conducive to risk taking, i.e., admitting the need for further information or clarification; and, it provides instant feedback to the presenter(s), in the form of the completed task sheets—as to where he is "hitting the mark" and where he is missing it. Thus, the presenter can correct his course and give feedback to the participants.

Schedules A–G illustrate the combination and alternation of large group presentations with small group activities and tasks. The array of schedules includes examples for half-day, one-day, and two-day workshops.

Schedule A

PARENT WORKSHOP

Parent Rights and Responsibilities in
the Education of Exceptional Children
WORKSHOP SCHEDULE

LG = large group
SG = small group

(LG)	9:00— 9:15	Coffee; Name Tags
(LG)	9:15— 9:30	Introductions; Workshop Schedule and Objectives
(LG)	9:30— 9:50	*Presentation:* "Legal Rights of the Handicapped: Educational Change Via Litigation and Legislation."
(SG)	9:50—10:15	*Activity I:* Discussion
	10:15—10:20	Break
(LG)	10:20—10:40	*Presentation:* "Due Process"
(SG)	10:40—11:05	*Activity II:* Discussion
	11:05—11:10	Break
(LG)	11:10—11:20	*Presentation:* "Action Strategies for Parents"
(SG)	11:20—12:00	*Activity III* (Personal Commitment: Group Strategies)
(LG)	12:00—12:30	Group Sharing; Evaluation; Wrap-up.

Schedule B

ACTIVITY/LEARNING CENTERS

(Science, Library, Activity Games, Arts and Crafts, Audio-Visual)

Objective: Participants will plan the layout, contents and at least three specific learning activities for a minimum of two activity centers.

Schedule:

1. *Educational Alternatives:* A group role playing exercise designed to stimulate participants to examine their own educational philosophy (concepts of open education; student directed learning, and so on).

2. Presentation	Room Environment Discussion
3. Small Group Activity	Task and Discussion on Designing and Planning an Open Learning Environment
4. Large Group	Feedback/Sharing
5. Presentation	Creating Activity Centers Discussion
6. Small Group Activity	Planning Content and Activities for Two Specific Learning Centers
7. Presentation	Story Starters, Activity Cards, and Learning Games (student-directed materials for Activity Centers)
8. Small Group Activity	Developing at least One Self-Instructional Product for Student Use in An Activity Center
9. Wrap-Up	Additional Ideas and Specific Suggestions for Student Self-Management in an Open Learning Environment

Time: ½ day or 1 day.

Schedule C

LEARNING ACTIVITY PACKAGES (LAPs)

Objective: Participants will develop a Learning Activity Package (LAP) to be used by a student independently. The LAP must include all of the following components:

1. Rationale
2. Objectives
3. Pretest
4. Learning Alternatives (at least 3)
5. Resources
6. References

Schedule:

1. Presentation	What is an LAP? Rationale, Scope, and Sequence; Examples and more Examples
2. Small Group Activity	Selecting a Topic and Developing a Rationale
3. Presentation	Review of how to write instructional objectives; Discussion
4. Small Group Activity	Specifying student objectives and developing a pretest.
5. Presentation	Instructional Alternatives (Learning Activities) Discussion and Examples

6. Small Group Activity   List Instructional Alternatives; Restructure Content into Student Format
7. Small Group Activity   Critique of LAP by Peers and Revision
8. Conclusion   Application of LAPs in the Classroom

Time: ½ day or 1 day.

Schedule D

PRECISION TEACHING

Schedule:

1. Presentation   Introduction;
Making Education Count
Discussion of Four Basic Steps
2. Small Group Activity   Task Activity on Basic Steps, Identifying Movement Cycles, and Pinpointing Behaviors
3. Presentation   It's All A Plot—Part A;
Introduction to the Behavior Chart;
Discussion
4. Small Group Activity   Practice Charting and Rate Calculation
5. Presentation   It's All A Plot—Part B
6. Small Group Activity   Comparison of Performance Rates and Case Study Examples
7. Presentation   It's All A Plot—Part C;
Discussion on Record Floor and Charting Conventions
8. Small Group Activity   Using Record Floor and Charting Conventions
9. Presentation   Short Cuts and Modifications;
The Ups and Downs of Charting;
Discussion of Phases, Aims, and Interventions.
10. Small Group Activity   Planning Interventions, Curriculum Materials, and Arranged Events
11. Presentation   Getting It Started in Your Classroom; Teaching Kids to Chart; Intervention and Case Study Examples.

Time: 1 or 2 days.

Schedule E

STRUCTURING THE CLASSROOM FOR SUCCESS
A WORKSHOP ON OPEN EDUCATION
(Time: 1 day)

Objective: Participants will develop some specific plans and ideas for initiating and implementing changes in their classrooms and with their students in one or more of the following areas:

1. Physical Room Environment
2. Activity/Learning Centers
3. Behavior Management Techniques
4. Individualizing Instruction

Schedule:

1. Presentation	Introduction
2. Activity	Educational Alternatives: A group role playing exercise designed to stimulate participants to examine their own educational philosophy (concepts of open education, student directed learning, and so on).
3. Presentation	Room Arrangement and Environment
4. Small Group Activity	Planning the Classroom Environment
5. Presentation	Creating Activity Centers
6. Small Group Activity	Planning the Contents and Layout of Activity Centers
7. Presentation	Behavior Management Techniques in the Open Classroom
8. Small Group Activity	Creating a Menu and Devising Ways of Scheduling
9. Presentation	Individualizing Instruction
10. Small Group Activity	Development of Activity Cards and/or Learning Games, tasks, and folders.
11. Presentation	Evaluating Learning Outcomes. How to Get It Started Tomorrow.
12. Small Group Activity	Contracting to Initiate at least one change in the classroom.

Schedule F*

BEHAVIOR MANAGEMENT

Workshop Objectives:

1. At the conclusion of the workshop, participants will be able to identify the major concepts of, and rules for, a Contingency Management System.
2. By the end of the workshop, participants will be able to plan each step necessary in setting up a Contingency Management System in the classroom.
3. Three weeks after the workshop, participants will have implemented a Contingency Management System. To be considered successful, the system designed by the teacher will include *all* of the following observable characteristics:
   3.1 Classroom divided into task area (where students work on academic tasks and assignments) and an *RE area* (where children go after task completion to engage in self-chosen reward activities).

*This schedule (and Schedule G following) is based on A. Langstaff and C. Volkmor, *Contingency Management* (Columbus, Ohio: Charles E. Merrill, 1975). A sound filmstrip package and book.

3.2 A posted *RE menu* or list of activities from which students can choose for their free time (RE time).

3.3 Nonverbal signal(s) which: (a) individual students can use to indicate need for teacher attention, (b) the teacher uses to signify the time for students to return to task area.

Sample Program:

1. Presentation	Pretest Introduction to Contingency Management Filmstrip 1 Contingency Management: Basic Principles.
2. Small Group Activity	HPB's: Pinpoint "natural reinforcers." Task I.
3. Presentation	How Contingency Management works in the Classroom Filmstrips 2 and 3 Discussion on Planning a Contingency Management Program, Menu, and Room Arrangement.
4. Small Group Activity	LPBs and HPBs. Creating a Menu and Room Arrangement. Tasks IV, V, VI, VII, Activity I.
5. Presentation	Planning schedule and developing tasks for a Contingency Management Program. Filmstrip 4 and discussion.
6. Small Group Activity	Developing a schedule and listing tasks. Activities II, III, IV.
7. Presentation	Getting the Program started: Signals, explaining program to students, helpful hints.
8. Small Group Activity	Task X on heading off problems.
9. Presentation	On to implementation! Adaptations, refinements.
10. Small Group Activity	List steps for first day implementation.
11. Small Group Activity	Posttest.
12. Presentation	Questions and answers.

Schedule G*

SAMPLE WORKSHOP SCHEDULE
TWO DAY WORKSHOP

(L) = Large Group   (S) = Small Group

Day 1

8:30—9:00 (L)   Pretest
Overview of Workshop

---

*This schedule is adapted from one originally designed and used by Bruce Weston, Director, California Regional Resource Center.

9:00—9:30 (S)	Communication Game
9:30—9:50 (L)	Filmstrip 1
	"Basics of Contingency Management"
	HPB/LPB
	Reinforcers (RE)
	Menu
	(Short presentation taken from Chapter 1)
9:50—10:10 (S)	Task I HPB/LPB
	Compare answers in group
10:10—10:20	RE
10:20—10:30 (L)	Filmstrip 2
10:30—11:00 (S)	Read Chapter 2 and discuss issues
11:00—11:20 (L)	Filmstrip 3
	Chapter 3—short presentation by teacher-presenter
	student LPBs + HPBs
	Examples of menus
11:20—11:40 (S)	Task IV and V
	Compare answers in group
11:40—12:00 (L)	Room Arrangement (Chapter 3)
	Examples: Teacher-presenter
12:00	Lunch
1:00—1:20 (S)	Task VI Diagram Classroom
	Compare answers in group
1:20—1:40 (L)	Filmstrip 4
	Chapter 4—Signals
	Schedules: Teacher-Presenter
	Examples
1:40—2:00 (S)	Activity II—Compare answers in group
2:00—2:15 (L)	Chapter 4
	Explaining the System: Teacher-Presenter
	Student Tasks—Examples
2:15—2:35 (S)	Activity III
	Compare answers in group
2:35—2:45	RE
2:45—3:00 (L)	Routines:
	Cleanup, Approximations, etc.
3:00—3:40 (L)	Questions and Answers

Day 2

8:30—8:50 (L)	Chapter 5—short presentation
	1st day preparation
	Teaching the System to students
8:50—9:10 (S)	List steps for 1st day implementation

9:10—9:50 (L)	Variations (taken from Chapter 6 in text):
	individualization
	saving up time
	checkmarks
	second week
9:50—10:00	RE
10:00—10:30 (L)	"Dealing with Undesired Behaviors"
	(taken from Chapter 5 in text)
10:30—10:50 (S)	Task X
	Compare and discuss answers in group
10:50—11:10 (L)	Contracting for Implementation
	Follow-Up Plans
	Back-Home Support
11:10—11:30 (S)	Posttest
	Teacher Contracts
11:30—12:00 (L)	Questions and answers

Small Groups

We have some very strong feelings about the use of small groups at conferences or workshops. Careful attention to the dynamics of the small-group process can "carry" a conference even when some of the other elements are less than perfect, such as the large group presentations, the setting, and so forth. Here are some basic principles, developed by Bruce Weston, director of the California Regional Resource Center, which seem to hold for us:

1. Choose your group leaders carefully. Their skill at facilitating someone else's learning is more important than their expertise in the skill or idea being taught.
2. The ideal size for a small group seems to be between five and ten. Less than five seems to make the participants feel uncomfortable. More than ten become cumbersome and slows the process.
3. Except at times when the conference process calls for a team interaction, assign people to small groups with people other than those from their own district or school if possible. This seems to forestall the natural tendency of persons of lesser status to defer to people of higher status in their district.
4. When appropriate to the content being presented, ask all of the non-teacher members of the group to assume the role of the teacher of a hypothetical class (if this is the focus of the content being presented).
5. Don't switch people from one group to another once the groups have begun. It is important that each group assume responsibility for its own

success as a group. If you step in and remove or add people to a group that has already begun to operate, you threaten this process.

6. After you have made it clear that you and the presenter(s) are available at any time for further information or clarification, stay out of the small groups unless specifically invited to come in. Group process seems to stop when an "outsider" comes in, even if the outsider's presence is well intended.

7. Keep others from entering the small groups. This can be particularly hard on "visiting firemen" who simply want to get an idea of how things are going.

Time Commitment

If you have looked at the schedules on the previous pages, you have probably noticed how carefully they are timed. We have been repeatedly reinforced for holding to such a schedule. Though it may look compulsive at first glance, our commitment is not to the clock, which is only a mechanical device, but to people. When we hold to the schedule (as long as it is reasonable) we are saying by our behavior that we are willing to be predictable.

Some Tips for Planning and Carrying Out Inservice

1. Remember, there are different levels of inservice—those aimed at awareness or information imparting, and those aimed at teaching a concept to be implemented in classrooms.
2. Plan carefully down to the last detail: equipment, location, content presentations, tasks, and handouts.
3. Communicate your inservice objectives to participants ahead of time.
4. If you are aiming toward adoption and implementation of a technique, arrange for participants to be actively involved in small group tasks requiring development and planning of how they will implement it.
5. Plan "helps" for participants after they leave the training session. This can be in the form of printed presentation summaries, handouts, bibliographies of selected readings, lists of sources for needed materials, and referrals to teachers and/or schools where the participants can see the idea or technique in action.
6. Prepare handouts—give participants something to take with them.
7. If there is prerequisite material, distribute it ahead of time so participants come prepared.
8. Tasks should be fairly short and focus on one, maybe two, small pieces of the content. Allow practice of skills learned.
9. Allow discussion time.

10. Keep to your time commitment.
11. Design opportunities for participants to apply new information and skills. (See examples of implementation tasks.) We have often brought a group of students to the workshop setting (or arranged for participants to go into a classroom) in order to try a new skill.
12. Provide immediate feedback to participants regarding their success.
13. Arrange for individual consultation and assistance until participants reach criterion on tasks.
14. Remember, teachers teach like they were taught. If we want teachers to change the way they teach children, we must change the way we teach teachers. This means *modeling* techniques and changing from the traditional presenter-dominated group lecture to a participant-centered mastery learning program.
15. Don't forget the importance of reinforcing teachers. Consider and try to arrange for such "rewards" as release time, inservice points, college credit, resouce books, instructional materials, added support by resource teacher, and praise and compliments for a job well done!
16. Try to involve principals in your training efforts. They can be a *major* reinforcer to keep things going back home.
17. Attend to the location or setting for your workshop. Try to arrange for a comfortable, quiet site away from phones and other interruptions.

Training Content for Regular Teachers and Resource Teachers

Every classroom teacher is a change agent. . . . As a classroom teacher, you hope that the final product of your efforts will be an individual who has achieved competence, self-esteem, and self-actualizing capabilities. To the extent that you succeed in approaching these goals, you are an agent of change. (Worell and Nelson, 1975, p. 3.)

Techniques for Regular Teachers

Hammill and Bartel (1975) suggest some things regular teachers can do to make mainstreaming easier and beneficial to all children—both normal and handicapped.

Regular teachers can:

1. Utilize individualized instruction, activity centers, and open educaton techniques which allow children to work at their own pace on various levels. (See resources at the end of this chapter.)
2. Design group activities in which all children can participate.

3. Provide human resources to allow for more individual attention—solicit parent volunteers, high school students, and peer and cross-age tutors.
4. Teach values as a regular part of the curriculum. Help children care about each other and learn to respond to others in need. (See resources at the end of this chapter.)

In an extensive review of the literature of current programs in mainstreaming across the nation, the following techniques rise to the surface as being critical skills for *all* teachers:

1. Behavior management techniques, including Precision Teaching (charting student progress) and self-management.
2. Instructional materials—selection and adaptation.
3. Peer and cross-age tutoring.
4. Room environment—activity centers directed toward individualized instruction.

Available data seem to indicate that teachers who refuse to accept responsibility for ''exceptional'' children also tend to avoid the responsibility inherent in the very concept of personalized instruction (Farrald, p. 112 in Kreinberg and Chow, eds., 1974).

Individualizing instruction is the *key* component in an overall educational program that meets the needs of all children. In summary, the major need areas for teacher inservice seem to center around the following:

1. *Assessment:* selecting an appropriate informal testing technique, application or testing, and analysis—including construction and use of criterion-referenced tests.
2. *Planning:* setting objectives, scheduling, selection of materals, and evaluation.
3. *Instruction:* small, large group presentations; continuous assessment; individual interactions; room environment and activity centers.
4. *Behavior Management Techniques.*
5. *Use of Aides:* for monitoring student completion of assignments or contract; administering diagnostic evaluations; monitoring continuous assessment procedures.
6. *Use of Volunteers or Parents:* for such activities as listening to reading; correcting papers with students for immediate feedback; dictating spelling; and charting student progress.

In addition, awareness level inservice needs to be conducted on such topics as ''Introduction to Mainstreaming Concepts,'' ''Identification and Screening of Handicapped and Potential Handicapped," "Attitudes Toward the Handicapped," and "Parent Involvement: Rights, Due Process, and Responsibilities."

Techniques for Resource Teachers

Some of the inservice training needs of Resource Teachers that have been raised include:

1. Additional skill in the development of individualized educational plans.
2. Information on the social/emotional or affective aspects of mainstreamed education.
3. More information on the school and community resources providing specialized help.
4. Vocational assessment and career education.
5. Consultation skills.

Following is an inservice training checklist designed to assess training needs among resource teachers. It was developed and used by the Humboldt-Del Norte Master Plan Office in Eureka, California. A similar checklist could be developed to assess the needs of regular class teachers.

In-Service Training Checklist

RESOURCE TEACHER

The following list includes most of the skills needed to be a Resource Teacher. Please review each skill and decide if (1) you need more training in this skill, or (2) you have sufficient training in this skill to serve as a consultant to train others. A program specialist will be available to review your needs with you.

Current Level of Knowledge	Need More Training		Can Train Others
Low 1 2 3 4 5 Hi			

PROCESS

_____	_____	Know which District staff member to contact to get support services.	_____
_____	_____	Know how to fulfill due process procedures (i.e., send out notices, obtain signatures, timelines, etc.)	_____
_____	_____	Understand purpose of Management Information System (computer forms) and can fill out forms correctly.	_____

Current Level of Knowledge	Need More Training		Can Train Others
Low 1 2 3 4 5 Hi			

Current Level of Knowledge	Need More Training		Can Train Others
_____	_____	Know how to use referral form and referral log.	_____
_____	_____	Ability to use Assessment Team process.	_____
_____	_____	Know how to work with community agencies.	_____

IDENTIFICATION

_____	_____	Implement a screening and/or referral system to identify learning handicapped children.	_____

ASSESSMENT

_____	_____	Know how to select, administer, and interpret formal tests such as: Keymath, Spache, PIAT, PPVT, MVPT, other (Please list) _____	_____
_____	_____	Know how to construct informal assessment procedures.	_____
_____	_____	Can administer informal inventories of academic skills.	_____
_____	_____	Can assess readiness skills.	_____
_____	_____	Can determine reading levels.	_____
_____	_____	Can specify areas of reading difficulty (decoding, oral reading fluency, phonics, etc.).	_____
_____	_____	Can determine level of academic performance.	_____
_____	_____	Can interview appropriate staff and parents.	_____
_____	_____	Can assess social/emotional problems in learning.	_____
_____	_____	Can do career aptitude and attitude evaluation.	_____
_____	_____	Can assess cultural factors influencing students' learning problems.	_____
_____	_____	Can perceive and record behavioral patterns in classroom observation.	_____
_____	_____	Can identify and record significant educational and affective behaviors in classroom observation.	_____

Current Level of Knowledge	Need More Training		Can Train Others
Low 1 2 3 4 5 Hi			

_____	_____	Can develop a readily understood behavioral information summary.	_____
_____	_____	Can plan and sequence assessment activities necessary for a particular child.	_____
_____	_____	Can identify needed resources (time, space, materials).	_____
_____	_____	Can develop learning styles profile of student.	_____
_____	_____	Can select appropriate instructional strategies.	_____

INSTRUCTIONAL PLANNING

_____	_____	Can organize assessment data for study of child's problem(s) into recommendations for an educational program.	_____
_____	_____	Can understand and use pertinent psychological test data for educational planning.	_____
_____	_____	Can break down an instructional task into simple, sequential learning steps and match task to child.	_____
_____	_____	Can write behavioral objectives.	_____
_____	_____	Can set up and document behavior modification program.	_____
_____	_____	Can discuss alternative remediation strategies with Assessment Team.	_____
_____	_____	Can select, locate, or construct materials for remediation strategies.	_____
_____	_____	Know how to set criteria for plan modification and exit.	_____

IMPLEMENTATION

_____	_____	Can implement an individualized program for each student based on written plan.	_____

EVALUATION AND REASSESSMENT

_____	_____	Know how to determine progress and success of student's educational program.	_____

Current Level of Knowledge	Need More Training		Can Train Others
Low 1 2 3 4 5 Hi			
_____	_____	Know how to modify instructional plan and program if necessary.	_____
		CONSULTATION	
_____	_____	Can demonstrate techniques to regular classroom teachers.	_____
_____	_____	Can demonstrate appropriate listening skills.	_____
_____	_____	Use of clarifying and information-gathering questions;	_____
_____	_____	Use of non-judgmental, non-punitive responses.	_____
_____	_____	Can use problem-solving/conflict-resolution skills.	_____
_____	_____	Ability to conduct parent conferences and counseling sessions for students.	_____
		COORDINATION	
_____	_____	Can establish communication and coordination with support personnel, agencies, parents, etc., and keep appropriate records of key persons and contacts made.	_____
		ADMINISTRATION AND MANAGEMENT	
_____	_____	Can establish necessary record-keeping systems to include: Calendar of RST activities Minutes of Assessment Team meetings Records of available resources and materials in district Pupil files with necessary forms.	_____
_____	_____	Can schedule time schedule to accommodate students and support services.	_____
_____	_____	Can conduct needs assessment.	_____
_____	_____	Can design and provide inservice based on the results of needs assessment.	_____
_____	_____	Can budget and record expenditures of management and support monies and RST funds.	_____

There are several packaged training materials already available on many of the content areas mentioned in this chapter. General programs designed to inform principals, administrators, and parents about mainstreaming models and processes, and more specific programs for training resource teachers and regular teachers in a variety of skills and techniques are listed in the resource section at the end of this chapter.

On the next few pages you will find a topical outline for a series of workshop sessions covering many aspects of a comprehensive service plan for handicapped children. Each segment could be presented as an overview in a half-day session or expanded to involve a week or more of in-depth inservice. This outline is based on a plan for inservice training which was conducted over a two-week period by the Master Plan Humboldt State University Inservice Consortium, Eureka, California. Session content is aimed at various personnel: administrators, program specialists, resource teachers, regular teachers, and parents.

Topical Outline of a Comprehensive Inservice on Instructional Programming

I. Identification and Referral

    a. Current issues in placement of students in special education
    b. Formal and informal screening systems
    c. Referral procedures
    d. Analyzing the referral information
    e. Due process/parent involvement

II. Support Services and Community Resources

    1. Identifying services and resources within the community
    2. Establishing and maintaining contact, communication, and cooperation

III. Assessment—Formal and Informal

    a. Identifying tools/instruments to assess and evaluate student strengths and weaknesses
    b. Selecting appropriate testing strategies
    c. Reliability, validity, item analysis
    d. Analysis, developing, and using criterion-referenced tests
    e. Using evaluation data to make educational hypotheses

IV. Assessment—Learning Style/Teaching Style/Environmental Considerations

    a. Defining learning styles and teaching styles and matching the two

    b. Identifying assessment techniques for determining learning and teaching styles

    c. Selecting instructional strategies to suit the learning styles of case students

V. Informal Assessment and Observation

    a. Techniques to sequence and document informal assessment

    b. Different types of observation as assessment

    c. Techniques to chart progress

    d. Using this data to plan effectively

    e. Interviewing

VI. Assessing Career Attitudes and Developing Career Education Experiences

    a. Using interviewing and career interest inventories to assess career attitudes

    b. Instructional strategies for career education

    c. Coordinating with other agencies

VII. Teaching Methods and Techniques—Reading

VIII. Evaluating Commercial and Teacher-Made Materials—Reading

IX. Teaching Methods and Techniques—Math

X. Evaluating Commercial and Teacher-Made Materials—Math

XI. Classroom Management

    a. Organizing materials

    b. Charting progress

    c. Reward systems

    d. Tutoring programs

XII. Individualizing Instruction

    a. Key features of individualized instructional programs

    b. Management strategies used in individualized programs

    c. Comparing instructional formats used in managing individualized instruction:

        Job sheets

        Learning stations

        Programmed instruction

        Contracts

XIII. Behavior Management

1. Pinpointing student behaviors in specific terms
2. Applying contingency management principles
3. Identifying "problem" behaviors and determining appropriate response

XIV. Instructional Plans

1. How to write
2. Specifying objectives and success criteria
3. Selecting methods/techniques
4. Specifying materials

XV. Implementation and Evaluation

1. Task analysis
2. Curriculum relevance
3. Supporting the classroom teacher
4. Evaluating student outcomes
5. Revising/updating the plan
6. Due process/parent involvement

XVI. Parent Involvement

a. Methods of encouraging parents to share feelings, problems, and concerns
b. Communication techniques
c. Activities for use at home

XVI. Due Process Rights and Responsibilities

a. School
b. Parents

XVII. Consultation Skills: Communication and Team Planning for Parents and Teachers

1. Active listening
2. Problem solving/conflict resolution

An in-depth description of some training sessions related to each of the five chapters in this book (*Introduction to Mainstreaming, Identification and Referral, Assessment, Instructional Planning,* and *Support Strategies*) is documented in a trainer's manual which accompanies this text. We have included presentation outlines, sample tasks and activities, sequenced schedules, and related references and resources to assist you in planning inservice experiences in your school district, county, or college classroom.

Study Questions and Activities

1. Select two groups, of three each, from the class to debate the pros and cons of: "Resolved—the mildly handicapped can be served more effectively by *indirect* as opposed to *direct* services from special education resource teachers." (See Chapter Five, Introduction.)

2. Have one class member assume the role of Ms. Vera Destraught, a first-year teacher with an overabundance of learning and behavior problems, and another class member assume the role as a resource specialist responding to Vera's request for help. Role play one or more of a series of conferences: (1) The first conference to define the problem(s); (2) The second conference to report the results of classroom observations and other informal assessments; (3) The third conference to plan joint responsibilities for instruction; and (4) The fourth conference to evaluate pupil progress. To lend variety, have class members take turns role playing different "teachers" (e.g., Mr. Manley Makismo, who hates to admit to his many problem pupils, or Mrs. Ima Intellect, who already has the "answers" to her pupils' many problems). Good luck!

3. Form discussion groups and share experiences with inservice workshops in which you have participated. Describe the workshops you have found the most beneficial and/or enjoyable. To what extent were the recommendations for effective inservice workshops presented in the text on design of tasks, schedules, and small group involvement validated by the group's experiences.

4. Recall the distinction between three types of inservice training experiences (increase awareness, improve skills, make classroom changes) listed in Chapter Five. Classify each of the "Content Strategies for the Regular Teacher" described into one of these three categories. Discuss the differing goals, emphases, and formats for each type and briefly outline the content of one specific workshop for each.

5. As a class project, class members should form work groups to develop inservice training workshops for regular class teachers. Each group should propose: (a) A topic for an inservice workshop; (b) The workshop objectives; (c) The schedule to be followed; (d) The media and materials for presentations; (e) The tasks for group involvement; and, (f) A rating sheet for evaluation of the workshop relative to stated objectives. The workshop should be evaluated by either presenting to a group of cooperating regular teachers and obtaining their feedback, or presentation of the developed

materials (objectives, media, tasks, rating sheet, etc.) to a panel of experts (e.g., regular teacher, principal, and resource specialist) for feedback. Develop a revised workshop design on the basis of the feedback obtained. Revised workshop materals may be reproduced and combined into a booklet which may be distributed to class members for future reference.

References

Bauer, H. The resource teacher—A teacher consultant. *Academic Therapy,* 1975, *10*(3), 229–304.

Beery, K., Brokes, A. L., Howlett, H., Jiguor, J. W., Lobree, V. A., Marshall, D. A., McCurdy, R. E., Racicot, R. H., Rolle, R. E. W., Stuck, R. L., Wardlaw, J. H., & Wiley, E. M. *The guts to grow.* Sioux Falls, S.D.: Dimensions (Adapt Press), 1974.

Berlin, I. N. Preventive aspects of mental health consultation to schools. *Mental Hygiene,* 1967, *51*(1), 34–40.

Dinkmeyer, D., & Carlson, J. *Consultation: A book of readings.* New York: John Wiley, 1975.

Dinkmeyer, D. The counselor as consultant: Rationale and procedures. *Elementary School Guidance and Counseling,* 1968: *2,* 187.

Dollar, B., & Klinger R. A systems approach to improving teacher effectiveness: A triadic model of consultation and change (Mimeo). Houston, Tex.: Houston Independent School District, n.d.

Egner A., & Paolucci, P. For the sake of children: Some thoughts on the rights of teachers who provide special education within regular classrooms. In Johnson, R., Weatherman, R., & Rehmann, A. M. (Eds), *Handicapped youth and the mainstream education.* Minneapolis: Audio Visual Library Service, University of Minnesota, 1975, 29–47.

Hammill, D. D., & Bartel, N. R. *Teaching children with learning and behavior problems.* Boston: Allyn and Bacon, 1975.

Haughton, D., & Enos, D. *Project and pert design for PREM* (Mimeo). Austin, Tex.: University of Texas, School of Education, Preparing Regular Educators for Mainstreaming Project, 1975.

Havelock, R. G. *The change agent's guide to innovation in education.* Englewood Cliffs, N.J.: Educational Technology Publications, 1973.

Jung, C., Howard, R., Emory, R., & Pino, R. *Interpersonal communications: Leader's manual* Portland, Ore.: Northwest Regional Educational Laboratory, Tuxedo, N.Y.: Xicom, 1972.

Klinger, R. *The KPLC as a model for individualized instructional support* (Mimeo). Houston, Tex.: Houston Independent School District, n.d.

Kreinberg, N., & Chow, S. (Eds). *Configurations of change: The integration of mildly handicapped children into the regular classroom.* Sioux Falls, S.D.: Adapt Press, 1974.

Lambert, N. *Similarities and differences between school-based and community-based consultation* (Mimeo). Berkeley: University of California, n.d.

McGinty, A., & Keogh, B. *Needs assessment for inservice training: A first step for mainstreaming exceptional children into regular education* (Mimeo). Los Angeles: Graduate School of Education, University of California, Los Angeles, 1975.

Pasanella, A., Volkmor, C., McIntyre, R., Watts, C., Weston, B., & Williams, T. *An odyssey: Success strategies for educational change agents.* Unpublished manuscript, 1975. Los Angeles, Calif.: California Regional Resource Center.

Savage W. Consultation services in local school systems. In K. Holly, *Consultant Handbook.* Duarte, Calif.: Duarte Unified School District, ESEA Title III Prospect: Clarity, 1975. Chicago: Midwest Administration Center, University of Chicago.

South Carolina Region V Educational Services Center. *The resource room: An access to excellence.* Lancaster, S.C.: Region V Educational Services Center, 1975.

Worell, J., & Nelson, C. M. *Managing instructional problems: A case study workbook.* New York: McGraw-Hill, 1975.

Resources: Teacher Training Programs

Introduction to Mainstreaming

Barnes, E. *Children learn together: The integration of handicapped children into schools.* Syracuse, N.Y.: Human Policy Press. (A slide-show) A powerful statement on mainstreaming including a discussion of the history of exclusion and segregation of disabled children and the recent forces—court decisions, parent power, changing attitudes—that are encouraging mainstreaming. It presents arguments for integration and responds to the concerns typically raised by teachers and parents. The slides demonstrate what is necessary for integration to succeed, including preparation, individualization, and range of specific supports and services to teachers. The slide-show consists of 132 slides and is available for $30.

Hale, S., McClain, N., & Samson, J. *SERT: Special education for regular teachers.* Special Education Services Department, Education Service Center, Region 10, and Special Education Department, East Texas State University, n.d. Eight modules in soft booklet form are designed to assist regular class teachers in dealing with special needs students mainstreamed into regular classrooms via the comprehensive special education plan for Texas. Each module is designed with pre- and posttests. The eight modules are:

1. Comprehensive Special Education
2. Formal Appraisal
3. Team Planning for Student Program Management
4. Informal Assessment
5. Organizing Content for Individual Differences
6. Materials Selection
7. Classroom Management
8. Evaluation of Instruction

Lexington, Massachusetts Public Schools. *Lexington teacher training program.* San Mateo, Calif.: Agency for Instructional Television, 1973. *Diagnosis and educational planning* is the first in a series of ten video tapes which comprise *The Lexington teacher training project: Integration of children with special needs in the regular classroom,* available from the Agency for Instructional Television. The project is designed to help regular classroom teachers deal with the vast differences between individuals in their classrooms, and to help special educators blend their skills into the regular classroom setting. The programs do not reveal in-depth information about instructional plans for particular problems, but the roles of psychologists, MDs and learning specialists are clearly portrayed. Some of the other programs in the series are:

Early assessment: Steps to planning: A teacher carries out activities which reveal differences in children's development in kindergarten. *After assessment:* Observations of a kindergarten classroom where activities are individualized to meet children's needs. *Every child can learn:* Math and reading teachers, working in a team with third and fourth graders, together with a learning specialist, demonstrated specific principles for adapting lessons for children with learning problems in an integrated classroom. *Together they learn:* Retarded primary level children, almost indistinguishable in the regular classes, work in different types of groups in an integrated program. The cassette is planned to show that the educable retarded can work with other children. *Every student is different: The high school.* This cassette suggests various ways by which a high school can provide for individual differences of students.

The programs are available in quadruples, 1 inch, 3/4 inch cassette and 1/2 inch video formats. Each program costs $200, and A.I.T. writes that, "Previews of representative lessons are available on request at no charge to those interested in considering this series for in-school use." Requests for information should be directed to the Agency for Instructional Television, Western Office, 1670 S. Amphlett Blvd., San Mateo, Calif. 94402.

Lott, L. A., Hudak, B. J., & Scheetz, J. A. *Strategies and techniques for mainstreaming: A resource handbook.* Monroe, Mich.: Monroe County Intermediate School District, 1975.

Region III Education Service Center. *Principals training program.* Austin, Tex.: Region III Education Service Center, 6504 Tracor Lane, Austin, Texas 78721. *What it is:* An extensive training package which develops the "rationale for returning the handicapped child to the regular classroom, alternate administrative and instructional arrangements for programming for handicapped students in the regular classroom" (including filmstrip presentations of the different models of the Resource Specialist concept) and "how to administer a building special education program," which discusses the team assessment procedure, instructional planning, and organization for delivery of services. *Contents:* This is a multi-media package. It contains two 16mm films, 8 filmstrips with cassettes, seven transparencies, a *Book of Readings,* a *Leader's Manual and Participant Manuals. Strengths:* Well organized. Task sheets are practical and oriented to the role of the principal in mainstreaming. Good introduction to mainstreaming and ways to deal with problems of implementation. Fosters understanding of the roles of all those involved in the mainstreaming process. The program is flexible and can be adapted to local needs ($350). Books and parts can be purchased separately.

Region XIII Education Service Center. *Teacher training program: Mainstreaming mildly handicapped students in the regular classroom.* Austin, Tex.: Region XIII Education Service Center, 1976. Price per kit is $375. A multi-media training package which focuses on skills, concepts and attitudes necessary to successfully mainstream, including: areas of individualizing instruction, utilizing alternate behavior management strategies, and interfacing the regular and special education. The program contains Facilitator Manual, Participant's Manual, seven filmstrips and tapes, games and puzzles, six audiotape cassettes, forty-one transparencies, and two 16mm films. The program phases (Mainstreaming Group Activities, Skill Building, Individualized Activities and Implementation Take Home Reinforcement) comprise 45–50 hours of instruction.

Classroom Management

Buckhalter, G., Presbie, R., & Brown, P. *Behavior improvement program.* Chicago, Ill.: Science Research Associates, 1975. An extensive and lucid presentation of classroom management and record keeping, using behavioristic principles, is presented in this inservice training package for teachers. There are twenty-four lessons (about ten minutes each) involving defining, observing, counting, charting, increasing, and decreasing classroom behaviors. The lessons are recorded on audio cassettes, accompanied by picture books which the participants view in sync with the tapes. Three of the tapes have accompanying filmstrips.

The package is programmed to meet the individual needs of the participating teachers. They are instructed in gathering baseline data on behaviors of their students. Then according to the frequency of the behaviors, the teachers are directed to those units of the program relevant to their problems. The program provides spirit masters for individual improvement charts and a large "class improvement chart" for the portrayal of group data.

The package would be helpful, through its organization and examples, for the resource teacher's inservice program for the regular education teacher. The package provides examples from K-12 classrooms and can readily accommodate actual school problems into the program.

In addition to the classroom behavior, there are lessons on bus, playground and lunchroom behaviors. There is also a lesson on involving parents in behavioral management systems.

The package may be purchased for $240.75 from Science Research Associates, 259 E. Erie St., Chicago, Illinois 60611. A filmstrip/cassette program used to introduce the program may be purchased for $21.40.

Center at Oregon for Research in the Behavioral Education of the Handicapped. *The PASS program.* Eugene, Ore.: Center at Oregon for Research in the Behavioral Education of the Handicapped, 1974.

An inservice program, with consultant's manual, teacher's manual and a filmstrip/ cassette program. The program is directed towards consultants, psychologists, counselors, or resource specialists able to conduct an inservice training program for four teachers. It is a 45-day training period, involving 6 two-hour meetings with the teachers and extensive classroom observation and consultation by the resource person.

The program for academic survival skills (PASS) concerns group managment of academic-related skills. It is for an entire class, having a general problem of work and study skills during one or two periods of the day. The resource person first observes the class to record the percentage of time all of the students are showing academic survival skills (e.g., listening to directions, attending to tasks, and so on). And the general objective is to have the kids acting academically 80% of the time that they should be.

The teacher is trained in defining the skills to the class, observing and timing their occurrence, charting the data and reinforcing the class as its academic survival skills improve. The gradual withdrawal of extrinsic reinforcement is also covered. The resource person is, more or less, caretaker of the inservice program using a "Manual for Consultants" as a guide. The teachers receive a training manual. There is a filmstrip/cassette program included which clearly explains the steps of the program and the roles of the resource person and the participating teachers. That program may be borrowed from CORBEH. The teacher's and consultant's guides cost $3 each. CORBEH is located at the University of Oregon, 1590 Willamette Street, Eugene, Oregon 97401.

Center at Oregon for Research in Behavioral Education of the Handicapped. *The class program.* Eugene, Ore.: Center at Oregon for Research in the Behavioral Education of the Handicapped, 1975. *Contingencies for learning academic and social skills:* a procedures manual, two filmstrip/cassette programs, is a program for "acting-out" children. It is designed to help teachers reduce the amount of time spent coping with disruptive kids. The teacher-consultant (psychologist, counselor, resource specialist) is responsible for a behavior rating scale on the child, and the consultant does classroom observations. Children observed to be "on-task" less than 80% of the time qualify for the *CLASS* program. The consultant acquires written agreements from the teacher, principal, parents and child before the program can be implemented. The program requires rewards and punishments to be consistent at home and school.

During Phase I (5 days), the consultant spends time with the child in the classroom, so that the teacher isn't required to neglect the rest of the class while the problem child is beginning a behavior modification program. Phase II (25 days) requires the gradual withdrawal of the consultant from the program.

A procedures manual for the consultant is included in the kit, along with two filmstrip/cassette programs. The first filmstrip offers an overview of the *CLASS* program, and the second is a fictionalized case study of a child going through it. The filmstrips offer sufficient information for psychologists, counselors, and resource specialists to determine if the program would be beneficial to their caseloads. They may be borrowed from CORBEH. The manuals for the consultants and the teacher manuals cost $3 each.

Langstaff, A. L. and Volkmor, C. B. *Contingency management.* Columbus, Ohio: Charles E. Merrill, 1975. This program is designed to train preservice and inservice

teachers, in both regular and special education, how to implement a Contingency
Management System. The complete program consists of a book and four sound-
filmstrips:
1. "Contingency Management: Basic Principles"
2. "Contingency Management in the Classroom"
3. "Planning a Contingency Management Program—I"
4. "Planning a Contingency Management Program—II"
All of the information needed to successfully implement a Contingency Management System is presented in the book and the filmstrips. The program is self-
instructional; it can be used by individuals or with groups. Chapters 1–4 of this
book provide further exploration of the ideas presented in the accompanying
filmstrip through:
1. Structured tasks and activities which develop skill in applying the principles of
   Contingency Management.
2. A short self-test on the filmstrip and text content.
Also included in the book are samples of classroom materials and suggestions for
adaptations and further reading on Contingency Management.

Social/Affective and Communication Skills

Gordon, T. with Burch, N. *T.E.T: Teacher effectiveness training.* New York: Peter
H. Wyden, 1974. This book, like Gordon's *P.E.T. Parent effectiveness training,*
concentrates on developing communication skills for better interpersonal relations
(in this case, between teacher and student) and for facilitating conflict resolution. In
addition to the T.E.T. inservice trainers' courses and teachers' courses are available
from Gordon's organization, Effectiveness Training:
Effectiveness Training Incorporated
531 Stevens Avenue
Solana Beach, California 92075
(714) 481–8121
Palomares, U. *Human development program (Magic circle),* LaMesa, Calif.: Human
Development Training Institute, 1975. The H.D.P. is a complete curriculum for
grades K-12, designed to encourage (1) awareness, (2) mastery, and (3) social
interaction. The developmentally sequenced curriculum of topics is for use in the
carefully structured setting of the "Magic Circle." The ground rules for Magic
Circle include: no "put-downs," equal speaking time, optional verbal participation,
among others. In upper grade settings the curriculum is referred to as *Inner change,*
not *Magic circle.* H.D.P. workshops are highly recommended prior to use of
curriculum:
Human Development Training Institute
7574 University Avenue
LaMesa, Calif., 92041
Volkmor, C. B., Pasanella, A. L., & Raths, L. E. *Values in the classroom: A
multi-media program.* Columbus, Ohio: Charles E. Merrill, 1977. A set of six
filmstrips and a work-test about the process of valuing and values clarification. The
entire program is based on the earlier work of Raths, Harmin, and Simon.

Precision Teaching

White, O.R., & Haring, N.G. *Exceptional teaching: A multimedia training package.* Columbus, Ohio: Charles E. Merrill, 1976. A multimedia program for teachers, concentrating on specific assessment and prescription procedures which can be used with a wide variety of exceptional learners. The diagnostic-prescriptive approach is demonstrated by *real teachers in actual classrooms.* The program consists of films, either 16mm or Super 8; audio cassette tapes; and work text.

Individualized Instruction

Mager, R. F., & Pipe P. *C.R.I: Criterion-referenced instruction: Analysis, design and implementation.* Training workshop of materials available from:

13245 Rhoda Dr.

Los Altos Hills, Calif. 94022

Volkmor, C. B., Langstaff, A. L., & Higgins, M. *Structuring the classroom for success.* Columbus, Ohio: Charles E. Merrill, 1974. This program shows how to function as a teacher and guide of an open classroom—how to create a more stimulating and more productive learning environment. Film, tapes, and text provide realistic experience with tested and proven techniques.

Behavior management principles are blended with ideas for decentralizing the physical room environment and setting up activity centers for individualized instruction.

The program provides a wide variety of semistructured activities to allow the reader to interact with the material. The text provides self-checking exercises to assist the student in understanding the concepts presented by the film and audio tapes. The filmstrip and book contents are:

1. Overview of Open Education
2. Room Environment
3. Creating Activity Centers
4. Behavior Management Principles
5. Behavior Management in the Classroom
6. Individualized Instruction.

index

Abeson, A., 9, 11, 32, 34, 35
Academic Readiness Scale, 43, 69
Academic skills, 118–21
  arithmetic, 120–21, 162, 166, 171
  reading, 119–20, 159, 164–66, 170–71, 188
  written language, 160, 166
Adamson, G., 12–13, 32, 34, 112–14, 142, 159, 205
  fail-save model, 12–13, 32, 34, 112–14
Adaptive education, 31
Affective behavior, 128–29
Affective education, 171–74
Affleck, J. O., 119, 121, 140, 189–90, 191, 205, 206
Agard, J. A., 8–9, 32, 33, 140, 151, 205
Allen, K. E., 142
Almy, M., 83, 88–90, 99, 138
Anastasiow, N., 120
Anderson, J., 174
Anecdotal records, 88–90, 136
Arithmetic, 120–21, 162, 171
  Cuisenaire Rods, 171
  Greater Cleveland Mathematics Program, 171
  Montessori, 171
  programmed, 171
  structural, 171
Assessment, 80–144, 238–39, 241–42
  academic skills, 118–121
  affective behavior, 128–29
  articulation, 122
  career needs, 124–27

Assessment *(Continued)*
  case studies, 131–36
  comprehension, 122–23
  interviews, 102–8
  language, 121–23
  observations, 83–102
  of perceptual-motor functioning, 123–24
  reporting needs, 129–36
  reward preferences, 127, 164
  school records, 108–9
  social behavior, 128–29
  speech, 122
  syntax, 123
  testing, 110–18
  vocabulary, 122
  vocational needs, 124–27
Auditory problems, 41, 70, 72–73, 123–24
  assessment of, 123–24
Axelrod, S., 99–100

Babikan, E., 143
Baker, E., 206
Ballard, J., 9, 34
Ball, G., 209
Bancroft, Judy, 75–79
Barber, L., 143
Barker, L. L., 207
Barnes, E., 246
Bartel, N. R., 111, 112, 119, 120–23, 138, 140, 170, 205, 206, 217, 235, 245
Basal reading series, 170

Basic Test of Reading Comprehension, 120

Bateman, B. D., 204

Bauer, H., 245

Baxter, I., 143

Beery, K., 8, 32, 212, 245

Behavioral Index of Communicative Disorders, 43, 69

Behavioral objectives, 169, 206–7, 239

Bender, L., 123, 138

Bennett, G. K., 138

Berlin, I. N., 245

Bessell, H., 174

Birch, J. W., 8, 9, 27, 29–30, 31, 32

Blashfield, R. K., 80–81, 138

Bloom, B. S., 118, 138

Body coordination, 160, 167

Boehm, A. E., 142

Bolick, N., 35

Boyd, J. E., 119, 138

Boyer, E. G., 142

Brabner, G., 119, 120, 138

Brandt, R. M., 43, 67

Brokes, A. L., 245

Brown, P., 248

Brown v. Board of Education, 14, 32

Buchanan, A., 143

Buckhalter, G., 248

Burch, Noel, 209, 250

Burgdorf, R. L., 11, 32

Burks, Harold, 43, 69

Burton, R. V., 142

Buswell, G. T., 120–21, 138

California Assembly Bill 4040, 18, 32

California Regional Resource Center, 164, 231–34

California Test, 121

Campbell, J. D., 24, 34, 82, 120, 121–22, 128, 142, 163, 174–75, 194–95, 205

Career Awareness Materials, 175

Career needs, 124–27, 160, 168–70, 174, 242

Carlson, J., 245

Cartwright, C. A., 24, 32, 34, 36, 37,

Cartwright, C. A. *(Continued)* 38, 40, 44–45, 54–57, 67, 82–83, 88–89, 98–99, 120, 121–22, 127, 128, 139, 142, 163, 174–75, 194–95, 205

Cartwright, G. P., 24, 32, 34, 36, 37, 38, 40, 44–45, 54–57, 67, 82–83, 88–89, 98–99, 120, 121–22, 127, 128, 139, 142, 163, 174–75, 194–95, 205

Cascade model, 10–13, 32

Case studies
   Leonard T., 62–64, 109, 131–34, 176–77
   Richard A., 65–68, 109, 134–36, 178–87

Casey, P. J., 11, 32

Cazier, V. O., 44, 70

Cegala, D. J., 207

Center for Vocational and Technical Education, 127, 144, 210

Central processing mechanisms, 21

Champagne, D. W., 205

Chow, S. H. L., 33, 245

Christie, L. S., 195–96, 205

Christopolos, F., 208

Civil Rights Act of 1964, 16

Classroom Inventory of Teacher Estimates for Special Service (CITES), 43, 69

Closed questions, 106–7

Cloward, R. D., 120

Clymer, T., 143

Cohen, M. A., 209

Cohen, S. A., 111, 120, 139

Communication skills, 216–17, 250

Computer Assisted Renewal Education (CARE), 27
   handbook, 172–73

Connolly, A. J., 143

Consulting teacher program, 27

Contingency management system, 230–32

Council for Exceptional Children, 35

Court decisions, 14–17, 224–25
   Brown v. Board of Education, 14, 32

Court decisions *(Continued)*
Diana v. State Board of Education, 16–17, 33
Larry P. v. Riles, 16–17, 33
Lau v. Nichols, 16, 33
Mills, v. DC Board of Education, 16, 17, 34
Wyatt v. Stickney, 16, 34
Criterion Referenced Measurement (CRM), 114–18, 192–96, 215, 241
Cromwell, R. L., 80–81, 138
Crutchfield, M., 144
Cuisenaire Rods, 171

Davis, M. D., 130, 141
Deno, E., 9, 10, 11–12, 27–29, 30–31, 32–33, 205
cascade model, 11–13, 32
Deno, S., 101, 139
Diagnostic Prescriptive Teacher (DPT) Program, 28
DIAL, 43, 69–70
Diana v. State Board of Education, 16–17, 33
Differential Aptitudes Tests, 126–27
Dinkmeyer, D., 174, 218, 245
Direct-teacher activities, 190
Dollar, B., 245
Drew, C. J., 207
Drier, H., 209
Due process, 14, 17, 19, 83, 237, 241, 243
Dunn, L. M., 9–10, 27, 33, 110, 122, 139
Duration recording, 90–91, 136

Educational assessment *(see* Assessment)
Educational planning, 148–92
Educational specialist, 8
Education for all Handicapped Children Act *(see* Public Law 94–142)
Egner, A., 214–15, 245
Eiseman, J. W., 208
Elkind, D. A., 67
Emory, R., 216–17
Enos, D., 245
Estrada, J., 67

Evaluating programs, 192–203, 239–40, 243
Event recording, 90–91, 136
Exemplary Center for Reading Instruction, 188

Fail-save model, 12–13, 32, 34, 112–14
Farr, R., 120, 139
Fernald method, 163, 171
Fink, R., 139
First Grade Screening Test, 44, 70
Ford, Gerald, 19, 146
Forness, S. R., 38, 67
Fourteenth Amendment, 14, 17
Fox, W. L., 207
Fremer, J., 207
Frequency recording, 90–91
Freston, C. W., 207
Fristoe, M., 139
Frostig Developmental Test of Visual Perception, 111, 123, 139
Frostig, M., 123, 139

Gallagher, N., 7–8
Ganyi, A. P., 207
Gartner, A., 208
General Special Education Resource Teacher Model, 28
Gibbons, B., 208
Giles, Marian, 44, 70
Gilhool, T. K., 6, 14, 33, 35
Gillingham Phonics, 171
Ginsburg, H., 67
Glasser, W., 174
Goldenberg, Dorothea, 43, 67–70
Goldman-Fristoe Test of Articulation, 122, 139
Goldman, R. M., 139, 205
Gonzales, M. A., 207
Gooden, B. L., 143
Goodman, L., 111, 140
Gordon, Thomas, 209, 250
Gottlieb, J., 8–9, 32, 33, 140, 151, 205
Graham, F. K., 123, 139
Greater Cleveland Mathematics Program, 171

Gronlund, N. E., 206–7
Gross, J., 101, 139
Gurski, Gabriele, 59
  Referral Analysis Chart, 59–61, 63, 64, 68

Hagen, E., 88, 142
Hale, S., 246
Hall, R. Vance, 92, 99–100, 139, 207
Halo effect, 43, 100
Halpern, A. S., 139
Hammill, D. D., 21–22, 25, 33, 45, 58, 67, 86, 110, 111–12, 119, 120, 122–24, 138, 139–40, 141, 170, 205, 206, 217, 235–36, 245
Haring, N. G., 121, 142, 143, 206, 251
Harmin, M., 129, 141, 209
Harms, T., 93, 140
Harrison School Center, 28
Harris, S., 207
Hass, J., 35
Hastings, J. T., 138
Haughton, E., 143, 209
Havelock, R. G., 220, 245
Hawkes, G. R., 67
Hawkins, R. P., 99–100
Hearing problems, 41, 70, 72–73, 123–24
  assessment of 123–24
Hewett, F. M., 38, 67
Higgins, M., 93–96, 251
Hobbs, N., 9, 33
Homme, L., 207
Housden, J. L., 117, 140, 207
Houston Plan, 28–29
Howard, R., 216–17
Howe, L. W., 209
Howlett, J., 245
Hoyt, F., 245
Hoyt, K. B., 210
Hudak, B. J., 247
Hulten, W. J., 209
Human Relations Kit, 175
Humboldt-Del Norte Master Plan Office, 237–40
Husek, T. R., 115, 141

Identification of handicapped, 36–45, 238, 241
  characteristics, 38–41
  decision points, 44–45
  screening instruments, 43–44
  screening process, 42
  screening techniques, 42–43
Illinois Test of Psycholinguistic Abilities, 111
Independent-child activities, 190–91
In-depth observation techniques, 41
Individualized reading, 170
Individual Learning Disabilities Classroom Screening Instrument, 44, 70
Information processing problems, 40
Inservice programs, 24, 26, 28–31, 220, 234–44, 246–51
Instructional integration, 9, 32
Integration, 8–9
  instructional, 9, 32
  social, 9, 151
  temporal, 9, 32
Intelligence quotient (IQ), 10, 16–17
Interviews, 102–8
  closed questions, 106–7
  improvement of, 106–7
  limitations of, 105–6
  nonverbal cues, 107
  open, 103–4
  open-ended questions, 106
  outcomes, 108
  structured, 103–4
  types of, 103–4
  uses of, 103–5
Irwin, L., 139
ITPA, 122

Jenkins, J. R., 20–21, 33
Jensen, Alan, 164
Jiguor, J. W., 245
John, L., 120–21, 138
Johnson, G. O., 9, 33
Johnson, R. A., 6, 33
Jung, C., 216–17, 245

Kanawha County, West Virginia, 29
Kanfer, F. H., 104–5, 140

Kanowitz, J., 105, 141
Kaufman, M. J., 8–9, 32, 33, 140, 148, 151, 205
Kendall, B. S., 123, 139
Kennedy, Carol, 164
Kent, R. N., 105, 141
Keogh, B., 246
Kibler, R. J., 207
Kinesthetic problems, 69–70, 73
Kirk, S. A., 122, 140
Kirk, W., 122, 140
Kirschenbaum, H., 209
Klein, S., 207
Klinger, R., 245
Kohler, M., 208
Kosekoff, J. P., 207
Kreinberg, N., 33, 245
Kukic, M. B., 8–9, 32, 33, 151, 205
Kunzelmann, H. P., 143, 209
Kunz, J. W., 11, 32

Lambert, Nadine, 44, 70, 246
Langstaff, A. L., 93–96, 127, 140, 230–31, 249–50, 251
Language experience approach, 170
Language problems, 40, 69, 121–23
assessment of, 121–23
LaPray, M., 119, 140
Laramore, D., 210
Larry P. v. Riles, 16–17, 33
Larsen, S. C., 111, 124, 140
Lau v. Nichols, 16, 33
LaVor, M. L., 9, 34
Law of the Hammer, 102–3
Lazerson, A., 67
Learning Activity Package (LAP), 228–29
Learning problems approach, 29
Least restrictive alternative, 11, 16, 19–20, 147
Least restrictive environment, 6–7, 19
Lefever, D. W., 139
LeGear, L., 117, 140, 207
Legislation, 17–20
California Assembly Bill 4040, 18, 32
Civil Rights Act of 1964, 16

Legislation *(Continued)*
Education for all Handicapped Children Act, 19, 32, 34, 83, 110, 142, 146–47, 192, 203, 225
Fourteenth Amendment, 14, 17
Massachusetts Chapter 776, 18, 33
Michigan Public Act 198, 18, 34
Public Law 94–142, 19, 32, 34, 83, 110, 142, 146–47, 192, 203, 225
Texas Senate Bill 230, 18, 34
Washington Special Education Code WAC 392–45, 18 , 34
Lerner, J. W., 205
Le Voci, J. P., 126, 140
Lewis, J., 125, 140
Lilly, M. S., 7, 9, 10, 12, 23–24, 33
zero reject model, 12, 23
Lippitt, P., 208
Lippitt, R., 208
Lister, J. L., 128–29, 140
Lobree, V. A., 245
Logan, D. R., 207
Lott, L. A., 247
Louisville, Kentucky, 29
Lowenbraun, S., 119, 121, 140, 189–90, 191, 205, 206

MacMillan, D. L., 9, 10, 17–18, 33
Madaus, 138
Mager, R. F., 207, 251
Mainstreaming
assessment, 80–144
court decisions, 14–17
definition of, 7–9
educational planning, 148–92
evaluation, 192–203
identification of handicapped, 36–45
implementation techniques, 20–27
influence of educators, 9–14
legislation, 17–20
models, 27–31
referral procedures, 45–68
resource teachers, 213–21
training programs, 221–44
Mangum, G. L., 210

Mann, P. H., 25, 27, 28–29, 30, 33, 37, 67, 144
Manpower Attitudes Test, 125–26
Mardell, Carol, 43, 69–70
Marshall, D. A., 245
Martin, G. L., 209
Maslow, P., 139
Massachusetts Chapter 766, 18, 33
Mayhall, W. F., 20–21
McCarthy, J. J., 122, 140
McClain, N., 246
McClung, M., 14, 33
McCurdy, R. E., 245
McGinty, A., 246
McIntyre, R., 246
McKenzie, H. S., 195–96, 205
McNeil, W., 11, 32
Meier, John, 44, 70
Meisgeier, C. H., 33
Melaragno, R. J., 208
Memory for Designs Test, 123
Mercer, J. R., 110, 140, 144
Meyen, E. L., 101, 141, 205
Meyers, C. E., 9, 10, 17–18, 33
Meyers, E. S., 144
Michigan Public Act 198, 18, 34
Miles, D. T., 125, 140, 207
Mills, B. C., 205, 206
Mills, D. D., 206
Mills, R. A., 205
Mills v. DC Board of Education, 16, 17, 34
Mingo, A., 209
Misclassification, 14, 16–17
Models, 27–31
    adaptive education, 31
    Computer Assisted Renewal Education (CARE), 27
    consulting teacher program, 27
    Diagnostic Prescriptive Teacher (DPT) Program, 28
    General Special Education Resource Teacher Model, 28
    Harrison School Center, 28
    Houston Plan, 28–29
    Kanawha County, West Virginia, 29

Models (*Continued*)
    learning problems approach, 29
    Louisville, Kentucky, 29
    Plano, Texas, 29–30
    Portland Public School's Prescriptive Education Program, 30
    Richardson, Texas, 30
    South Carolina Regional V Educational Services Center, 27, 30, 34, 51–53, 67, 130, 141, 195, 196–201, 205, 219, 246
    Stratistician Model, 30–31
    Tacoma, Washington, 31
    task analysis approach, 29
    Tucson, Arizona, 31
Modified Reward Preference Assessment, 127
Molloy, L., 11, 34
Montessori, 171
Motor problems, 69, 70, 73, 77–78, 123–24
    assessment of, 123–24
Myers, P. I., 206

Natchman, W., 143
Nelson, Calvin C., 43, 69
Nelson, C. M., 161, 163, 172, 206, 216, 235, 246
Newcomer, P., 141
Norm-referenced tests, 115–17
Northway, M. L., 141
Nyberg, David, 129, 141

Observations, 83–102
    advantages of, 85
    anecdotal records, 88–90, 136
    duration recording, 90–91, 136
    event recording, 90–91, 136
    frequency recording, 90–91
    improvement of, 100–101
    involving measurement, 90–92
    limitations of, 100
    outcomes of, 101–2
    Participation Chart, 99
    placheck, 90, 92, 136
    skills, 86–88

Observations *(Continued)*
  time sampling, 90–92, 136
  types of, 88–93, 136
Occupational Awareness Test, 126
Occupational Preference Test, 126
Ohio Trade and Industrial Education
  Services, 127
O'Leary, K. D., 105, 141
Open-ended questions, 106
Opinions About Work, 125
Opper, S., 67

Palomares, U., 174, 209, 250
Panyan, M. C., 207
Paolucci, P., 214–15, 245
Participation Chart, 99
Pasanella, A. L., 209, 246, 250
Pate, J. E., 44, 70
Peabody Picture Vocabulary Test, 122,
  139
Pennsylvania Association for Retarded
  Children (PARC), 14, 17, 34
Perception check, 217
Perceptual-motor problems, 40, 69,
  123–24
  assessment of, 123–24
Perez, F. I., 33
Perscriptive Instructional Activities
  Form, 126
Phillips, J. S., 140, 141
Pino, R., 216–17
Pinson, N. M., 210
Pipe, P., 251
Placheck, 90, 92, 136
Plano, Texas, 29–30
Plase, D., 67
Popham, W. H., 115, 141
Portland Public School's Prescriptive
  Education Program, 30
Presbie, R., 248
Preschool Evaluation Form, 75–79
Pritchett, E. M., 143
Problem behaviors, 38–41
  hearing, 41, 70, 72–73
  information processing, 40
  language, 40, 69

Problem behaviors *(Continued)*
  motor, 69–70, 73
  perceptual-motor, 40, 69
  retrieval, 40
  social-emotional, 41, 69, 70
  speech, 40
  storage, 40
  vision, 41, 70, 72
Process testing, 111–12
Programmed reading, 170
Public Law 94–142, 19, 32, 34, 83, 110,
  142, 146–47, 192, 203, 225
Pupil Behavior Rating Scale, 44, 70

Racicot, R. H., 245
Raffeld, P., 139
Raths, L. E., 129, 141, 209, 250
Rausch, H. L., 102–3, 142
  Law of the Hammer, 102–3
Ray, R. S., 141
Reading, 119–20, 159, 164–66, 170–71,
  188, 209
  basal series, 170
  Fernald, 171
  Gillingham Phonics, 171
  individualized, 170
  language experience approach, 170
  programmed, 170
  Spalding Phonics Approach, 171
Rechs, J. R., 207
Referral Analysis Chart, 59–61, 63, 64,
  68
  case studies, 64, 68
Referrals, 45–68, 241
  analyzing, 59–62
  case studies, 62–68
  informal, 57–58
  Referral Analysis Chart, 59–61, 63,
    64, 68
  sample forms, 47–58
  self, 58
  suggestions for, 58
Rehabilitation Research and Training
  Center, 125
Reid, E., 205
Reinforcement Inventory, 127

Reissman, F., 208
Resource teacher
  as consultant, 218–19
  as inservice trainer, 220
  characteristics, 215–16
  communication skills, 216–17
  establishing rapport, 217–18
  professional skills, 215
  responsibilities of, 213–15
  training experiences, 220–21
Retrieval problems, 40
Rewards, 127, 164, 174–75, 242
  activities, 175
  attention, 174
  food, 174
  knowledge of results, 174–75
  token economies, 175
Reynolds, M. C., 130, 141
Richardson, Texas, 30
Risley, T. R., 92, 141
  placheck, 90, 92
Rocky Mountain Educational Laboratory, 125–26, 141
Rolle, R. E. W., 245
Rosler, M., 67
Ross, R., 119, 140
Rubina, T. J., 7, 34
Russ, Gene, 164

Sabatino, D., 21, 34, 80, 82, 130, 141
Salvia, J., 112, 142
Samson, J., 246
San Diego Quick Assessment, 119
Saslow, G., 104–5, 140
Savage, W., 218, 246
Scelza, C., 7–8
Schaefer, Florence, 164
Scheetz, J. A., 247
Schiefelbusch, R. L., 206
School adjustment, 160, 168
School records, 108–9
  case studies, 109
Screening Checklist for Classroom Teachers, 44, 70
Screening instruments, 43–44, 69–71
  Academic Readiness Scale, 43, 69

Screening instruments *(Continued)*
  Behavioral Index of Communicative Disorders, 43, 69
  Classroom Inventory of Teacher Estimates for Special Service (CITES), 43, 69
  DIAL, 43, 69–70
  First Grade Screening Test, 44, 70
  Individual Learning Disabilities Classroom Screening Instrument, 44, 70
  Pupil Behavior Rating Scale, 44, 70
  Screening Checklist for Classroom Teachers, 44, 70
  Teacher Rating Scale for the Identification of Handicapped Children, 44, 70–71
  Walker Problem Behavior Identification Checklist, 44, 71
Screening techniques, 42–43
  checklists, 42–43
  rating scales, 42–43
Self-concept, 160, 167–8, 171–72
Semel, E. M., 142
Semmel, M. I., 86, 141
Shaw, S. F., 24, 34
Shaw, W., 24, 34
Siegel, E., 161–62, 205
Siegel, R., 161–62, 205
Simon, A., 142
Simon, S. B., 129, 141, 209
Simpson, D., 125, 140
Skill testing, 112
Skindrud, Karl, 102–8
Slingerland, B. H., 122, 141
Slingerland Screening Tests, 122, 141
Smith, C. W., 141
Smith, R. M., 119, 120–21, 123, 141, 206
Social and Prevocational Information Battery, 125
Social-emotional problems, 41, 57, 69, 70, 75, 128–29
  assessment of, 128–29
Social integration, 9, 151
South Carolina Regional V Educational

South Carolina *(Continued)*
  Services Center, 27, 30, 34, 51–53, 67, 130, 141, 195, 196–201, 205, 219, 246
Spalding Phonics Approach, 171
Special Education Resource Teachers (SERT), 28
Speech problems, 40, 122
  assessment of, 122
Spencer, E. F., 120–21, 141
Spinazola, C., 24, 34, 82, 120, 121–22, 128, 142, 163, 173, 174–75, 194–95, 205
SRA
  achievement test, 121
  materials, 175
Stanford-Binet, 111
Stanford Test, 121
Starlin, C., 143, 209
Stellern, J., 111–12, 127, 142
Stewart, F., 43, 69
Storage problems, 40
Stratistician Model, 30–31
Strauss, J. S., 80–81, 139
Streifel, S., 207
Structural arithmetic, 171
Stuck, R. L., 245
Suiter, P., 144
Sullivan, Paula, 164
Systematic observation methods, 42
System FORE, 110, 208

Tacoma, Washington, 31
Task analysis, 29, 114–15, 161–62, 206–7, 215, 243
Teacher Rating Scale for the Identification of Handicapped Children, 44, 70–71
Temporal integration, 9, 32
Terminal behavior, 114, 137, 159, 161–62, 189
Testing, 110–18, 143–44
  Basic Test of Reading Comprehension, 120
  California Test, 121
  Criterion Referenced Measurement

Testing *(Continued)*
  (CRM), 114–18
  Differential Aptitudes Tests, 126–27
  Frostig Developmental Test of Visual Perception, 111
  Goldman-Fristoe Test of Articulation, 122
  Illinois Test of Psycholinguistic Abilities, 111
  ITPA, 122
  Manpower Attitudes Test, 125–26
  Memory for Designs Test, 123
  norm-reference, 115–17
  Occupational Awareness, 126
  Occupational Preference, 126
  Opinions About Work, 125
  Peabody Picture Vocabulary Test, 122, 139
  process, 111–12
  San Diego Quick Assessment, 119
  skill, 112
  Slingerland Screening Tests, 122
  Social and prevocational Information Battery, 125
  SRA Achievement Test, 121
  Stanford-Binet, 111
  Stanford Test, 121
  task analysis, 114–15
  terminal behavior, 114
  Test of Language Development (TOLD), 122
  Wechsler Intelligence Scales, 111
  Work Cases, 126
Test of Language Development (TOLD), 122
Texas Senate Bill 230, 18, 34
Thorndike, R. L., 88, 142
Thurber, G., 143
Time sampling, 90–92, 136
Toker, A., 7–8, 34
Towle, M., 162, 205
Training experiences, 220–44
  comprehensive program, 241–43
  content preparation, 221
  for regular teachers, 235–37
  for resource teachers, 237–41

Training experiences *(Continued)*
  schedules, 226–33
  small groups, 233–34
  task design, 221–26
  time commitment, 234–35
Tubesing, D. A., 107, 142
Tubesing, N. L., 107, 142
Tucson, Arizona, 31

Valett, Robert, 43, 69
Van Etten, G., 12–13, 32, 34, 112–14,
    142, 159, 205
  fail-save model, 12–13, 32, 34,
    112–14
Vasa, S. F., 43, 69, 111–12, 127, 142
Vision problems, 41, 70, 72, 123–24
  assessment of, 123–24
Vocational needs, 124–27, 160, 168–70,
    174, 209–10
Volkmor, C. B., 93–96, 127, 140, 209,
    230–31, 246, 249–50, 251

Walker, Hill, 44, 71
Walker Problem Behavior Identification
    Checklist, 44, 71
Wardlaw, J. H., 245
Ward, M. E., 24, 34, 82, 120, 121–22,
    128, 142, 163, 174–75, 194–95,
    205
Washington Special Education Code
    WAC 392–45, 18, 34
Watts, C., 246

Webb, W. W., 44, 70
Wechsler Intelligence Scales, 111
Weinberg, R. A., 142
Weintraub, F. J., 9, 34
Weld, L., 141
Weston, Bruce, 231–34, 246
Wheeler, A. H., 207
White, O. R., 121, 142, 143, 251
Whittlesey, J. R. B., 139
Why Work Series, 175
Wiederholt, J. L., 21–22, 25, 33, 45, 58,
    67, 111, 140
Wiig, E. H., 142
Wiley, E. M., 245
Willems, E. P., 102–3, 142
  Law of the Hammer, 102–3
Williams, T., 246
Worell, J., 161, 163, 172, 206, 216, 235,
    246
Work Cases, 126
World of Work Kit, 175
Written language, 160, 166
Wyatt v. Stickney, 16, 34

Yarrow, M. R., 142
Yonkers Career Education Project, 126,
    140
Yoshida, R. K., 9, 10, 17–18, 33
Ysseldyke, J. E., 24, 32, 37, 67, 111,
    112, 142

Zero reject model, 12, 23